Secular Religions in France 1815–1870

UNIVERSITY OF HULL PUBLICATIONS

SECULAR RELIGIONS IN FRANCE
1815-1870

BY

D. G. CHARLTON

Published for the UNIVERSITY OF HULL by the
OXFORD UNIVERSITY PRESS
LONDON NEW YORK MELBOURNE
1963

Oxford University Press, Amen House, London E.C.4

GLASGOW NEW YORK TORONTO MELBOURNE WELLINGTON
BOMBAY CALCUTTA MADRAS KARACHI LAHORE DACCA
CAPE TOWN SALISBURY NAIROBI IBADAN ACCRA
KUALA LUMPUR HONG KONG

Printed in Great Britain

'Le vieux monde se dissout, les vieilles doctrines s'éteignent; mais, au milieu d'un travail confus, d'un désordre apparent, on voit poindre des doctrines nouvelles, s'organiser un monde nouveau; la religion de l'avenir projette ses premières lueurs sur le genre humain en attente, et sur ses futures destinées . . .'
—F. Lamennais, *Esquisse d'une philosophie*, Paris, Pagnerre, 1840–46, 4 vols., iii. 273.

Preface

NON-CHRISTIAN thought in nineteenth-century France is not uncommonly regarded as, above all, critical and destructive of established ideas, whether in religion and philosophy or in politics and economics; this was an age of revolutions, intellectual no less than political. Yet that was only one side of a complex, ambivalent whole. Again and again criticism gave way to construction, revolution to counter-revolution, and destruction became but the preparation for new intellectual achievement. This was a century of remarkable creative enterprise, no less outstanding for what it built than for what it demolished, more so, one is tempted to say, than any age since the Renaissance, for its vigour was manifest over so wide an area: in the expansion of science—what one writer has indeed called 'the counter-revolution of science'; in the rise of new political and economic doctrines, in particular socialism and modern democracy; and, to an equal extent, in philosophy. For these years gave birth to the metaphysical systems of Hegel and other German idealists, soon influential in France, to the positivist philosophy of Comte, Taine, and others, to countless metaphysical theories of history and progress. It is too rarely emphasized that the nineteenth century was an age that longed for infallibility—and found it, whether in the papal infallibility asserted in France by Bonald, Maistre, and Lamennais and proclaimed later by the Pope himself, or in the infallibility of science announced by the adherents of 'scientism', or in the metaphysical infallibility of Hegelian absolutism, or in the infallibility of historical evolution as expounded by Marx and a hundred other philosophers of history. The truly scientific attitude, the rigorously critical spirit constantly yielded to prophetic fervour and messianic expectation, and any destructive mood was more than countered by a deeply sincere desire to build new philosophies—new religions, indeed—to replace the beliefs that had been abandoned. A critical reaction against many of the ideas to be considered here supervened in French thought from about 1870 (which has therefore been taken as a convenient *terminus ad quem* here), but the previous fifty years or more constituted in contrast what may be called the constructive phase of the century's philosophical life. One cannot but be impressed and even astonished at the unusual richness and diversity of the systems propounded during these years, at the vigorous proliferation of substitutes for Christianity. Others have examined the *political* 'messianism' of the age but its *philosophical* 'messianism', as expressed in the many philosophical 'substitute-religions' that were everywhere announced, has been more neglected. This book seeks to provide an introductory survey of this phenomenon and to study a representative selection of these religious substitutes. It is directed in the first instance to the student of French literature and civilization, but I hope it will also be suitable for the general reader. And since it deals with what, in my submission, is the most arresting feature of the philosophical scene at this time, it may also serve in some degree as an introduction to the age's intellectual trends as a whole. Whereas books in English are readily available on French thought in earlier centuries and on both political and theological ideas in the nineteenth century, the background of non-Christian philosophical ideas at this time is nowhere conveniently presented to my knowledge, except for G. Boas's *French Philosophies of the Romantic Period*, which ends at about 1830, A. L. Guérard's *French Prophets of Yesterday*, and J. A. Gunn's *Modern French Philosophy*, both of which concentrate on the Second Empire and after, and, although still of considerable value, were written forty years ago or more.

Considerations of space, not to add limitations of knowledge, have imposed two restrictions which should be made explicit. I have by design so defined my subject as to exclude all but passing references to political and social thought and to theological developments, each of which would demand another book. Whilst, as I have tried to indicate, there were constant interactions between them and philosophical thinking, the distinctions are difficult to make only in a few marginal cases—such as Michelet's 'religion of justice', centred upon the Revolution and France, which I have finally excluded as being primarily a political credo, whereas, for example, the Saint-Simonian cult, though no less political, also expressed itself in a fully organized 'church'. It should also be added that the Ideologue group of philosophers is likewise largely absent, for their main works come before 1815, my *terminus a quo*.

My method has been to concentrate on salient themes in the period's intellectual development rather than to devote each chapter to a particular group or thinker; the cross-references in the footnotes and the Index may help those who would have preferred the second approach. The reader should also note that whilst there is in general a chronological progression within the separate chapters, this is not the case as between them. Each concerns the whole period under review, but to emphasize the chronological facts a brief list of the principal thinkers of the age is included. Lastly, it should be mentioned that a more comprehensive, though still selective bibliography is provided than might seem warranted in a book of limited introductory scope; this has been done to help readers wishing to consult more detailed guides to particular subjects and authors.

My survey can make claim to only occasional scholarly originality, and I am conscious of a deep indebtedness to the scholars whose specialist works I have consulted. I would wish to express my gratitude for the help I have drawn from them and also the hope that I have not simplified their conclusions more than is inevitable in a compressed presentation. At the same time, I have been struck in the course of my work by the absence of any recent *œuvres de synthèse* on several major topics. We lack, for instance, general accounts of the decline of Christian belief in nineteenth-century France, the fortunes of pantheism and, in particular, Spinozism, the impact of Darwinian and other evolutionary theories, and also any contemporary appreciation of the eclectic philosophers, especially of the much-maligned Victor Cousin. Perhaps my own brief treatments of these and other similarly neglected subjects may interest others, if only by their shortcomings, in undertaking more intensive study.

Chapter III and the pages on Renan in Chapter V contain in greatly abridged form material published in my book, directed to a more specialist reader than this, on *Positivist Thought in France*

Preface

during the Second Empire; I am grateful to the Delegates of the Clarendon Press for permission to utilize it here.

Lastly, I am happy to be able to acknowledge here the more personal debts I have contracted. My greatest obligation is to Professor P. Mansell Jones, who, with characteristic kindness, has read the work twice in its entirety, offered invaluable and meticulous guidance and criticism, and been a source of constant encouragement. My sincere thanks are also due to Professor Garnet Rees who has likewise given me very useful advice and comment on the whole book and been unfailingly generous in helping and encouraging me. I am also very grateful to other friends and colleagues who have discussed difficulties with me, and particularly to Professor John Lough for his helpful comments at a late stage in my work; to the Librarians of the Universities of Hull and Toronto and their staffs for their ready assistance; to the University of Hull for the financial help which facilitated my visits to other libraries; to its Publications Committee for its kindness in accepting this work for inclusion in its series and to its Secretary, Mr. P. A. Larkin, for his prompt and friendly advice; and to the officials of the Oxford University Press for their helpfulness during the process of publication. Above all I am indebted to my wife, both for preparing the Index and in numerous other ways.

Hull, 1962   D. G. C.

Contents

Abbreviations

THE following abbreviations are employed:

R.D.M.   *Revue des Deux Mondes*
R.H.L.F.   *Revue d'histoire littéraire de la France*
R.L.C.   *Revue de littérature comparée*
R.M.M.   *Revue de métaphysique et de morale*
Rev. Philos. *Revue philosophique de la France et de l'étranger*

Unless otherwise stated the place of publication of works cited is Paris and italics in quotations are those of the author cited.

List of Principal Thinkers

1. Traditionalist Catholics
   - J. de Maistre (1753–1821)
   - L. de Bonald (1754–1840)
   - R. de Chateaubriand (1768–1848)
   - F. de Lamennais (1782–1854)

2. Ideologues
   - A. L. Destutt de Tracy (1754–1836)
   - G. Cabanis (1757–1808)
   - F. P. Maine de Biran (1766–1824)
   - M. J. Degérando (1772–1842)

3. Eclectics
   - P. Laromiguière (1756–1837)
   - P. P. Royer-Collard (1763–1845)
   - V. Cousin (1792–1867)
   - Th. Jouffroy (1796–1842)

4. Socialistic Reformers
   - H. de Saint-Simon (1760–1825)
   - C. Fourier (1772–1837)
   - É. Cabet (1788–1856)
   - P. Enfantin (1796–1864)
   - P. Leroux (1797–1871)
   - P. J. Proudhon (1809–1865)
   - L. Blanc (1813–1882)

5. Liberals
   - J. Michelet (1798–1874)
   - E. Quinet (1803–1875)
   - A. de Tocqueville (1805–1859)
   - E. Scherer (1815–1889)

6. Positivists
   - (H. de Saint-Simon (1760–1825))
   - A. Comte (1798–1857)
   - É. Littré (1801–1881)
   - C. Bernard (1813–1878)
   - E. Renan (1823–1892)
   - H. Taine (1828–1893)
   - Th. Ribot (1839–1916)

7. Neo-Criticists
   - A. A. Cournot (1801–1877)
   - J. Lequier (1814–1862)
   - C. Renouvier (1815–1903)

8. Idealists
   - É. Vacherot (1809–1897)
   - F. Ravaisson (1813–1900)
   - J. Simon (1814–1896)
   - Paul Janet (1823–1899)
   - J. Lachelier (1832–1918)
   - A. Fouillée (1838–1912)

I

Introduction

LÉON BRUNSCHVICG once remarked that vast speculative theories of history were the 'darling vice' of the nineteenth century.[1] Truth to tell, vast synthetic systems of any kind were sure of a ready hearing in France during the half-century and more of social upheaval and intellectual confusion that followed the Revolution and the advent of industrialization. Sensitive to the disruptions of economic, political, scientific, and industrial change—almost obsessed, indeed, by the dangers of historical development—thinkers sought above all to reconstruct—and to reconstruct, first and foremost, philosophically, religiously. For it is ideas that govern history, they believed: social unity can be founded only upon philosophical or religious unity. To their eye the eighteenth century appeared a critical, intellectually destructive era, whose results were manifest in the vicious anarchy of the Reign of Terror.

> O dix-huitième siècle, impie et châtié!
> Société sans dieu, qui par Dieu fus frappée![2]

Hugo's lines sum up a widespread view. Nor was the omnipotence of ideas taken for granted by thinkers alone. Fearful of their social repercussions, successive governments—during the Restoration, under Louis-Philippe, during the Second Empire—intervened to censor or prosecute the over-bold, and to suppress or control philosophical teaching in the universities. Educational reforms in 1821, for instance, were introduced with the following declaration of principle: 'Les bases de l'éducation des collèges sont la Religion, la Monarchie, la légitimité et la Charte.'[3] Cousin,

---

[1] 'History and Philosophy', in *Philosophy and History—Essays presented to E. Cassirer*, Oxford, Clarendon Press, 1936, p. 30.

[2] V. Hugo, *Regard jeté dans une mansarde, Les Rayons et les ombres*, IV.

[3] *Ordonnance* of 27 February 1821, cited by M. Leroy, *La Pensée de Sainte-Beuve*, Gallimard, 1940, p. 124.

Guizot, Jouffroy, Quinet, Michelet, and others, all had their courses suspended at one time or another. Even moderates like the eclectics were bitterly charged with corrupting the young—and that not only in Catholic journals but in the Chambre des Pairs itself.

To provide the new society with an ideological synthesis—this was the aim of thinkers of every shade of opinion, from extreme Left to equally extreme Right. Consequently, the first half of the century sees, as Bréhier notes, 'une extraordinaire floraison de doctrines amples et constructives qui prétendent révéler le secret de la nature et de l'histoire et faire connaître à l'homme la loi de sa destinée, individuelle et sociale'.[1] It may be the great *summum* of Catholicism, presented afresh by the traditionalists—Bonald, Joseph de Maistre, the younger Lamennais, Chateaubriand. It may be the vast metaphysical structures of Hegel and his fellow ideal-ists in Germany, quickly made known in France by Cousin and his eclectic disciples—who themselves devised a spiritualistic 'natural religion' drawn in part from Hegel and in part from that equally all-embracing metaphysician, Spinoza. It may be the 'positive philosophy' of Auguste Comte, whose principal works alone extend in the commonest editions to some eleven lengthy volumes. It may be the 'religions' of humanity, of Nature, of science, or of progress of other social thinkers—such as Saint-Simon and Enfantin, whose joint *œuvres* in the definitive edition amount to forty-seven volumes in all. It may be the many and varied social and political theories—falling for the most part out-side our scope—that are devised by 'social Catholics', humanitar-ians, socialists, utopians, collectivists. All these thinkers expound in detail and at length a philosophy to end all philosophies; all soar —in this resembling the Romantic poets—to a messianic oratory, a tone of prophetic revelation; all are persuaded that the fate of a nation can be swayed by ideological truth and error.

For us today it is in some ways difficult to share or appreciate the excitements of this system-making. It provoked in the end an extensive critical reaction, fully expressed from about 1870 but gathering momentum earlier. A more sceptical, analytical ap-

[1] É. Bréhier, *Histoire de la philosophie*, t. ii—*La Philosophie moderne*, Alcan, s.d., p. 573.

proach replaces the apocalyptic mood of the preceding fifty years; faith in all-inclusive philosophies gives way to a more cautious, moderate, pragmatic attitude; thinkers descend from the clouds of speculation and take up the more humdrum tasks of epistemological analysis. The later nineteenth century, as Bréhier well remarks, is sceptical about discovering final ends and first causes:

l'attention du philosophe se transfère à l'exercice de la pensée qui connaît ou de la volonté qui agit et sur les conditions formelles de cette pensée ou de cette volonté. . . . L'esprit, las de chercher un objet imaginaire, se replie sur lui-même pour observer les lois de son exercice.[1]

And to a large extent twentieth-century philosophy, above all in Britain and America, has continued this reaction—witness the spread of logical positivism and linguistic analysis, both anti-metaphysical in outlook. It is true that in France Bergsonians and existentialists have lent a certain fresh impetus to metaphysics— but the former in order to reject the rationalist and scientific methods of nineteenth-century thinkers, the latter to proclaim the absence of objective metaphysical meaning in the world.

Yet though products of a mood quite dissimilar to ours, the ideas of earlier-nineteenth-century philosophers have continued to influence our thought and social organization. The Catholic authoritarianism of Joseph de Maistre has been revived by Bourget, Barrès, Charles Maurras. Marxism—a highly typical synthesis of the period, compounded of Hegelian metaphysics and positivistic social theory—now determines the fortunes of a third or more of the world's population, whilst another third at least is imbued with the hopes of nineteenth-century humanism and socialism. Even in the strictly philosophical realm our problems are in large part theirs, although we may pose them in different terms—the limits of the scientific methods; the relations of science and religion; the sources of moral obligation and the relation of religion and ethics; the scope and methodology of social science and psychology; the reality and freedom of the self; the validity of

[1] ibid., p. 910.

the idea of progress and the possibility of a speculative philosophy of history; and many others. To this extent we cannot but be implicated in their arguments. Moreover, these thinkers are facing what has been called the characteristic predicament of the nineteenth century—but which is perhaps no less acute in our own: that of 'honest unbelief', of the religious temperament estranged from the Christian faith. The present survey has this as a principal theme: it studies men's differing responses to a situation in which they no longer accept Christianity but still believe that religious commitment of one sort or another is essential—even where they interpret 'religion' as little more than an ethical, political, or metaphysical system.

If the urgency and concern animating these alternatives to Christianity should seem a little unusual to a modern reader, it is worth recalling the immediate intellectual background. For the men of 1815 the various religious cults of the Revolutionary period were a very recent memory. In fact, these cults closely prefigured the social religions we shall examine, both in their underlying assumptions and in their details.[1] Only about twenty years before our period begins, the Republican Calendar had replaced the Gregorian, parish churches in Paris had become Temples of Reason, and the Paris Commune, closing the churches of all other sects, had declared that it would 'recognize no other religion than that of Truth and Reason'. Robespierre's reaction to this kind of non-deistic creed anticipated the ideas of Saint-Simon, Comte, and others later. When he proclaimed that 'atheism is aristocratic' and, repeating Voltaire, that 'si Dieu n'existait pas, il faudrait l'inventer', he was appealing to the conviction they were to express that without a sound religious basis no society can prosper. His own 'Culte de l'Être Suprême' shows us what dogmas he thought indispensable in a social religion—the existence of God, the immortality of the soul, the moral obligation to carry out one's

[1] For details of the Revolutionary religions, cf., amongst many studies, the works of A. Mathiez, especially *La Révolution et l'église*, Colin, 1910, and *La Théophilanthropie et le culte décadaire*, Alcan, 1903, and A. Aulard, especially *Le Culte de la raison et le culte de l'Être suprême*, Alcan, 1892. For a brief discussion, cf. P. Trahard, *La Sensibilité révolutionnaire (1789–1794)*, Boivin, 1936, ch. vii.

social duties. God provides supernatural sanction for morality, and immortality rewards the moral agent, and Robespierre also realized that the common people need the stimulus of ceremonies if they are to share (in Rousseau's words about his civil religion) those 'sentiments of sociability, without which it is impossible to be a good subject and a faithful citizen': hence the provision of frequent festivals, with hymns and civic chants, in honour (to choose at random from a long list given by decree) of liberty and equality, justice, courage, love, infancy, agriculture, posterity, as well as the Supreme Being. After Robespierre's fall, greater liberty allowed the creation of yet further 'churches'. The Directoire encouraged, for example, the 'Culte décadaire' based upon patriotism, with festivals celebrating such objects as youth, the married, the aged, and the sovereignty of the people, and utilizing (alongside both Catholics and other sects) renamed churches in Paris—the Temple of the Supreme Being (Notre-Dame), the Temple of Agriculture (Saint-Eustache), the Temple of Gratitude (Saint-Germain-l'Auxerrois), the Temple of Victory (Saint-Sulpice), and some dozen others. The government also favoured the deistic cult of theophilanthropy, founded in 1795 and accepted by Bernardin de Saint-Pierre and the painter David amongst others, which again centred on moral values such as justice and solidarity and erected over its altars such humanistic proclamations as: 'Le bien est tout ce qui tend à conserver l'homme et le perfectionner.' [1] Worship took place in the family circle, or in simple temples, or amid Nature, and its saints included Socrates, Rousseau, Washington, and—for this was a more tolerant group than most—Saint Vincent de Paul.

Against this background, Saint-Simon's 'Temple of Newton' or Comte's 'Positivist Calendar', for instance, look rather less improbable and artificial than they might appear to us at first sight. Only just before or at the time of Napoleon's Concordat with the Pope, promulgated in 1802, did these cults lose governmental support. Only in April of that year—to take a single instance—

---

[1] Cited by J. Vinson, *Les Religions actuelles*, Delahaye et Lecrosnier, 1888, p. 526. Theophilanthropy continued throughout the century and, as late as 1888, Vinson notes, it had 85,000 adherents (p. 528).

was Sunday re-established as the official day of rest and worship. And the very decline of these cults might well seem to socially conscious anti-Catholics to present a challenge. Michelet and others were deeply to regret the failure of the 'religious Revolution'. '[La Révolution] ferma un moment l'église [he writes] et ne créa pas le temple.'[1] Where the revolutionaries had failed, others might perhaps succeed.

Nor was it only specific, revolutionary cults that had found favour during the Revolutionary and Napoleonic years. Even before 1789 there were many symptoms of a movement of opinion away from the mocking atheism of Holbach and Helvétius and towards the religious sensibility of Rousseau's *Profession de foi*. The arguments of Chateaubriand's *Génie du christianisme* and Ballanche's *Du sentiment* (1801) were foreshadowed (as Masson and Monglond abundantly show[2]) by numerous Christian apologists —from Père Fidèle's *Le Chrétien par le sentiment* (1764) to Madame de Genlis's *La Religion seule base du bonheur* (1787), Lamourette's *Les Délices de la religion* (1788) and Necker's *De l'importance des opinions religieuses* (1788). Rousseau's appeals to feeling, to the 'utility' of religion, to its aesthetic and emotional values, when constantly reiterated by other writers, helped to revive men's sense of 'religious need' and, reversing the *philosophes'* separation of ethics and religion, encouraged the belief professed by Bernardin de Saint-Pierre and many others: 'Pas de vertu sans religion.'[3] Occultism shared in this renewed enthusiasm; referring to 1780, one contemporary noted: 'Jamais les Roses-Croix, les adeptes, les prophètes, et tout ce qui s'y rapporte, ne furent aussi nombreux, aussi écoutés.'[4] In 1796 Bonald could declare: 'La religion naît de toutes parts', whilst Paul Didier hailed in 1801 a 'retour à la reli-

---

[1] J. Michelet, *Histoire de la révolution française*, Lacroix, 1868, 6 vols., v. 403–4. For a similar view, cf. E. Quinet, *Le Christianisme et la révolution française*, *Œuvres complètes*, Pagnerre, 1857–60, 12 vols., t. iii, ch. xiii and xv; and L. Ménard, *Lettres d'un mort*, Librairie de l'Art indépendant, 1895, pp. 92–93.

[2] P. M. Masson, *La Religion de J.-J. Rousseau*, 2ᵉ éd., Hachette, 1916, 3 vols., t. iii— *Rousseau et la restauration religieuse*; and A. Monglond, *Le Préromantisme français*, Grenoble, Arthaud, 1930, 2 vols., t. ii, ch. i.

[3] B. de Saint-Pierre, *Études de la nature*, cited by Masson, op. cit., iii. 146.

[4] Cited by A. Viatte, *Les Sources occultes du romantisme*, Champion, 1928, 2 vols., i. 181, from the *Mémoires* of the Baronne d'Oberkirch.

gion'.[1] It may be true that the Napoleonic Church was 'more a matter of external observance than true piety' and that the Catholic revival of the early nineteenth century was 'opportunist' and 'political' in its motives, yet the 'retreat from Voltairianism' was none the less clearly marked well before 1815.[2] Romantic religiosity, the misfortunes of the Revolution and the Terror, an ashamed desire, perhaps, to expiate their crimes, social conservatism, and the self-interest of aristocrat and priest, all conspired to the same end. From 1800 onwards one finds a strong campaign waged against *la philosophie*, and even some of the leading inheritors of eighteenth-century sensationalism, Degérando, Laromiguière, and Maine de Biran, had moved by 1814 to a distinctly spiritualist philosophy, if not to the Catholic faith itself. Even Cabanis abandoned his unyielding agnosticism shortly before his death. In his *Lettre à M. Fauriel sur les causes premières*, written about 1806–7, though still critical of much in established religion, he approved of 'la religion simple et consolante' of Franklin and Turgot and conceded that man's desire for a future life springs from 'les plus nobles sentiments du cœur humain' (and may perhaps be justified, moreover), that his other religious ideas too may derive from his innate 'way of feeling', and that religions have at least been useful to past societies by linking and bringing together their citizens. He even tentatively embraced a stoical, semi-pantheistic 'religion' of his own.[3] This general change of attitude towards religion undoubtedly favoured Christianity above all, but it also prepared the minds of unbelievers to seek and examine alternative religious creeds.

Secular thinkers were to be still more directly encouraged in their system-building by particularly unwelcome features of the

[1] L. de Bonald, *Théorie du pouvoir*, Constance, 1796, 3 vols., ii. 4. On Didier, cf. Masson, op. cit., iii. 272.

[2] R. Fargher, 'The Retreat from Voltairianism, 1800–1815', in *The French Mind—Essays presented to G. Rudler*, Oxford, Clarendon Press, 1952, pp. 223–4. On Napoleon's active opposition to the Ideologues, cf. G. Boas, *French Philosophies of the Romantic Period*, Baltimore, Johns Hopkins U.P., 1925, ch. i.

[3] *Œuvres philosophiques de Cabanis*, P.U.F., 1956, 2 vols., ii. 262, 267, 292, 261, 294–5. Cf. F. Picavet, *Les Idéologues*, Alcan, 1891, pp. 273 ff. For evidence that this spiritualistic revival was not confined to Paris, cf. L. Trénard, *Lyon: De l'Encyclopédie au préromantisme*, P.U.F., 1958, 2 vols., ii. 679–731.

resurgence of Catholicism itself. What the restoration of public worship under the Consulate and the Concordat with the Pope had begun was greatly reinforced by the return of the Bourbon monarchy and of *émigré* bishops. The nobles too had learned the cost of the Voltairean principles with which they or their fathers had toyed in the 1780's. King, Church, and aristocracy were now at one in their determination to found the new régime on the 'union of throne and altar', and the reactionary policies started by Louis XVIII were even more zealously continued after 1824 by Charles X. Many of the appropriated lands were restored to the Church; divorce was abolished; Sabbath observance was severely enforced; religious burial was refused to revolutionaries as well as heretics and actors; sacrilege was made punishable by imprisonment and even death. New religious communities increased in number, and the Jesuits illegally re-entered France, tacitly welcomed by the government, and promoted the secret and influential group of the *Congrégation* in Paris and the provinces devoted to the support of the Bourbons. The universities were reorganized under the control of the Gallican bishop Frayssinous; the École de Médecine was first suppressed and then re-formed to exclude eleven non-Catholic professors; certain courses were abolished in the faculty of law as being dangerous; in the faculty of letters the lectures of Cousin, Guizot, and Villemain were suspended; the École Normale was closed. King and Church were re-embarked on the well-tried policy of repression, but now in a novel atmosphere of liberalism. As a result, the 1820's were a time of increasing anti-clerical feeling, with the unpopularity of the clergy at its height, and the Revolution of 1830 was as anti-Catholic as it was anti-royalist. This situation affected secular thinkers in two ways in particular: first, it heightened their opposition to Catholicism and thus their determination to supplant it; secondly, it diminished the possibility of a compromise, of their accepting a modified form of Christianity. Whereas such compromise philosophies abounded in England in the nineteenth century, in France Catholic intolerance was matched by atheist intransigence. Furthermore, popular detestation of the Church around 1830 made it not altogether foolish to believe that Catholicism was at last dying;

Stendhal was not alone in predicting (as he did in 1822) that the Church had a mere twenty-five years to live.[1] The challenge to build new systems was thus the more urgent.

Intellectually also the French Catholic scene prior to 1830 offered little to attract minds that respected scientific method and logical reason and believed in progress and social improvement. It was not so much that the intellectual standard of the clergy remained low and their seminaries poor in quality and old-fashioned in syllabus and method until at least 1840.[2] Rather it was that even the Church's most persuasive apologists were stressing arguments which could only be singularly unappealing to predominantly rational thinkers. Chateaubriand's *Le Génie du christianisme* (1802) offers a first example. Christianity's truth is vouched for, he argues, by its capacity to satisfy man's innermost nature and desires, by its useful and beneficent influence upon society, and by the rich aesthetic heritage it has inspired. This Romantic apologetic could certainly commend itself to the many spiritual descendants of Rousseau, as we have already remarked, but its weakness for more hard-headed thinkers lay in its pragmatism. What is inspiring or consoling is not necessarily true, nor is what is beautiful; the appeal to social utility might speak to those who had wearied of political change and upheaval but could hardly convert idealistic reformers—men who recalled, moreover, the Church's pre-revolutionary conservatism. As early as 1788 Rivarol remarked that religion's 'utility', not its 'truth', had become its apologists' primary concern.[3] Well might Senancour later insist upon the real issue!

Pour persuader de la vérité d'une religion, . . . il ne s'agit point de voir s'il y a lieu de désirer qu'elle soit vraie. . . . Établissez la vérité, l'incontestable vérité des choses que vous annoncez. Elles sont belles sans doute, elles sont morales et poétiques, mystérieuses et pittoresques.

[1] A similar view was held, for instance, by Hugo, Vigny, Michelet, Quinet, Auguste Barbier, Heine, and others. Cf. also Sainte-Beuve, 'Le Père Lacordaire', *Nouveaux lundis*, Michel Lévy, 1863–70, 13 vols., iv. 392 ff.

[2] For evidence of this, cf. L. Foucher, *La Philosophie catholique en France au dix-neuvième siècle*, Vrin, 1955, pp. 11–15: 'L'on peut dire que pendant le premier quart du XIXᵉ siècle et au delà, le clergé français manqua en général de temps, de moyens, de maîtres pour une solide formation philosophique et théologique.'

[3] Rivarol, *Lettres à M. Necker*, in *Œuvres complètes*, Collin, 1808, 5 vols., ii. 169.

Mais ce n'est pas du tout de cela qu'il s'agit: prouvez qu'elles sont vraies.[1]

Still more clearly, and with the same invocation of utility rather than philosophical truth, the leading traditionalists of this period were advancing reasons for belief that inevitably repelled radical minds. Bonald's *Théorie du pouvoir politique et religieux* (1796) and *La Législation primitive* (1802) preach that monarchy is the sole natural form of government—a restatement of the divine right of kings that won him Napoleon's approval—and that the Catholic religion is the only stable foundation for French society. Opposing the Cartesian method of systematic doubt, he appeals to the necessity of an authority to curb the unruly desires of sinful man and the pride of individual reason, he hymns the wisdom enshrined in tradition, and points us back to the divine revelation given not only by Christ but, much earlier, to primitive humanity. Joseph de Maistre's *Considérations sur la France* (1796), followed by *Du Pape* (1819) and *Les Soirées de Saint-Pétersbourg* (1821), argue the same position, though in a more lively style. The Revolution was God's punishment of France's rejection of lawful authority, namely the monarchy, which is divinely ordained. Still more influential than these works was Lamennais's *Essai sur l'indifférence en matière de religion* (4 vols., 1817–23). He too attacks all those, be they atheist, deist, or Protestant, who follow the principle of free examination and deny the existence of authority and of assured knowledge in the sphere of religion. Their sceptical 'indifference' leads to social dissolution, for the great religious truths and the moral values they promote are the bedrock of a stable society. Moreover, individual reason, inner experience, and the senses are all alike distorted by illusion and error, Lamennais points out; how then can they be our religious guides? We must act in this realm as we do in ordinary life: accept the testimony of others and the common experience of our society as embodied in its traditions.

Ôtez la foi, tout meurt: elle est l'âme de la société, le fonds de la vie humaine. Si le laboureur cultive et ensemence la terre, si le navigateur traverse l'Océan, c'est qu'ils croient, et ce n'est qu'en vertu d'une

[1] Senancour, *Rêveries sur la nature primitive de l'homme*, Droz, 1940, 2 vols., ii. 79.

croyance semblable que nous participons des connaissances transmises, que nous usons de la parole, des aliments mêmes. . . .[1]

The 'general reason', the authority of mankind as a whole, must replace personal reason as our judge of truth in regard to religion also. And since all races in all ages have believed in a deity, God's existence is the first 'certitude de fait' (as opposed to logical certainty) that we should accept. This ingenious but far from convincing apologetic, like that of Bonald and Maistre, ran counter to the firmest principles of nineteenth-century free-thought, however. Perhaps the only elements in Lamennais's earlier outlook which could be welcomed by a progressive mind were his beliefs in the separation of church and state and in a rudimentary form of Christian Socialism—but both beliefs were condemned by the Papacy during the 1830's! Many radicals could admire the Lamennais of the *Paroles d'un croyant*, but this condemnation confirmed in their minds all the lessons taught by the previous two decades: both in practice and in intellectual outlook Catholicism was unchanged and quite unsuited to the needs of the modern age. The social and economic problems posed by the industrial revolution; the rise of liberalism and democratic aspiration; the philosophical challenges that came with the progress of the sciences—to all these salient features of the nineteenth century the Church as a whole remained coldly unresponsive. There are exceptions to this generalization, of course: a few Catholics did attempt to adapt their faith to the new intellectual and political situation, and increasingly so after about 1830. This was true to some extent of Ballanche and Buchez and of the talented disciples who gathered around Lamennais at La Chesnaie and Juilly, Lacordaire, Montalembert, Gerbet, Charles de Coux, and others. First through the short-lived journal *L'Avenir*, then through books, sermons, and lectures (such as Lacordaire's famous *Conférences de Notre-Dame* in 1835), later through their influential organ, *Le Correspondant*, these 'Liberal Catholics' contributed to an undoubted revival of belief, especially amongst the upper and bourgeois classes.[2] Yet they were

---

[1] Cited by Foucher, op. cit., p. 36.

[2] P. Spencer notes also the respect in which they were held by Second Empire intellectuals. (*Politics of Belief in Nineteenth-Century France*, London, Faber, 1954, p. 151.)

an obvious minority, ambiguously regarded by the Church's leaders, their moderation countered by the intolerant orthodoxy of such Catholic journals as *L'Ami de la Religion* and, later, Veuillot's *L'Univers*, and even they failed to perceive the force of many of the arguments advanced against Christianity.[1] Amongst the French Protestants, both Calvinist and Lutheran, the liberal tradition was stronger. The orthodox movement of *Le Réveil* led by the Monod brothers was more than balanced by the liberalism of Samuel Vincent, the Coquerels, Colani, Albert Réville, Pressensé, and Auguste Sabatier. It was, for example, in the *Revue de théologie*, founded at Strasbourg in 1850, that the German biblical critics were first discussed, well before Renan's *Vie de Jésus*, in the same open spirit as was to be manifest in England in the Oxford *Essays and Reviews*.[2] But whilst Protestantism might attract such thinkers as Constant, Quinet, Renouvier, Louis Ménard, and, at moments, George Sand, Renan, and Taine, it was too weak numerically, too geographically localized, to seem in the eyes of most Frenchmen a workable compromise between Catholicism and agnostic freethought. Hence, whereas in England the story of the nineteenth-century 'honest doubters' is above all one of attempts to *adapt and revise* Protestant Christianity, the comparable story in France is chiefly concerned with men's attempts to *replace* Catholic Christianity.

[1] Cf. Spencer, op. cit., p. 178.
[2] This is not a fortuitous comparison. Certain articles from this *Revue* were translated into English to reinforce the Oxonians' position; cf. *The Progress of Religious Thought as illustrated in the Protestant Church of France*, with an introductory essay on the 'Oxford Essays and Reviews' by J. R. Beard, London, Simpkin, 1861.

II

Religious Doubt and Aspiration

1. *The Decline of Christian Belief*

IF we often associate the nineteenth century with philosophical criticism rather than construction, this is chiefly because of the widespread loss of Christian belief, in intellectual circles, for which it is notorious. One might describe the sixteenth and seventeenth centuries as, in this regard, a time of tentative unbelief, an unbelief often as irrational and unscientific as it claimed Christianity to be: witness, for example, the Italian 'naturalists' or Cyrano de Bergerac. The late seventeenth and the eighteenth centuries might be termed an age of aggressive, rationalistic unbelief, deeply antagonistic to the Church, confident that religion is superstitious folly and a hindrance to human progress. Yet it was the nineteenth-century criticisms of Christianity which were incomparably the most powerful and disturbing in their impact, the more so in that they claimed to be based on a scientific foundation rather than on the sometimes callow rationalism of certain at least of the *philosophes*, the more arresting, also, in that they often came from men who were reluctant to break with the old faith, sympathetic to the religious attitude to life, but persuaded almost against their will of the falsity of the Christian creed.

This decline of Christian belief is the essential background for the essays of constructive philosophy we are to survey. For these are undertaken, in considerable measure, in order to replace the Christian religion—a religion believed untrue, or incomplete, or maleficent, and yet thought of as the prototype of something greatly valuable in human life, whether for social, moral, psychological, or other reasons. Furthermore, the new philosophies of the century derived very commonly from a Christian atmosphere: their doctrines often ran closely parallel to the Christian, and some of them, indeed, purported to offer 'the true Christianity' or 'a new Christianity'.

13

The principal arguments advanced by the nineteenth-century doubters and unbelievers are well known, and a fairly brief summary may thus suffice. One may remark first the grounds for rejecting the dogma of the literal inerrancy of the Bible. Geology, the study of fossils, and the work of Laplace, Lamarck, and, later, Darwin, all reveal that the world is far older than the six thousand years or so calculated from the Bible narrative: it follows that the Bible cannot be literally infallible—unless, of course, one shares the view held by Cuvier amongst others that God has given the rocks and fossils the appearance of great age in order to test our faith. Again, if biologists are correct in alleging that man has evolved from the animals, the Creation story of Genesis must be historically false. Biblical scholars and philologists likewise point to inaccuracies, absurdities, and contradictions in the Scriptures and call even Christ's 'inerrancy' into question: for example in Mark XII He appeals to Psalm CX as the word of David, whereas it can now be shown that David was not its author. Again, if the story of the Flood is literally true, how is it that beasts which cannot swim or fly are found in the Americas, and whence jumped the kangaroos of Australia, unknown in the Old World? Historians in their turn claim that, by ordinary academic criteria, there is quite inadequate independent evidence for the Gospel stories, nor, some of them add, is there any sign of Divine Providence at work in human history: natural explanations are wholly sufficient. The study of other religions, moreover, reveals the frequency of miraculous events parallel to those recounted in the Gospels—virgin births, resurrections, ascensions. If these be true, what becomes of the uniqueness of Christianity? If these be false, the mere product of man's myth-making proclivity, may not the Gospel narratives be of similar origin?

The English Protestant in the twentieth century who has long since abandoned any belief in the literal infallibility of the Bible may be puzzled that such considerations as these should have seemed so deadly to religion or that works like D. F. Strauss's *Life of Jesus* (1835), rendered into French by Littré and into English by George Eliot, Lyell's *Antiquity of Man* (1863), and the Oxford *Essays and Reviews* (1860) should have created so much concern.

But in nineteenth-century Europe this belief was shared by Protestants and Catholics alike; for example, only in 1864 did the British Privy Council decide (in the case of Dr. Williams and Dr. Wilson) that the Anglican clergy were not obliged to hold or teach it.

The cases of Renan and Scherer, amongst many others, well illustrate the centrality this biblical fundamentalism had for nineteenth-century Christians. Edmond Scherer (1815–89) began his career as a dogmatic Calvinist. He read theology at Strasbourg, completed his doctoral thesis—on *La Dogmatique de l'Église réformée*—in 1843, obtained a Chair at the Neo-Calvinist École Libre de Théologie at Geneva in 1845 and eventually became Professor of Biblical Exegesis there. His teaching was particularly strict in its emphasis on the plenary inspiration of the Bible— ironically, in view of what was to happen. For from 1848 his doubts on just this dogma began to grow, and by the end of 1849 he felt obliged to resign. He now believed that errors and contradictions abound even in the New Testament, and that as an historical document it has all the marks of human fallibility, nor, he argues, does it ever claim to be inspired. For a time he remained an orthodox believer on every other point and continued to give free, independent lectures on theology for the next ten years, years during which he was allied with the Liberal *Revue de théologie* founded in 1850 by Colani, Pressensé, and others. Faith in Christ Himself is untouched by science and scholarship, Scherer maintains, and the Gospel has its true centre not in infallible history but in 'the person and character of Jesus Christ'; '[l'Évangile] régénère l'homme en le plaçant dans l'atmosphère spirituelle de la confiance, de la liberté et de l'amour.' [1] Yet gradually fresh doubts—about the existence of free will and the supernatural— forced him still farther from Christianity, and by 1861, when he wrote on Hegel in the *Revue des Deux Mondes*, he seems to have concluded that Christianity is irreconcilable with his belief that all our knowledge is relative. Recalling the death of Pan, he sadly acknowledges 'la fin d'un autre âge, le dernier

[1] 'De l'inspiration de l'écriture' (1853), *Mélanges de critique religieuse*, Cherbuliez, 1860, p. 34.

soupir d'un autre dieu'; 'l'absolu est mort dans les âmes, et qui le ressuscitera?'[1]

Looking back, he himself can recognize that the decisive step was taken in 1849, for it was then that he rejected all possibility of absolute knowledge, of that absolute for which man 'thirsts' just as he 'thirsts for the infinite'. The 'revolution' in religious thought (he writes in 1851) 'n'est pas seulement dans la méthode et dans l'argumentation, elle est dans le fond des choses, dans la conception théologique même'. 'La crise de la foi' lies in 'un ébranlement de la foi d'autorité'—for the Protestant, the authority of the Bible. He who had earlier opposed free examination now argues: 'La raison et le sentiment religieux de l'homme sont devenus la règle et le juge souverain de l'appréciation en matière de foi.'[2] And this consecration of the individual judgement and the rejection of all other authority become the starting-point for his progress towards universal relativism. Well might he assert that the study of the Bible, apparently so innocent and legitimate, is 'le dissolvant le plus actif de la croyance'![3]

A parallel and still more celebrated example on the side of Catholicism is offered by Ernest Renan (1823–92). A Breton, born into a deeply religious environment, he entered his first seminary in 1838 to train for holy orders. Within a few years, whilst at the seminary at Issy, he began to be troubled by philosophical doubts concerning the reality of the supernatural. In 1843 he moved to Saint-Sulpice, and here he received his first training in philology and biblical scholarship. The following year he learned German and began to read in the original such scholars as Strauss. By October 1845 he had abandoned his faith, left Saint-Sulpice and broken with the Church. As with Scherer, the decisive issue was the literal infallibility of the Scriptures. He cannot accept this tenet, yet he is convinced that it is an essential part of Catholic belief. His *Souvenirs d'enfance et de jeunesse* provide a lucid, if sometimes rather romantic commentary on this crisis:

[1] 'Hegel et l'hégélianisme', *R.D.M.*, 15.2.1861, p. 855. For a summary of his argument on free-will, cf. *Mélanges de critique religieuse*, pp. 106–7; the ideas here were first advanced in an article of 1853, 'Du péché'.
[2] 'La Crise de la foi', ibid., pp. 3, 7–9.
[3] Cited by O. Gréard, *E. Scherer*, Hachette, 1890, p. 151.

Mon initiation aux études allemandes me mettait . . . dans la situation
la plus fausse; car, d'une part, elle me montrait l'impossibilité d'une
exégèse sans concessions; de l'autre, je voyais parfaitement que ces
messieurs de Saint-Sulpice avaient raison de ne pas faire de concessions,
puisqu'un seul aveu d'erreur ruine l'édifice de la vérité absolue et la
ravale au rang des autorités humaines, où chacun fait son choix, selon
son goût personnel. Dans un livre divin, en effet, tout est vrai, et, deux
contradictoires ne pouvant être vraies à la fois, il ne doit s'y trouver
aucune contradiction. . . .

But contradictions and errors abound in the Bible, Renan argues:
'il s'y trouve des fables, des légendes, des traces de composition
tout humaine'. And unfortunately no compromise is possible: 'Une
seule erreur prouve qu'une Église n'est pas infaillible; une seule
partie faible prouve qu'un livre n'est pas révélé.'[1] Hence he left the
Church, and he stresses that metaphysical doubts about the Trinity, the Incarnation, and other dogmas played no part in his deci-
sion. 'Mes raisons furent toutes de l'ordre philologique et critique;
elles ne furent nullement de l'ordre métaphysique, de l'ordre
politique, de l'ordre moral.'[2] For the rest of his career he will
approach the Bible, in works like his *Histoire des origines du christianisme* (7 vols., 1863–81)—the first volume being his notorious
Vie de Jésus—and his *Histoire du peuple d'Israël* (5 vols., 1887–93),
in the scientific, independent manner he would adopt for any
secular text.

Yet Renan's disclaimer about metaphysical questionings is misleading, for he brought to bear upon his philological study a philosophical belief that was an important factor in his loss of faith—
and that of many other intellectuals. Trained to be critical and
scientific—by his priestly teachers—he came to hold that only
scientifically verified knowledge could be acceptable to a modern
mind. The supernatural and the miraculous have never been thus
verified, he contends; on the contrary, many allegedly miraculous
events can now be explained scientifically, whilst reports of others
are the product of human superstition, error or, even, fallible eye-
sight. 'Ce n'est pas d'un raisonnement [he concludes], mais de

[1] *Souvenirs d'enfance et de jeunesse*, éd. 'Collection nouvelle', Calmann Lévy, s.d.,
pp. 256–7.   [2] ibid., p. 262.

17

tout l'ensemble des sciences modernes que sort cet immense résultat: Il n'y a pas de surnaturel.'[1] From this premiss followed his later interpretation of Christ as merely the greatest of 'the sons of men', his wholly naturalistic account of the Gospel events and his explanation of many of the miracles as illusions, deceits, or myths added by Christian tradition. 'Aucun des miracles dont les vieilles histoires sont remplies ne s'est passé dans des conditions scientifiques,' he says in the introduction to *La Vie de Jésus*.

Jusqu'à nouvel ordre, nous maintiendrons donc *ce principe de critique historique*, qu'un récit surnaturel ne peut être admis comme tel, qu'il implique *toujours* crédulité ou imposture, que le devoir de l'historien est de l'interpréter et de rechercher quelle part de vérité, quelle part d'erreur il peut recéler.[2]

And in the preface to a later edition he adds—revealing the priority of this philosophical bias over even his philological scruples: 'C'est parce qu'ils racontent des miracles que je dis: "Les Évangiles sont des légendes; ils peuvent contenir de l'histoire, mais certainement tout n'y est pas historique." '[3]

This philosophical belief was, of course, widespread in the nineteenth century, as it had been amongst the *philosophes* in the eighteenth. Religion deals essentially with the unobservable, and thus we can never *know* whether it is true or false—'for knowledge is of things we see'. Some positivists—John Stuart Mill, Comte, Spencer, for example—held that we can form our own *beliefs* and themselves suggested that the existence of God may be more probable than not. Others, like Littré, held that even beliefs about the unobservable are philosophically 'meaningless', since, as twentieth-century logical positivists were to put it, the meaning of a proposition is the means of its verification; if it cannot be verified, it cannot, on this definition, have meaning. Two other philosophical arguments were also relevant. First, the so-called metaphysical proofs of God's existence are logically unsound. Secondly, the order and regularity found by the scientific study of nature

[1] *L'Avenir de la science—Pensées de 1848*, 23e éd., Calmann Lévy, 1929, p. 47.
[2] *La Vie de Jésus*, 24e éd., Calmann Lévy, 1895, p. xcv and p. xcviii, my italics.
[3] ibid., p. vi.

makes the occurrence of miracles highly improbable: there seems to be no place for supernatural intervention in a world that is apparently ruled by natural laws.

The belief that religion is unscientific and therefore unworthy of credence affected many minds, but still more powerful in their effect were ethical considerations. Although many historians have given greater stress to the scientific, philological, and philosophical grounds for unbelief, moral rejection of Christianity appears to have been in fact primary for all but professional philosophers. The ethical arguments fall under three headings. First, certain Christian doctrines are immoral—notably, the dogma of eternal punishment in Hell for those who are not saved, and also the substitutionary theory of the Atonement, which holds that Christ died in order to satisfy God's inexorable demand that human sin be punished—even if 'the price of cancelled sin' be paid by an innocent substitute. Both doctrines offended against the contemporary rejection, in legal and moral thought alike, of punishment that is wholly retributive and not also reformative; both rest upon an ethically repugnant conception of God as a Shylock demanding his 'pound of flesh', without mercy, willing that the innocent (whether Christ on the Cross or unbaptized babies in Hell) should suffer although they are guiltless. For Catholics the moral challenge here may be softened by the Roman rejection of the still more savage doctrine of Election and by the idea of a Purgatory where all may yet win their way to Heaven, but it cannot wholly be avoided. Amongst doubters it was often an insuperable difficulty—as witness both Romantic and Parnassian writers. Implicit in Vigny's *La Femme Adultère* and *Le Déluge*, moral questioning of God is explicit in *Le Mont des Oliviers* and, as early as 1821, in *La Prison*, whilst in *Stello* he expresses his horror at Joseph de Maistre's treatment of the problem of suffering.[1] Musset, though more wistful about his doubts, is no less trenchant:

> Mon juge est un bourreau qui trompe sa victime. . . .
> (*L'Espoir en Dieu*)

whilst of the Catholic Church he declaims:

[1] *Stello*, ch. xxxi and xxxii.

Quelle pagode ils font de leur Dieu de vengeance!
Quel bourreau rancunier, brûlant à petit feu!
Toujours la peur du feu.—C'est bien l'esprit de Rome.[1]

Lamartine likewise rejected the Christian doctrine of Hell, and Michelet in later life opposed the Church on primarily moral grounds: its teaching on the fate of children who die without baptism is immoral; its distinction of saved and damned is a blasphemy against God's goodness; and its doctrine of original sin a blasphemy against childhood.[2] About the same time Leconte de Lisle, in such a poem as *La Vision de Snorr*, satirizes the barbarity of Christian teaching about Hell, whilst in *Le Nazaréen* Christ on the Cross is seen in the same light as in Vigny's *Mont des Oliviers*:

Plein d'angoisse, il cria vers les sourdes nuées.

Eternal punishment is the more revolting, poets and thinkers alike submit, in that man is not wholly responsible for his acts. He is determined, be it by those forces of heredity and environment that psychologists and sociologists were beginning to study, be it by those 'fatal' impulses of passion and desire of which the Romantics felt themselves a prey. It was this scepticism as to man's free-will that led Scherer, for example, still further from Christian belief. In an article 'Du péché' (1853), he points out that if the Christian idea of the Fall is true and sin is inherited, then the individual's freedom is considerably diminished—and sin can no longer be rightly called sin at all. And, apart from this theological consideration, he comes to think that free-will is 'l'inévitable *illusion* de la conscience du moi'.[3] Vigny developed a parallel theory in *Satan Sauvé*: God has created us with physical needs that lead us to crime—for which He, not we or Satan, is to blame;

Un mal universel accable la nature,
Une douleur profonde est dans la créature . . .
Tout se débat en vain dans la chaîne de fer
Dont un seul a lié le ciel, l'homme et l'enfer.

---

[1] *La Coupe et les lèvres*, acte iv, sc. 1, in Musset, *Poésies complètes*, Gallimard, 1957, p. 186.
[2] Cf. G. Monod, *Les Maîtres de l'histoire—Renan, Taine, Michelet*, Calmann Lévy, 1894, p. 246.   [3] *Mélanges de critique religieuse*, pp. 106–7, my italics.

Yet again, Leconte de Lisle, in *La Fin de l'Homme*, with heavy irony makes Adam say:

> Et maintenant, Seigneur, vous par qui j'ai dû naître,
> Grâce! Je me repens du crime d'être né . . .
> Seigneur, je suis vaincu, que je sois pardonné!

It is not only the Christian doctrines that clash with our higher moral notions: the world itself is far from evidencing the alleged goodness of its Creator. The signs of divine bounty to which Rousseau, Bernardin de Saint-Pierre, and Chateaubriand appealed are more than matched by Nature's cruelty and impassivity: disease kills or maims the innocent; children and animals, guiltless of sin, die in pain; creature preys on fellow creature. Nature, 'red in tooth and claw', suggests a divine tyrant rather than a loving Father.

> On me dit une mère, et je suis une tombe,

writes Vigny, echoed by Leconte de Lisle, Louise Ackermann, Sully Prudhomme, and others later. Vigny even instances our religious doubts as evidence of God's malevolence: Christ in the Garden prays for certainty—

> Mais le ciel reste noir, et Dieu ne répond pas.
> (*Le Mont des Oliviers*)

The human condition, he submits in the same poem, is bounded by 'mal et doute':

> Mal et Doute! . . .
>   . . . C'est l'accusation
> Qui pèse de partout sur la création!

Darwin's *Origin of Species* (1859) rendered this 'problem of evil' still more acute, but it certainly did not originate with him. Even on the scientific level, Lamarck, years before, had presented hardly less oppressive a picture. Sainte-Beuve's Amaury, in *Volupté*, sums up the French biologist's outlook, as given in his lectures, by saying:

La nature, à ses yeux, c'était la pierre et la cendre, le granit de la tombe, la mort! La vie n'y intervenait que comme un accident étrange et singulièrement industrieux, une lutte prolongée, avec plus ou moins de succès et d'équilibre çà et là, mais toujours finalement vaincue; l'immobilité froide était régnante après comme devant.[1]

Finally, the political, social, and moral practice of the Christian Churches—and especially the Roman Church—was alleged to be no less immoral than their doctrines. Intolerant and absolutist, corrupt, worldly and intriguing, socially apathetic except in support of the monarchy and aristocracy, preoccupied with the observance of rites and dogmas rather than with the spirit of Christian charity: these were the charges made by social reformers, Romantic and Parnassian poets, positivist and eclectic philosophers, and historians like Michelet and Quinet. A recent historian of 'social Catholicism' before 1870 has concluded that, with a minority of honourable exceptions, French Catholics ignored the sufferings brought by the Industrial Revolution:

la plupart des catholiques français ne comprennent pas ou ne veulent pas comprendre l'intérêt prépondérant qu'il y aurait pour l'Église de France à regagner la classe ouvrière en participant à ses tentatives d'émancipation.[2]

The Church's alliance with conservatism seemed to socially conscious thinkers one of its most damning characteristics. So strong was this hatred of 'la bête écarlate', indeed, that much of the rejection of Christianity was in reality a rejection of the Catholic Church. Some observers—more logically—drew a sharp distinction between Roman teaching and practice and the 'true', 'pure' religion of Christ Himself. Almost every writer of liberal political and social sympathies came to oppose Catholicism, stirred into antagonism by such Papal acts as the brutal suppression of political liberalism in the Vatican States in the 1830's as well as its intolerant practices and teaching in France itself. Nor was this antagonism softened by that doctrinal intransigence of Rome which was to reach its culmination in the *Syllabus* of 1864 and the declaration of Papal infallibility in 1870. The French free-thinker might look

---

[1] *Volupté*, Garnier, s.d., pp. 134–5.
[2] J. B. Duroselle, *Les Débuts du catholicisme social en France (1822–70)*, P.U.F., 1951, p. 702.

wistfully at the Non-conformists and Quakers of Britain or the Lutherans in Germany, but he was forced by his national situation into opposing all organized Christianity.

Such were the principal sources of unbelief which the science of the later nineteenth century only served to renew. Darwinism not only demoted man to the status of an animal, denying his pretensions to be God's special preoccupation, and running counter to the Creation story given in Genesis. It illustrated yet further the cruelty of Nature, and also its wastage and inefficiency. Equally, it greatly weakened the argument from Design, already undermined philosophically by Hume and Kant: human and animal adaptation to environment results not from divine planning but from the age-long, ruthless process of the survival of the best adapted. Physiological and psychological studies indicated another line of attack: mind and body are so intimately connected that it is impossible to believe either that man has a soul (which has never, in any case, been observed) or that this soul could survive bodily death.

Persuasive Christian replies to all these objections have not been lacking, especially in our own century. But for an English Protestant it is one of the tragedies of the nineteenth-century French scene that the Catholic response to this intellectual challenge was less an attempt at reasoned argument than ecclesiastical repression and bitter abuse at the level of journalists such as Veuillot. An honest doubter like Quinet, distressed by German biblical criticism, could only note, in 1842, that the Catholics still talked of Voltaire, Locke, and Reid instead of this living difficulty.[1] In 1845 Renan writes plaintively to the Abbé Cognat, a few weeks before his final break:

Ah! si j'étais né protestant en Allemagne! . . . Là était ma place. Herder a bien été évêque, et certes il n'était que chrétien; mais, dans le

---

[1] *La Controverse nouvelle* (1842), in *Les Jésuites, etc.*, Pagnerre, 1857, p. 334. This charge is confirmed by a recent Catholic historian, Jean Leflon (*Histoire de l'église*, t. xx, *La Crise révolutionnaire, 1789–1846*, Bloud et Gay, 1949, pp. 362–3): 'Jusqu'en 1842, la France ne possède aucune école de hautes études ecclésiastiques. . . . On continue à rompre des lances avec les jansénistes, les quiétistes, les philosophes du XVIIIᵉ siècle: on pourfend les vieilles erreurs; on résout les anciens problèmes, sans se douter que l'évolution historique en offre de plus redoutables.'

catholicisme, il faut être orthodoxe. C'est une barre de fer; il n'entend pas raison.[1]

It is doubtful if even the 'Liberal Catholic' thought of this and the following decade—in men like Montalembert—rendered this situation less agonizing, whilst from the *Syllabus* of 1864 the Roman Church was firmly set for the rest of the century, excepting only the brief period of the *Ralliement*, on the road of suppression rather than discussion. Such a policy could hardly fail to strengthen the view that a rational mind can never accept Catholicism. Many of the best and most humane thinkers of the century were forced into opposition to Christianity. Who shall say if the consequences of this unhappy severance have even yet fully worked themselves out in French intellectual and political life?

2. *The Religious Aspirations of Nineteenth-Century Doubters*

Non-Christian, anti-Catholic though many nineteenth-century secular thinkers might be, and often enthusiastic about the conquests of science, they were usually far from irreligious in their general attitude. It would be quite false to imagine that they were content with unbelief or unconcerned with the intellectual and emotional vacuum left by their rejection of the Christian faith. Isolated thinkers did not even concede that they had in fact rejected it; basically, nothing is changed, they argued. One must abandon a few outdated dogmas, a few primitive misconceptions, and effect a few 'translations' of religious 'myths' and 'symbols' into the intellectual language of the modern age, but nothing 'essential' need be jettisoned. D. F. Strauss himself took this view, prefacing his *Life of Jesus* by saying, perhaps a little too suavely:

The author is aware that the essence of the Christian faith is perfectly independent of his criticism. . . . The supernatural birth of Christ, his miracles, his resurrection and ascension, remain eternal truths, whatever doubts may be cast on their reality as historical facts.[2]

In France, Catholic dominance made such a position far less com-

---

[1] *Souvenirs d'enfance et de jeunesse*, pp. 337–8.
[2] D. F. Strauss, *The Life of Jesus*, London, Chapman, 1846, 3 vols., vol. i, p. xi.

mon, but echoes of it are perhaps heard in certain 'natural religions'—that of Victor Cousin, for example, or of Lamartine.

Far more of the doubters openly abandoned Christianity, but did so with distressed reluctance. Regret for lost faith, the emptiness of religious scepticism: these are common themes in nineteenth-century writing, so much so that Sainte-Beuve—who himself sadly described, like Matthew Arnold in *Dover Beach*, the ebbing of the sea of faith—could allege that the 'conflict of mind and heart' in regard to religion became a fashionable pose in the mid-century years.[1] Gérard de Nerval once described himself as '[un] enfant d'un siècle sceptique plutôt qu'incrédule':[2] the phrase could be applied to many of his fellow writers.

> . . . Ma raison révoltée
> Essaie en vain de croire et mon cœur de douter—

thus Musset in often-quoted lines from *L'Espoir en Dieu* (1838), and earlier, in *Rolla* (1833), whilst disavowing belief, he had bitterly condemned the Voltaireans:

> Pour qui travailliez-vous, démolisseurs stupides,
> Lorsque vous disséquiez le Christ sur son autel?

Vigny was equally distressed by the intellectual uncertainty which afflicts humanity: man's doubts, we saw, are even a symptom of God's malevolence in his eyes. The Parnassians were hardly less sensitive, as witness Leconte de Lisle, well described as 'un athée obsédé de divin'.[3] We are, he declaims in *Dies Irae*,

> . . . consumés d'une impossible envie,
> En proie au mal de croire et d'aimer sans retour;

and he despairingly asks:

> Où sont les Dieux promis, les formes idéales,
> Les grands cultes de pourpre et de gloire vêtus?

His friend Ménard, Sully Prudhomme, and Louise Ackermann, amongst other Parnassians, shared his concern. However confirmed

[1] *Nouveaux lundis*, Michel Lévy, 1863–70, 13 vols., v. 14.
[2] *Les Filles du feu*, Champion, 1931, 2 vols., i. 290.
[3] P. Flottes, *Leconte de Lisle, l'homme et l'œuvre*, Hatier-Boivin, 1954, p. 129. Cf. H. Elsenberg, *Le Sentiment religieux chez Leconte de Lisle*, Jouve, 1909.

a positivist, the poetess feels that, in losing Christian faith, 'nous avons tout perdu';

> Nous restons sans espoir, sans recours, sans asile,
> Tandis qu'obstinément le Désir qu'on exile
> Revient errer autour du gouffre défendu.[1]

'Mon doute insulte en moi le Dieu de mes désirs,' cries Sully Prud-homme, and Ménard, even amidst his youthful enthusiasm for science, deplores the abandonment of belief that it seems to him to entail.[2] One can also recall, amongst the novelists of the same period, Flaubert, with his interest in Spinozist metaphysics and Spencer's 'unknowable', his preoccupation with Saint-Antoine, and his unexpectedly sympathetic portrayal of the religious ceremony witnessed by Bouvard and Pécuchet, whilst, still later, Pierre Loti regrets his failure to rediscover faith (*Jérusalem*) and declares the unique value of Christianity and its 'mythes adorables' (*Matelot*).

In more philosophical circles one finds a similar reaction—a saddened, earnest heart-searching as Christian belief yields (in a characteristic phrase of Scherer's) to 'cet empire absolu qu'exerce le vrai sur les esprits honnêtes'. And Scherer adds, thinking of men like Colenso: 'Si l'essence de la religion est le juste et le vrai, on peut dire que les hommes dont nous parlons deviennent incré-dules par dévouement à la religion même. . . . Tel est le spectacle vraiment tragique auquel assiste le XIXᵉ siècle!'[3] Renan's *Souvenirs d'enfance et de jeunesse* testify to a parallel unhappiness, and so, too, does the case of Théodore Jouffroy (1796–1842). Jouffroy, one of the most independent of Cousin's colleagues, was brought up as a Catholic, but lost his faith as a youth, and thereafter sought an alternative creed in eclectic philosophy. In a famous passage he describes a night at the École Normale when he was twenty, during which he realized the full extent of his scepticism. Renan, speaking of the students at his seminary at Issy in 1842, before his own break

---

[1] *Œuvres de Louise Ackermann—Ma vie; Premières poésies; Poésies philosophiques*, Lemerre, 1885, p. 92, *Le Positivisme*.

[2] R. F. A. Sully Prudhomme, *Œuvres—Poésies*, Lemerre, 1925-6, 6 vols., ii. 22 (*La Prière, Les Épreuves*); L. Ménard, *Poèmes et rêveries d'un païen mystique*, Librairie de l'Art indépendant, 1895, pp. 35-36 (*Prométhée délivré*, 1843).

[3] E. Scherer, 'Les Confessions d'un missionnaire' (1863), *Mélanges d'histoire religieuse*, 2ᵉ éd., Michel Lévy, 1865, pp. 275-6.

with the Church, tells us: 'Les belles pages de ce désespéré de la philosophie nous enivraient; je les savais par cœur.' [1] Jouffroy's words—words, one might say, of an agnostic Chateaubriand!— may be strange reading for seminarists but are worth quoting here, for they capture a widely shared nineteenth-century mood.

Je n'oublierai jamais la soirée de décembre où le voile qui me dérobait à moi-même ma propre incrédulité fut déchiré. J'entends encore mes pas dans cette chambre étroite et nue où longtemps après l'heure du sommeil j'avais coutume de me promener; je vois encore cette lune à demi voilée par les nuages, qui en éclairait par intervalle les froids carreaux. Les heures de la nuit s'écoulaient, et je ne m'en apercevais pas: je suivais avec anxiété ma pensée qui de couche en couche descendait vers le fond de ma conscience, et, dissipant l'une après l'autre toutes les illusions qui m'en avaient jusque-là dérobé la vue, m'en rendait de moment en moment les détours plus visibles.

En vain je m'attachais à ces croyances dernières comme un naufragé aux débris de son navire; en vain, épouvanté du vide inconnu dans lequel j'allais flotter, je me rejetais pour la dernière fois avec elles vers mon enfance, ma famille, mon pays, tout ce qui m'était cher et sacré· l'inflexible courant de ma pensée était plus fort; parents, famille, souvenirs, croyances, il m'obligeait à tout laisser; l'examen se poursuivait plus obstiné et plus sévère à mesure qu'il approchait du terme, et il ne s'arrêta que quand il l'eut atteint. Je sus alors qu'au fond de moi-même il n'y avait plus rien qui fût debout.

Ce moment fut affreux; et quand vers le matin je me jetai épuisé sur mon lit, il me sembla sentir ma première vie, si riante et si pleine, s'éteindre, et derrière moi s'en ouvrir une autre sombre et dépeuplée, où désormais j'allais vivre seul, seul avec ma fatale pensée qui venait de m'y exiler et que j'étais tenté de maudire. Les jours qui suivirent cette découverte furent les plus tristes de ma vie. . . .

. . . J'étais incrédule, mais je détestais l'incrédulité; ce fut là ce qui décida de la direction de ma vie. Ne pouvant supporter l'incertitude sur l'énigme de la destinée humaine, n'ayant plus la lumière de la foi pour la résoudre, il ne me restait que les lumières de la raison pour y pourvoir. [2]

---

[1] *Souvenirs d'enfance et de jeunesse*, p. 217.
[2] 'De l'organisation des sciences philosophiques—Deuxième partie', *Nouveaux mélanges philosophiques*, 3e éd., Hachette, 1872, pp. 83–85. On the controversy aroused by this and similar passages, cf. J. Pommier, *Deux études sur Jouffroy et son temps*, Alcan, 1930.

This final paragraph, too, is characteristic: faith has gone but the concern with the 'enigma of human destiny' remains, and the desire for a unifying philosophy. Nineteenth-century thinkers were, in general, keenly aware of both the moral and social utility and the private consolations of religious or at least philosophical belief. Émile Durkheim's acknowledgement of the social value of religions and William James's belief in their psychological value were foreshadowed throughout the century. Cousin, for example, in this at one with Catholics and social reformers alike, can assert: 'Dans toute époque du monde la religion est le fond moral de cette époque; c'est la religion qui en fait les croyances générales, et par là les mœurs, et par là encore, jusqu'à un certain point, les institutions.' [1] For social reformers like the Saint-Simonians, Comte, Pierre Leroux, and Étienne Cabet, as for the revolution-aries before them, religion was prized as a cult to spur the masses in society to moral action. As already remarked, they, like tradi-tionalist Catholics such as Maistre and Bonald and eclectics such as Cousin, saw the chaos and horror of the Revolution as warnings against irreligion. They also recognized our personal need for belief, what they interpreted as 'the desires of the *heart*', of the emotions rather than of man's other faculties, and this view was repeated by numerous writers of the age—sometimes, it is fair to add, with a truer 'inwardness' and reverence for the spiritual than most of the reformers manifested. Very few were happy with what Musset calls 'the sterile milk of impiety'; very few were merely hard-headed, scientifically minded and unemotional materialists.

This is witnessed at the most basic level by the widespread, al-most platitudinous respect for 'the religious sentiment' in man, the sense of reverence, awe, and elevation as he surveys the wonders of Nature or broods upon himself and his destiny. Religion, thinks Saint-Simon, has existed since man first distinguished between cause and effect. Michelet believes it is born 'presque toujours d'un vrai besoin du cœur', whilst Leroux declares: 'L'homme a un besoin naturel de religion et de culte, et . . . il est religieux parce qu'il est raisonnable.' 'Il ne faut . . . pas chercher à éteindre la

[1] *Cours de l'histoire de la philosophie moderne*, 2ᵉ série, t. ii, Didier et Ladrange, 1847, p. 85.

métaphysique ou le sentiment religieux de l'homme, mais l'éclairer et le faire monter plus haut,' claims Claude Bernard. For Renan, 'ce qui est de l'humanité, ce qui par conséquent sera éternel comme elle, c'est le besoin religieux, la faculté religieuse'.[1] And although this view—at once a product and an axiom of the historical study of religions developed by the *philologues* during the century—might not commit these thinkers to any detailed creed, it nevertheless represented a distinct warming towards religion compared with the earlier outlook of Holbach or Helvétius.

Three examples may serve to illustrate further this revised attitude. Benjamin Constant (1767–1830) is better known as a novelist but was preoccupied throughout his life with religious thought. He first planned his book on Roman polytheism as a youth, though it was only to be published in 1833, after his death, and his original intention was to show, following Helvétius, that pagan religion is superior to Christianity. But over the next twenty-five years, during which he worked spasmodically at it, the book underwent a marked change. Its author, Constant writes to a friend in 1811, was no longer 'ce philosophe intrépide, sûr qu'il n'y a rien après ce monde, et tellement content de ce monde qu'il se réjouit de ce qu'il n'y en a pas d'autre'. He now feels that 'un peu de science mène à l'athéisme, et plus de science à la religion', and he expresses his surprise at Holbach's 'inexplicable thirst for destruction'.[2] By 1804 at the latest he had started a second and more influential work, *De la religion considérée dans sa source, ses formes et ses développements*, a book stimulated by his contacts with German religious scholars and partly written in Göttingen, and eventually published in five volumes from 1824 to 1831.

Constant attacks three positions in particular: the view that religion is mere superstition; the idea, found especially in 'natural religions', that religion can be based primarily upon reason; and the ecclesiastical assertion that dogmas are given by divine revelation and are thus rightly enforced by Church authority upon

---

[1] H. de Saint-Simon, *Œuvres choisies*, ed. Lemonnier, Brussels, Van Meenen, 1859, 3 vols., i. 205; J. Michelet, *La Bible de l'humanité*, Flammarion, s.d., p. 45; P. Leroux, *D'une religion nationale*, nouv. éd., Boussac, 1846, pp. 23–24; C. Bernard, *Pensées, Notes détachées*, Baillière, 1937, p. 64; E. Renan, *L'Avenir de la science*, p. 483.

[2] B. Constant, *Œuvres*, Gallimard, 1957, pp. 1645, 1404.

individual adherents. His arguments against the first two of these are most relevant here. His claim is that religion is 'a need of the soul', that religious belief stems from a 'religious sentiment' possessed by every man, 'indestructible', 'a fundamental law of his nature', 'universal', distinguishing man from the animals. For the sake of religion, man, throughout the ages, 's'interdit le plaisir, abjure l'amour, se précipite dans les souffrances et dans la mort'. In the face of the universality of this feeling, Constant asks, can we believe that it is only 'une grande erreur'? [1] Against those who argue that man is religious because of a superstitious fear of the world around him, he points out that animals also feel terror of the unknown and are yet not religious: man's very fear of the 'occult powers' is a symptom of his innate religious awareness. It is also an error, he continues, to seek the 'origin' of religion—or of society and language, likewise—for to do so assumes wrongly that men once existed without these things: in reality, all three are 'inhérents à l'homme'. 'L'homme n'est pas religieux parce qu'il est timide; il est religieux parce qu'il est homme.' [2] Man may have become 'maître de la nature visible et bornée', but we all thirst from time to time for 'une nature invisible et sans bornes'; 'dans le silence de la nuit, sur les bords de la mer, dans la solitude des campagnes' the individual forgets himself, feels himself 'entraîné dans les flots d'une contemplation vague, et plongé dans un océan de pensées nouvelles, désintéressées, sans rapport avec les combinaisons étroites de cette vie'. Thus he concludes:

le sentiment religieux est la réponse à ce cri de l'âme que nul ne fait taire, à cet élan vers l'inconnu, vers l'infini, que nul ne parvient à dompter entièrement, de quelques distractions qu'il s'entoure, avec quelque habileté qu'il s'étourdisse ou qu'il se dégrade. [3]

Churches and their dogmas, rituals and ceremonies are, by comparison, of minor importance—'des formes que prend le sentiment intérieur et qu'il brise ensuite'. Man is his own best priest. [4] Not that religious institutions and rites are superfluous; but they are essentially 'variable and transitory', and they become evil

---

[1] Constant, *Œuvres*, pp. 1420, 1400–1.
[2] ibid., pp. 1407, 1410.   [3] ibid., pp. 1413, 1415.   [4] ibid., pp. 1405–6.

when religious castes seek to prolong their life, giving them 'un caractère dogmatique et stationnaire qui refuse de suivre l'intelligence dans ses découvertes, et l'âme dans ses émotions que chaque jour rend plus épurées et plus délicates'. This leads to persecution of unbelievers, and they in their turn become more fanatical and extreme than they would wish and appear to attack the religious feeling itself, whereas their opposition is really only to a now outdated religious form.[1]

Madame de Staël (1766–1817), friend of Constant, and bred like him in the intellectual environment of the *philosophes*, shared his religious preoccupation. In the final Part of *De l'Allemagne* (1810), most famously, she offers an account of contemporary German views on religion and 'enthusiasm', views which she shared. Feeling is the heart of religion, she claims: 'c'est au sentiment de l'infini que la plupart des écrivains allemands rapportent toutes les idées religieuses'. This 'sentiment' is 'positive and creative' and 'the true attribute of the soul', and it is also the source of our aesthetic delight and of 'all our sacrifices of self-interest'. Her description of its birth could have been signed by Constant and the Romantics alike:

Quand nous contemplons le ciel étoilé, où des étincelles de lumière sont des univers comme le nôtre, . . . notre pensée se perd dans l'infini, notre cœur bat pour l'inconnu, pour l'immense, et nous sentons que ce n'est qu'au delà des expériences terrestres que notre véritable vie doit commencer.

At such moments, she adds, the divine lives in us: 'l'enthousiasme signifie *Dieu en nous*'; 'quand l'existence de l'homme est expansive, elle a quelque chose de divin'.[2]

With Constant and Madame de Staël, indeed, we are in that tradition of religious thought which ran from the *Profession de foi* of Rousseau's Vicaire Savoyard and Bernardin de Saint-Pierre's *Études de la nature*, through several of the Revolutionary cults and the occultists of the turn of the century, through (in more Catholic channels) the apologetic works of Chateaubriand, to almost every

---

[1] ibid., pp. 1411, 1419, 1421–2.
[2] *De l'Allemagne*, nouv. éd., Garnier, s.d., 2 vols., ii. 233–4, 295.

Romantic writer—Hugo, Musset, Lamartine, George Sand, most clearly—and beyond to thinkers like Renan. The main elements of this tradition are seen even in *La Vie de Jésus*, as when Renan writes in one of its *Préfaces*:

Fausses quand elles essayent de prouver l'infini, de le déterminer, de l'incarner, si j'ose le dire, les religions sont vraies quand elles l'affirment ... Le dernier des simples, pourvu qu'il pratique le culte du cœur, est plus éclairé sur la réalité des choses que le matérialiste qui croit tout expliquer par le hasard et le fini.[1]

The affirmation of the infinite; the denial that dogmas can fully encompass this infinite; the emphasis upon the 'heart' as the best guide for the religious life—these were assertions shared by all these writers, as studies, often critical, of the 'religion of the Romantics' have made abundantly clear.[2] 'La croyance en Dieu est innée en moi; le dogme et la pratique me sont impossibles...'[3] Here is an affirmation, made by Musset in 1840, that was characteristic of them all, and whilst orthodox Christians may regret its second part, it is important not to overlook the genuine turning to religion embodied in the first.

A final example may be found in Edgar Quinet (1803–75), historian, epic poet, ardent Republican (who found exile in Belgium and Switzerland during the Second Empire), and scholar under German influence of ancient civilizations. Here again one meets an uneasy division between religious aspiration and doubt as to many of the traditional doctrines of Christianity. Quinet is convinced that every aspect of life in any society is determined by its religion and that the history of religions is the central thread of man's development over the ages; from religion derive, 'comme autant de conséquences nécessaires, les institutions politiques, les arts, la poésie, la philosophie, et, jusqu'à un certain point, la suite même des événements'. Man, he urges, 'poursuit l'infini d'une poursuite éternelle, changeant de temple, de sanctuaire, de société, sans changer de désir'.[4] Hence one of his best-known

---

[1] *La Vie de Jésus*, p. xxxi.   [2] Cf. Bibliography, p. 221 below.
[3] Musset, *Lettre à la duchesse de Castries* (1840), *Correspondance* (1827–1857), Mercure de France, 1907, p. 177.
[4] *Le Génie des religions*, *Œuvres complètes*, Pagnerre, 1857–60, 12 vols., i. 12, 10.

works, *Le Génie des religions* (1842), traces the progress achieved in this religious 'pursuit' from its primitive origins, through the Chinese, Indian, Persian, Egyptian, Babylonian, and Hebrew religions, to the creeds of Greece and Rome. And just because he holds that religious belief is so all-directive in man's life, he is the more acutely aware of his own uncertainties. Even as he surveys these religions of the past, he will examine 'cette poussière divine' to find whether there remains 'quelque débris de vérité, de révélation universelle' which he might make his own.[1] Nor will he be satisfied with some 'compromise' creed based on reason alone, such as the theism of Voltaire, or with any of the metaphysical systems which claim to preserve religion's 'essentials' whilst offering in fact the mere intellectual shell of a religion. Thus he rejects emphatically the attempt of Hegel and Strauss to translate Christianity into abstract terms—'le Dieu tout personnel du crucifix' into 'le Dieu-Substance', the God of Jacob and St. Paul into the God of Parmenides, Descartes, and Spinoza—and to offer men 'un christianisme sans Christ'. He believes that genuine, 'existential' religion is being challenged above all in his day by German pantheism—a doctrine he detests for its subordination of human freedom to impersonal cosmic forces and its implicit deification of man, as well as for its intellectualism.[2] He is equally critical of Kant's *Religion within the Limits of Pure Reason* (1793), even though he admires its stress upon morality. Reviewing it in 1841, he writes: 'Dès les premiers mots du livre, vous mesurez tous les ravages du scepticisme, l'homme sans Dieu ...'; true spirituality is replaced by 'l'orgueil d'une bonne conscience'; God, instead of being 'le principe, la source de vie', becomes merely 'la conséquence, le corollaire et le terme des choses'.[3] Quinet will reject these masquerading philosophical substitutes. 'Je ne suis point de ceux [he tartly declares] qu'une formule métaphysique console de toutes les ruines.' Rather will he hope for a rebirth of authentic religion, for 'l'éclair qui doit tout éblouir, et ramener la paix que le monde a perdue'.[4]

---

[1] ibid., i. 13.   [2] 'Examen de la Vie de Jésus' (1838), ibid., iii. 345–7.
[3] 'Lettre sur Kant' (1841), ibid., x. 291–2.
[4] 'Examen de la Vie de Jésus', ibid., iii. 287, and *Le Génie des religions*, ibid., i. 14.

Side by side with scepticism, in fact, there thrived the idea that the nineteenth century was a time of philosophical upheaval from which a new creed would emerge. It might be a revised form of Christianity, as attempted earlier by Rousseau's *Profession de foi*, or as announced by Lessing in his *Education of the Human Race* (1785) —a book that was to be a 'bible' of the Saint-Simonians. Others foresaw the coming of a new religion—Chateaubriand in his *Essai sur les révolutions* (1797) and Madame de Staël in *De l'Allemagne* (1810). Yet others looked for either possibility, like Joseph de Maistre, who in 1796 predicted that 'either a new religion is about to be formed or Christianity will be rejuvenated in some extraordinary fashion'.[1] But whatever the prediction, this generation, like most others, felt itself at a turning-point in intellectual history. Stendhal's Bishop of Besançon in *Le Rouge et le noir* is reiterating an almost commonplace comparison when he remarks: 'La fin du paganisme était accompagnée de cet état d'inquiétude et de doute qui, au dix-neuvième siècle, désole les esprits tristes et ennuyés.'[2] Quinet even draws a parallel with the disciples' state of mind after Christ's Crucifixion and concludes:

Aujourd'hui le monde entier est le grand sépulcre où toutes les croyances, comme toutes les espérances, semblent pour jamais ensevelies. . . . Mais . . . du sein de nos ténèbres, le Dieu éternellement ancien, éternellement nouveau, renaîtra vêtu d'une lumière plus vive que celle du Thabor.[3]

Later too, in 1857, Poitou stresses the urgency with which religious questions are being discussed: 'nous sommes entrés dans une époque de crise, de transformation ou de rénovation religieuse'.[4] The same sense of impending revival is no less marked in social thinkers. Leroux, hailing the 'second Renaissance'—the discovery of Oriental civilization—claims it will achieve 'la destruction du christianisme en faveur d'une religion nouvelle'.[5] George Sand

---

[1] *Considérations sur la France*, nouv. éd., Lyon and Paris, Pélagaud, 1862, p. 73.
[2] *Le Rouge et le noir*, ch. xxix.   [3] 'Examen de la Vie de Jésus', op. cit., iii. 352.
[4] E. Poitou, *Les Philosophes français contemporains et leurs systèmes religieux*, 2ᵉ éd., Charpentier, 1864, p. i (1ᵉʳᵉ éd., Durand, 1857). A good parallel case on the rationalist side is offered by F. Huet, *La Révolution religieuse au dix-neuvième siècle*, Michel Lévy, 1868; the old philosophies are also disintegrating, he adds (pp. 305-6 and *passim*.).
[5] Cited by R. Schwab, *La Renaissance orientale*, Payot, 1950, p. 260.

declares that, following the ruin of Catholicism, 'une philosophie nouvelle, une foi plus pure et plus éclairée, va se lever à l'horizon',[1] whilst Hugo, in the preface to *Les Feuilles d'automne* (1831), describes a similar scene: '. . . au dehors comme au dedans, les croyances en lutte, les consciences en travail; de nouvelles religions . . .; les vieilles religions qui font peau neuve . . .' Saint-Simon, Comte, and numerous other enthusiasts of progress likewise felt they were on the brink of a new age of synthesis, of the final epoch of history. 'La société a besoin [writes an observer in 1828] d'une doctrine nouvelle ou renouvelée, d'une philosophie ou d'une religion, qui, remplaçant dans les consciences une foi qui n'y fait plus rien . . . apportent aux âmes une moralité dont elles ne sauraient se passer longtemps.'[2]

These hopes and predictions were not to be disappointed. The nineteenth-century reader was offered a rich assortment of alternative creeds, motivated now by thoughts of social utility, now by a genuine spiritual yearning, and the rising interest in religion was manifested in many ways: the keen curiosity about Catholicism aroused in the 1830's by apologists like Lacordaire, whose lectures packed Notre-Dame to overflowing; amongst the intellectually minded, enthusiasm for the metaphysical constructions of Spinoza, Hegel, and other German philosophers; amongst the less intellectually minded, the spread of occultism and a profusion of minor religious leaders and sects, from the religion of the 'Mapah' and the Église Française of the Abbé Châtel to the 'little religions of Paris' studied at the very end of the century by Jules Bois;[3] equally marked, the expansion of freemasonry; amongst educated readers of both rational and mystical bents, a ready interest in studies of non-Christian religions. Some of these diverse substitutes for Christianity conceived of religion as basically, in Matthew Arnold's words, 'morality touched with emotion', others were more metaphysical in emphasis; some lavishly incorporated occultist and quasi-mystical elements, others were more spartan. But almost all were united in claiming the term 'religion'

[1] *Lélia*, Calmann Lévy, s.d., 2 vols., ii. 156.

[2] P. Damiron, *Essai sur l'histoire de la philosophie en France au XIXᵉ siècle*, 3ᵉ éd., Hachette, 1834, 2 vols., ii. 78.

[2] J. Bois, *Les Petites Religions de Paris*, Chailley, 1894.

for their own system, and perhaps no other century has so enthusiastically misappropriated and redefined the concepts of the Christian creeds or invented so many synonyms for 'God'—*l'Idéal, le Grand Tout, le Grand Être*, even, it sometimes seems, *l'Inconnaissable*. To take only two preliminary examples here, we find Vigny —without any sense of incongruity, it would appear—presenting his stoical philosophy in the guise of 'la religion de l'honneur', complete with its 'altar', its 'Saints and Martyrs'. 'C'est une Religion mâle [he affirms of his wholly naturalistic and very limited belief], sans symbole et sans images, sans dogme et sans cérémonies. . . .'[1] Michelet's cult of patriotism offers a much more arresting instance. 'Nous avons perdu nos dieux!' he declares in *Le Peuple* (1846). Yet we need 'un Dieu, un autel . . . un Dieu, en qui les hommes se reconnaissent et s'aiment'—for faith is 'la base commune d'inspiration et d'action'.[2] He proceeds in all seriousness to cast France for this elevated role—as a religion of fraternity that fulfils the unaccomplished promises of Christianity, as a new 'pontiff' more enlightened than the Pope of Rome, as God's spokesman to humanity, as a 'first gospel', as the instrument of man's salvation: 'ma patrie peut seule sauver le monde'.[3] Education is to spread the doctrine of 'la France, comme foi et comme religion', of 'la patrie' 'comme dogme et principe', 'puis . . . comme légende', a legend centred on France's two 'redemptions' through Joan of Arc and the Revolution.[4] And above all, 'pour suprême leçon', this teaching will reveal to the young people of France 'l'immense faculté de dévouement, de sacrifice, que nos pères ont montrée, et comme tant de fois la France a donné sa vie pour le monde'.[5] Michelet also adds that whilst education can do most to implant this faith 'in the very heart of the child', it should be supplemented by a whole 'culture religieuse, morale, agissant

[1] *Servitude et grandeur militaires*, Conard, 1914, liv. 3, ch. x.
[2] *Le Peuple*, ed. L. Refort, Didier, 1946, pp. 229, 259.
[3] ibid., pp. 246, 267, 268, 271. Michelet is, of course, far from alone in holding this faith; something like it inspired generations of French radicals. It was one example amongst many of the century's 'political messianism', of which, Talmon concludes, 'the real victor was . . . nationalism'. (J. L. Talmon, *Political Messianism: The Romantic Phase*, London, Secker & Warburg, 1960, p. 513.
[4] *Le Peuple*, pp. 247, 267
[5] ibid., p. 268.

par les assemblées, les bibliothèques populaires, les spectacles, les fêtes de tout genre, surtout musicales'.[1]

In later chapters we shall consider a representative selection of systems which sought to provide a complete replacement for Christianity, a theology as well as an ethic: 'social religions' like those of Saint-Simon and Comte; 'metaphysical religions' like the 'natural religion' of Cousin and his eclectic followers, the doctrines of Renan and Étienne Vacherot, and various pantheistic systems; occultist creeds and 'neo-pagan' beliefs derived from the world-religions popularized by the *philologues* of the age. And whilst other systems propounded to the nineteenth-century reader might not purport to be complete 'religions', they too borrowed the language of prophetic fervour and offered a comprehensive explanation of man's situation and destiny. Such, most notably, were the cults of science and of progress. We shall look later at a number of current theories of history and progress, each presenting a broad, synthetic interpretation of the entire human past and an all-embracing programme or prediction for the future. Above all, however, this was the century of science. It was supremely science that both destroyed the old ideas and inspired the new. The scientific spirit, whether to criticize or to encourage, hovered over almost every creed we shall survey, 'religions' and philosophies of history alike. And even science itself inspired in some of its admirers an almost religious devotion. The following chapter therefore concerns this major preoccupation of the age's thought.

[1] ibid., pp. 249, 269.

III

The Cult of Science

1. Science in Nineteenth-Century France

A RECENT historian has claimed for the 'scientific revolution' of the late-seventeenth and eighteenth centuries that 'it outshines everything since the rise of Christianity and reduces the Renaissance and Reformation to the rank of mere episodes, mere internal displacements, within the system of medieval Christendom'.[1] In the nineteenth century this 'revolution' continued at an ever-quickening pace. The sciences in France recovered swiftly from the interruptions of 1789 and the Reign of Terror. In 1795 the Académie des Sciences, suspended in 1793, was revived as part of the Institut. In 1808 the École Normale was reorganized and became a famous centre of scientific education and research, especially under Pasteur's influence later. In the fields of biology and zoology, the Jardin du Roi was reconstituted in 1793, and chairs were given to such men as Lamarck and Étienne Geoffroy Saint-Hilaire. Most important of all, in 1794 the École Polytechnique was created, mainly for work in the applied sciences, and with its highly distinguished teaching staff became internationally famous, a model for technological universities in other countries, and the nursery of a whole century of French scientists and thinkers, including Sadi Carnot, Comte, numerous Fourierists and Saint-Simonians, amongst them Enfantin, and later Renouvier and Sorel. Its atmosphere was one of enthusiastic confidence in the powers of science and the benefits of technological organization—benefits which such pupils as Comte and the Saint-Simonians would later seek to extend to the field of 'social engineering'. The École Polytechnique has indeed been described as 'the source' of the 'scientistic hubris', the over-confidence in science, we must study later in this chapter.[2] University faculties of

---

[1] H. Butterfield, *The Origins of Modern Science*, London, Bell, 1949, p. viii.

[2] Cf. F. A. Hayek, *The Counter-Revolution of Science*, Glencoe, Ill., The Free Press, 1952, pp. 105–16.

science were slower to reform themselves, but none the less nine-teenth-century science was to outdo even the age of Newton in the richness of its discoveries. In the first half of the century alone, in physics Ampère ('the Newton of electricity', as J. C. Maxwell termed him) created electrodynamics, Carnot founded thermo-dynamics and enunciated its first two laws, and Malus and Fresnel drastically revised the theory of light and hence the science of optics. Chemists like Gay-Lussac, Chevreul, J.-B. Dumas, and Charles (husband of Lamartine's beloved Elvire) were no less active, and in biology and zoology the work of Lamarck and Saint-Hilaire on evolution was outstanding, whilst hardly less so were Cuvier's creation of palaeontology and the advances in physiology of Magendie, teacher of Claude Bernard. The later years of the century saw even more immediately impressive developments—Berthelot's founding of thermochemistry and chemical mechanics; Pasteur's work on microbes and bacteria and his invention of inoculation and milk-pasteurization; Bernard's pioneering studies in the biochemistry of the nervous system, especially in its relation to digestion and secretion; the discovery by Pierre and Marie Curie of radium, narrowly preceded by Becquerel's discovery of the radioactivity of uranium.

Many scientific ideas and theories were to be invoked indi-vidually in the philosophical disputes of the century, but cumu-latively their impact was still more forceful. The feeling grew that only scientific knowledge is reliable, that only the observable can be known. In the eighteenth century awareness of scientific de-velopments, despite the popularizing works of Fontenelle and his successors, had still been confined to a relatively small minority. In the nineteenth century science began to capture the educated, if not the popular imagination—as witness, to mention only one of a host of instances, the frequency of a scientist or doctor as the hero of late-nineteenth-century dramas. Foreign scientists like Lyell, Faraday, Darwin, and Maxwell became hardly less famous or notorious than their French colleagues, and throughout the cen-tury striking discoveries emphasized the authority and progress of science. It might be the unearthing of fossils and bones near Paris as far back as 1808, from which Cuvier (hailed by Balzac in *La*

Peau de chagrin as 'the greatest poet of our century') reconstructed extinct animals; or Le Verrier's prediction in 1846 of the existence of a new planet, Neptune, dramatically verified within a few days at almost the exact position calculated; or the launching of motor-propelled balloons above Paris in 1872 (an occasion celebrated by Sully Prudhomme in *Le Zénith*). And in daily life itself, with the spread of industrialism, railways, gas-lighting, better heating, and less primitive surgical treatment, the power of science was manifest. Although isolated figures like Baudelaire protested that true civilization does not lie in 'steam and gas', the idea grew that science can ensure an unlimited physical progress. Hugo's *Plein Ciel*, saluting the ascent of the *aéroscaphe*, is not untypical:

> Où va-t-il, ce navire? Il va, de jour vêtu,
> A l'avenir divin et pur, à la vertu,
>   A la science qu'on voit luire,
> A la mort des fléaux, à l'oubli généreux
> A l'abondance, au calme, au rire, à l'homme heureux. . . .

Thanks to science a material utopia is round the corner.

But this was not all. In the nineteenth century the 'human sciences' took their place beside the natural sciences—not only the physiology of man and the theory of his evolution, but also sociology, psychology, a more scientific history, especially of previous civilizations and religions, and anthropology. Whereas eighteenth-century scientists had dealt primarily with the non-human, in the nineteenth century—as Taine rather menacingly remarks—'la science approche enfin, et approche de l'homme; c'est à l'âme qu'elle se prend, munie des instruments exacts et perçants dont trois cents ans d'expérience ont prouvé la justesse et mesuré la portée'.[1] How far this scientific study of man could legitimately go remained in dispute throughout the century (and still does), and this question itself proliferated more detailed problems that were to be the subject of hot debate. Is human behaviour wholly determined—and therefore wholly reducible in principle to scientific laws? Does physiological psychology show the idea of a 'soul' or 'mind' to be a superfluous hypothesis? Are there 'laws of human

---

[1] *Histoire de la littérature anglaise*, 18° éd., Hachette, s.d., 5 vols., iv. 388.

history' from which assured conclusions about the future can be drawn and on which a scientific social planning can be based? Is man no more than a superior animal? Are our moral convictions merely the product of our particular society and our particular stage in human evolution?

The disquieting consequences opened up by these and other questions were hidden from many of the nineteenth-century enthusiasts for science. More commonly, the development of sociology, psychology, and history provoked a rather unthinking confidence that man's moral and social lot, as well as his material condition, could be perfected through science, or greatly improved at the least. It was not only a Comte or Renan who thought this. Hugo continues *Plein Ciel*—'the supreme expression of the nineteenth-century belief in human perfectibility', as Hunt remarks[1]—with the assertion:

> Il va, ce glorieux navire,
> Au droit, à la raison, à la fraternité,
> A la religieuse et sainte vérité
> Sans impostures et sans voiles,
> A l'amour, sur les cœurs serrants son doux lien,
> Au juste, au grand, au bon, au beau. . . .

The hero of Ponsard's drama, *Galilée* (1867), speaks for his creator when he hymns:

> Science, amour du vrai, flamme pure et sacrée,
> Sublime passion par Dieu même inspirée. . . . (ii, 1)

For Sully Prudhomme science and conscience together will lead us to 'la Cité future', the city of justice. Zola—even more dazzled—believes that 'la poursuite de la vérité par la science est l'idéal divin que l'homme doit se proposer': it will allow man to be 'maître du bien et du mal', 'régler la vie, régler la société, résoudre à la longue tous les problèmes du socialisme, apporter surtout des bases solides à la justice . . .' Not everyone would agree with Berthelot that 'le triomphe universel de la science arrivera à assurer aux hommes le maximum possible de bonheur et de moralité', but very many would have endorsed a slightly

[1] V. Hugo, *La Légende des siècles*, ed. H. J. Hunt, Oxford, Blackwell, 1945, p. 234.

more modest amendment.[1] Nor was it only Zola and his disciples in the literary field who wished to be co-workers with the scientists. Much earlier, Balzac, captivated by Saint-Hilaire's studies of animal species, could hope to show the various human 'species' produced by differing social environments, whilst Stendhal—a disciple of the Idéologues—pursued with a psychologist's objectivity, as Taine was admiringly to stress, '[son] métier d'observateur du cœur humain'. Flaubert, whatever his reservations about scientific progress, declared that 'le grand art est scientifique et impersonnel' and studied the workings of environment and determinism in the life of Emma Bovary with all the documentation and objectivity of a scientist. Leconte de Lisle, though despising the poems in praise of scientific invention of Maxime Du Camp, turned for inspiration to the 'science' of *philologie*. The Goncourts, even more, used the novel as 'un instrument d'enquête sociale', as in *Germinie Lacerteux*, or to present a 'clinical' study of love, as in *Renée Mauperin*, whilst the aim of the young Paul Bourget in *Physiologie de l'amour moderne* is evident from the title itself. A 'scientific' subject-matter, a 'scientific' treatment and approach —these were literature's testimony at this time to the immense prestige of science.

The two salient beliefs that nineteenth-century science as a whole engenders in the thought of its age are, first, the complete reliability and the fruitfulness of the scientific methods and, secondly, the possibility—with whatever limiting conditions—of creating a 'science of man' that shall radically ameliorate human life and even human nature. We must now consider those thinkers who work up these beliefs into a complete philosophy, the philosophy of positivism.

2. The Positivist Philosophy

The basis of the positivist philosophy is the view that all genuine knowledge must be of the scientific type, that is to say must be based upon observation and experiment. Consequently, we can only know (the truths of logic and mathematics apart) phen-

---

[1] É. Zola, *Le Docteur Pascal*, Charpentier, 1928, p. 47, and *Le Roman expérimental*, Charpentier, 1923, p. 24; M. Berthelot, 'Science et morale', *Revue de Paris*, 1.2.1895.

omena and the laws of relation and succession of phenomena, for these and these alone can be empirically verified. Positivism thus denies the validity of such alleged ways of knowing as intuition and *a priori* reasoning (prior to observation, as opposed to the *a posteriori* reasoning employed in the sciences), and it equally denies that we can have any knowledge about religion or metaphysics, since these are by definition largely concerned with a realm that is said to exist *behind* phenomena, in a world that can never be observed. It was Comte, in France, who gave the classic definition of this position.

Dans l'état positif [he says], l'esprit humain, reconnaissant l'impossibilité d'obtenir des notions absolues, renonce à chercher l'origine et la destination de l'univers et à connaître les causes intimes des phénomènes, pour s'attacher uniquement à découvrir, par l'usage bien combiné du raisonnement et de l'observation, leurs lois effectives, c'est-à-dire leurs relations invariables de succession et de similitude.[1]

This view, one may note, also assumes that in fact phenomena are related and are determined—so that if *B* has constantly been seen to follow *A* in certain conditions, we are entitled to suppose that, given exactly the same conditions, *B* will again follow *A*. This was conceived in the nineteenth century to be a working assumption of the sciences and therefore it was assumed by positivism also, although such a thinker as John Stuart Mill was somewhat worried about the problem of the validity of induction. This assumption may harden into the assertion that we *know* that phenomena are invariably related and determined, as in Taine's thought, for example, but such a claim goes beyond the limits of verification. It thereby deserts the proper positivist standpoint which supports Hume in thinking that we can never know that there is a *necessary* connexion, as opposed to a regularity of succession, between phenomena.

3. Henri de Saint-Simon and Auguste Comte

Although Comte is usually regarded as the 'father' of positivism, its general attitude can be traced back even to such seventeenth-century thinkers as Bacon, Hobbes, Gassendi, Bayle, and

[1] *Cours de philosophie positive*, 2e éd., Baillière, 1864, 6 vols., i. 9-10.

Locke, and was greatly developed by eighteenth-century thinkers —the *philosophes* from Fontenelle to Condillac and Condorcet and British empiricists such as James Mill, Bentham, and Hume—and in the early nineteenth century by the Idéologues. Even Littré, defending Comte's originality, admitted that his master's thought was anticipated by Turgot, Condorcet, Kant, and Saint-Simon,[1] whilst Renan resented the 'exaggerated reputation' of Comte, 'érigé en grand homme de premier ordre pour avoir dit, en mauvais français, ce que tous les esprits scientifiques, depuis deux cents ans, ont vu aussi clairement que lui'.[2] It is probable, indeed, that the novelty of Comte's thought and its influence in France have often been overestimated and that (as one historian claims) 'le comtisme n'est qu'un épisode, parmi beaucoup d'autres, du développement du positivisme'.[3] The essence of positivism lies in the whole empiricist tradition and especially in the eighteenth-century philosophy of sensationalism. 'Nous n'avons point d'idées qui ne nous viennent des sens,' declared Condillac. Nineteenth-century positivists explored and expanded this point of view.

The first to do so was Henri de Saint-Simon (1760–1825), whose grandfather was a cousin of the author of the *Mémoires*. He began his career as a soldier, fighting with the Americans in the War of Independence. Later, during the French Revolution, he engaged in financial speculations that ended in his imprisonment until after the fall of Robespierre. It was only in middle age in fact that he turned to the intellectual pursuits that were to gain him a lasting European fame. From about 1798, having quarrelled with his business partner, he became increasingly possessed by a sense of mission to redirect human affairs at what he felt was a turning-point in history. His first work appeared when he was forty-two, to be followed by a considerable number of articles and books, some of them later being written wholly or in part by his disciples, including the young Auguste Comte.

[1] *Auguste Comte et la philosophie positive*, 2ᵉ éd., Hachette, 1864, pp. 38–97. On Comte's indebtedness to earlier thinkers, cf. H. Gouhier, *La Jeunesse d'A. Comte et la formation du positivisme*, Vrin, 1933–41, 3 vols.

[2] *Souvenirs d'enfance et de jeunesse*, éd. 'Collection nouvelle', Calmann Lévy, s.d., p. 219. Cf. also his *Discours et conférences*, 9ᵉ éd., Calmann Lévy, 1928, pp. 75–76.

[3] G. Cantecor, *Comte*, nouv. éd., Mellottée, s.d., p. 169.

His general outlook was derived from the *philosophes*, especially Condorcet, and was perhaps strengthened also by contact, after he finally settled in Paris, with scientists of the École Polytechnique and the École de Médecine. Even his first, rather confused work, the *Lettres d'un habitant de Genève* (1803), reveals the direction his thought was taking. He claims that mankind's one true common interest lies in the progress of the sciences and he proposes a social reorganization, centred upon a cult of Newton, which will give far greater authority and influence to the scientists. It is these notions that he expands in his next works, the *Introduction aux travaux scientifiques du dix-neuvième siècle* (1807–8) and his *Mémoire sur la science de l'homme* (1813). Although praising his predecessors—from as far back as Socrates down to Condorcet—he claims that the Encyclopaedists in particular were destructive rather than creative and that we now require to construct a new system to replace the Christian outlook they destroyed. Saint-Simon is persuaded that history and progress are primarily determined by the advance of knowledge and ideas and that social unity must rest on intellectual unity, and consequently he insists that the sciences must be unified and given a systematic philosophical basis. And it is no less imperative to extend the scientific method to encompass the study of man and human society, what he calls 'la science de l'homme'. This new 'social science' will be based upon physiology, he claims, a branch of science which is itself in need of a stricter scientific approach, in his view, but he does not doubt that both studies can follow astronomy, physics, and chemistry, and move from the merely 'conjectural' to the fully 'positive' stage. Moreover, once this is achieved, morals, politics, and philosophy can likewise become wholly scientific and social life be reorganized in a rational way. To these ends he also proposes a new encyclopaedia of all existing knowledge and the creation of academies of moral and social scientists (and also of artists), to be set up side by side with Napoleon's recently established Academy of natural scientists; progress cannot but be hastened if once the best scientists, scholars, and artists are allowed greater influence. Saint-Simon sees his own task, one might say, as that of a general director of studies.

Much of his later writing was in part the work of disciples like Thierry and Comte, so that it is not easy to know which ideas are truly Saint-Simon's. Certainly the works he produced in collaboration with them, such as *De la réorganisation de la société européenne* (1814) and *Du système industriel* (1821) seem more lucid, hard-headed, and organized than his own earlier books. Furthermore, these later publications are concerned above all with political, economic, and religious questions rather than with the philosophical development of his position. But one may conclude, though the question is admittedly complex, by saying that he provided the general ideas and preoccupations of the positivist philosophy which others would make more detailed, more precise, and more forceful. Chief amongst these thinkers was Auguste Comte, who began his career as secretary to Saint-Simon. And whilst one may well debate the extent of his originality, one cannot deny that Comte gave nineteenth-century positivism its fullest and most weighty exposition.

Born in 1798 and educated at the École Polytechnique, Comte devoted his whole life from the age of nineteen, when he joined Saint-Simon, until his death in 1857 to elaborating his 'positive philosophy'. He first sketched it in various youthful *opuscules*, the best known being the first version of the *Système de politique positive* (1824), but its most famous expression was in the *Cours de philosophie positive* (1830–42), based on lectures given privately to his followers in Paris. This is the work which affected Littré and Mill so deeply and, after Harriet Martineau's abridged translation in 1853, English writers like Frederic Harrison, G. H. Lewes, and George Eliot.[1] In later life, after a brief but intense relationship with Clotilde de Vaux (1844–6) which made him especially aware of the primacy of emotion in human life, he turned more exclusively to social ethics and the creation of a new 'religion of humanity'. Still without regular employment and living largely on the subscriptions of his disciples, Comte now became the high

[1] On Mill, cf. his own *Autobiography* and *Auguste Comte and Positivism* and I. W. Mueller, *John Stuart Mill and French Thought*, Urbana, Illinois U.P., 1956. On George Eliot, cf. B. Willey, *Nineteenth-Century Studies*, London, Chatto & Windus, 1949.

priest of his 'positive' cult and its dogmatic theologian, with works like *Le Catéchisme positiviste* (1852), the second version of the *Système de politique positive* (1851–4), and the only completed volume of the *Synthèse subjective* (1856).

Comte was the greatest systematizer of the positivist tradition: both his masterly syntheses and the authoritarianism and absurdities of his religion stemmed from his *esprit de système*. The search for unity motivated his attempts to organize the sciences and their methods, to detect the directing forces of history and to develop a social theory applicable to every realm of life—work, thought, political organization, religion, and art. And although, ironically, some—including Mill and Littré, his most influential disciples— have alleged a radical division between what he termed his two careers (the first as a new Aristotle, the second as a new St. Paul, in his own words), his entire thought has cohesion. Feeling and a concern for morality may tend in his later works to replace reason and a concern for the sciences, but throughout his aim is to establish a philosophical basis for the sciences and for a scientific ordering of society. His lifework is already explicit in his *Plan des travaux scientifiques nécessaires pour réorganiser la société*, written in 1822.

His work can be divided into three main compartments: his philosophy, his religion (to be discussed in Chapter IV), and his sociological ideas. These ideas fall outside our scope, except for their philosophical implications, but probably constitute his most lasting achievement; although Mill believes 'he has done nothing in Sociology which does not require to be done again, and better', later thinkers like Durkheim have acknowledged him (though with reservations) as a founder of social science.[1]

His most renowned philosophical notion is his *loi des trois états*, expounded in the opening chapter of the *Cours*. The human mind, in every department of thought, moves in turn through three 'states'—'l'état théologique, ou fictif; l'état métaphysique, ou abstrait; l'état scientifique, ou positif'. Furthermore, the nature of society at any period is determined by the intellectual stage it has

[1] J. S. Mill, *Auguste Comte and Positivism*, 2nd ed., London, Trübner, 1866, p. 124. For a brief discussion of Durkheim's reservations, cf. A. W. Gouldner, 'Introduction' to É. Durkheim, *Socialism and Saint-Simon*, transl. Sattler, London, Routledge, 1959, pp. ix–xv.

reached. In the first, seen in antiquity and in the Middle Ages up to the fourteenth century, theocracy and a military outlook are found, whilst in the third sociocracy and an industrial outlook predominate, and in between, in the second stage, stretching from the fourteenth century to 1789, one sees a gradual decomposition of the old order and a building-up of a new order to be fully reached in the third stage. In the theological state man aspires to absolute knowledge, desires to know 'la nature intime des êtres, les causes premières et finales de tous les effets qui le frappent', and represents phenomena (thunder or plagues or good crops, for example) as the result of the direct action of supernatural agents. Comte also sub-divides this stage into fetichist, polytheist, and monotheist phases. In the metaphysical state— which is only a modification of the theological, he observes— there is the same illegitimate search for primary causes and absolute knowledge, but the 'supernatural agents' are replaced by abstractions, 'par des forces abstraites . . . conçues comme capables d'engendrer par elles-mêmes tous les phénomènes observés'. Thus the peculiar error of this state is to attribute existence and causal force to what are merely our own abstract notions: good examples would be the *philosophes'* use of 'Nature', Hegel's 'Absolute', Renan's 'Ideal', and many nineteenth-century uses of 'progress' and 'evolution' as if they were directive powers in human history, independent of man himself. Comte stresses that both these states are inevitable and are also useful at their own point in man's development, but they must ultimately be surpassed, and in the scientific or positive state men more modestly confine themselves to a 'relative knowledge', knowledge of phenomena and their 'invariable relationships', eschew the false abstraction of the metaphysicians, and no longer seek to know the first causes or the final end of the universe. The law of gravitation is the type of our only possible knowledge: it renders coherent and predictable a great variety of phenomena and to that extent explains them— but it says nothing about the nature of 'weight' and 'attraction' in themselves, a problem, Comte adds, that can only be left 'to the imagination of the theologians and the subtleties of the metaphysicians'.

From this starting-point Comte moves to his most significant addition to the positivist tradition: his extension of the scientific method to the study of societies, the founding of a 'social physics', a task which he describes as 'le premier but de ce cours, son but spécial'. Although Saint-Simon preceded him here, Comte considers much more deeply the methodology of social science. He first classifies the existing sciences in their order of complexity—mathematics, astronomy, physics, chemistry, and biology or physiology—and urges that this corresponds with the order in which they emerged historically and also with their increasing utility for man. He also discusses their methods in detail, seeking to show up the theological and metaphysical elements still remaining in them—to such effect that Mill could praise his 'wonderful systematization of the philosophy of all the antecedent sciences . . . which, if he had done nothing else, would have stamped him . . . as one of the principal thinkers of the age':[1] he was, in fact, a leading practitioner in his time of the philosophy of science. But in general these five sciences have moved into the positive state: it is time for the sixth science, sociology, to take the same step away from its theologico-metaphysical infancy, just as astronomy did from astrology or chemistry from alchemy. He does not want a science of psychology, one notes: that would merely be a mixture of physiology and sociology. The new science must reject abstract ideas, breaking, for instance, with the Benthamite notion of a social science deduced from general laws about 'universal human nature'; it must gather more facts and perfect new techniques of investigation.[2] Above all, going beyond mere 'empiricism', it must co-ordinate these facts and in the light of the laws of social action it discovers, it must take on the predictive function of a true science, defining in particular the limits and nature of political action. Social phenomena, he asserts, are 'aussi susceptibles de prévision scientifique que tous les autres phénomènes quelconques'—though he recognizes that the predictions may be less precise than in other sciences since the facts are more complex.[3] Sociology will resemble the other sciences in its methods as well as its aims. Observation is the basic method; experimentation is possible in so

---

[1] Mill, *Comte*, p. 53.   [2] *Cours*, iv. 213-16.   [3] ibid., iv. 226.

far as we can note what happens when some special factor, like a revolution, interferes with the regular course of events; comparison also can be fruitful—between human and animal societies and between co-existing human societies. But in particular Comte looks to a new method, peculiar to sociology, which he elevates as 'le principal artifice scientifique de la nouvelle philosophie positive': this is the historical method.[1] He divides the laws of social science into two kinds: the laws of 'social statics' and those of 'social dynamics'. By studying human history and the development of societies up to the present, we can both verify the former laws and discover the latter: we can distinguish those physical, intellectual, moral, and political trends that have progressively become more dominant from the other trends that have grown weaker. This will eventually allow us to predict the ultimate ascendancy or decline of a given set of trends. Moreover, these conclusions can be 'verified': they must be such as our prior knowledge of man renders probable.[2] There has been a decline in the amount of food men eat, but a law that men would finally cease to eat at all would be belied by the fact (as Comte solemnly notes) that all organisms require some food if they are to survive. Or if a law implied that in most men reason predominates over desire or altruism over egotism, we should know—in virtue of our prior acquaintance with human nature—that the law must be false and that history had been misinterpreted. This 'verification' was warmly greeted by Mill who named it 'the Inverse Deductive Method': 'by means of it empirical generalizations are raised into positive laws, and Sociology becomes a science'.[3]

The same positivist approach is reaffirmed in his later works, especially in his *Discours sur l'ensemble du positivisme* (1848), a useful and unwontedly succinct summary of his whole outlook. Here he also refutes the charges of atheism, materialism, and fatalism brought against positivism.[4] Atheism is as much a metaphysical theory as theism. Like Mill, Comte suggests that the hypothesis of an intelligent Will behind the universe is rather more reasonable

[1] *Cours*, iv. 322–8.   [2] ibid., t. iv, '48ᵉ leçon'.   [3] Mill, *Comte*, p. 86.
[4] In *Système de politique positive*, Mathias, Carilian-Goeury et Dalmont, 1851–4, 4 vols., i. 46–55; cf. Mill, *Comte*, pp. 14–15, 114.

than the atheist hypothesis, but neither view can be verified by observation and thus we can have no knowledge, as opposed to belief, either way. He also argues against materialism, less effectively, claiming that scientists have wrongly transferred to sociology the materialistic assumptions of the non-human sciences. Fatalism he rebuts by distinguishing between science's acceptance of the invariability of natural laws and fatalism's claim that man lacks free-will. Man *is* able—and this is central to his own dreams of social action—to modify events to some extent as he chooses. (What he does not admit, however, is the possibility of *chance* variations in the natural order.)

Here too—as in the *Cours* itself—his ultimate aim is evident: to legislate for society. 'Science, d'où prévoyance; prévoyance, d'où action': this is his guiding principle throughout.[1] Like the traditionalists and eclectics and like Saint-Simon and other socialists, he wishes to build a more stable society, to replace the state of 'crisis' left by the Revolutionary era by 'order'. Like them also he believes a firm intellectual basis is needed—and is provided by the *Cours*. Science and philosophy are mainly valuable as a preparation for action, and his own goal is less truth for its own sake than laws to guide social reorganization.[2] Hence he is led to erect his *système de politique positive*, linked with a dogmatic ethic based on love of man, and his 'religion of humanity': positive sociology is to be the political dictator of the new state, and the cult of humanity is to draw men together and prompt them to altruistic action. And by 1848 he is amending his former classification of the sciences by adding *la morale* as a seventh science and claiming that the later sciences, being more useful to man, are more 'eminent'—a value-judgement he had eschewed earlier.

In his later thought Comte undoubtedly abandons positivism at many points (as we shall also see in studying his religious and ethical views): the social prophet replaces the social scientist. This was Littré's contention and led him to break with his master. Mill, too, admired the *Cours* and drew much from it, but considered the later works radically 'false and misleading'. Yet the *Cours*

---

[1] *Cours*, i. 51.   [2] ibid., vi. 633-6.

itself is unfaithful to positivism and contains the seeds of his future beliefs: this we must now illustrate.

First, Comte is all too often uncritical and unscientific in his attitude to facts. It is significant that he should so impatiently attack 'empiricism', by which he means the impartial gathering of facts without a theoretical basis.[1] He quite fairly argues that we must come to the work of observation with preconceived hypotheses in mind or it will prove fruitless, but it is hard not to feel that in his own practice his hypotheses sometimes ceased to be tentative and became theories to be justified, come what might. He has frequently been accused of selecting the facts that support his views and neglecting those that do not. He also criticizes specialized research and the search for truth as an end in itself, and whilst one may sympathize with some of his strictures here, it often seems that he himself wants quick results even in a difficult field and would perhaps prefer false laws to no laws at all.[2] By 1848 he is even re-defining the 'positive' approach as generalized good sense directed to a social purpose.[3]

Secondly, he bases his system upon certain assumptions which he never justifies. He affirms, for instance, that ideas govern human history—and on this he bases his claims that the *loi des trois états* applies to every aspect of human life and society and also that a sound philosophy is the indispensable foundation for a sound polity. Yet this view was being challenged in his own day —by Marx and others—and demands a substantiation that Comte never gives. Again, he assumes that the evolution of humanity has been rigidly determined: each stage was inevitable. This is the keystone of his belief that sociology can discover invariable laws, upon which scientific prediction and legislation can depend. But he never shows that his laws are more than a pattern he himself is imposing on history or, alternatively, that they are justified by their predictive success. Yet again—in part arising from this—he assumes that sociology can be fully scientific. Having earlier admitted the imperfections of its methods—even saying at the end

[1] Cf., for example, *Cours*, i. 12; iv. 300, 304; vi. 531, 600.
[2] Cf., amongst other examples, ibid., i. 26–27; iv. 325–6; vi. 546, 600, 639; and *Système, Préface*, i. 17.   [3] *Système*, i. 57–58.

of the forty-ninth lesson of the *Cours*, for example, that it will always remain somewhat inferior to the other sciences—he later claims far too great a certainty for its conclusions: by the end of the *Cours* he is attributing to it 'autant de positivité et plus de rationnalité qu'aucune des sciences antérieures déjà jugées par ce Traité.[1] It is in a similar spirit that he contends that *l'état positif* is the final stage of man's development.

'It is one of M. Comte's mistakes that he never allows of open questions,' Mill suggests.[2] His *esprit de système* and his preoccupation with social planning together explain both his infidelity to positivism and also such features of his thought as the reduction of historical change to a few dominant laws, the dogmatism of his social theories, and the meticulous and authoritarian organization of his religion. They account above all for his claiming too much for the scientific methods, too wide a range and too much certainty and authority. Under their pressure Comte moved from positivism to a different position, sometimes termed scientism, which greatly exaggerates both the potential range and the reliability of scientific discovery.

4. Comte's Disciples: Émile Littré

Comte's disciples can be conveniently divided into two groups: those who accepted his entire system, the 'orthodox positivists' who belonged to the Positivist Church of Humanity, and the 'dissident positivists' who accepted the teaching of the *Cours* (with minor reservations) but rejected his later thought as being itself unfaithful to positivism. The former were little known even in their own day and were perhaps more numerous abroad than in France. The latter, more eminent group, included, in England, John Stuart Mill and G. H. Lewes and, in France, Émile Littré.

Littré (1801–81) is best known as a philologist, author of the *Histoire de la langue française* (1862) and the *Dictionnaire de la langue française* (1863–78), but this devoted savant also wrote on biology and physiology and translated Strauss, Schiller, Dante, and Hippocrates. He was also a member of the Académie des Inscriptions et Belles-Lettres and of the Académie Française, he frequently

[1] *Cours*, vi. 547. [2] Mill, *Comte*, pp. 14–15.

contributed to many leading reviews, and after 1870, first as *député*, then as *sénateur*, he became a notable Left-wing political figure. He was also a philosopher, overshadowed for us by Comte, but in his own age highly influential, as witness the abusive contemporary attacks on him: Monsignor Dupanloup even resigned from the Académie Française when Littré was elected to it.

Littré did not read Comte's *Cours* until he was thirty-nine. He had been completely negative in his outlook, he says, having long since renounced theology and, later, metaphysics: 'l'ouvrage de M.Comte me transforma'. He found a standpoint that gave direction and order to his scientific studies and a philosophy that brought him 'serenity': 'elle suffit à tout, ne me trompe jamais, et m'éclaire toujours'.[1] He amply repaid his debt by becoming the leading propagandist of positivism in the Second Empire. Having written an *Analyse raisonnée du 'Cours'* in 1845 and applied its ideas to social problems in books in 1849 and 1852, in 1863 he published *Auguste Comte et la philosophie positive*, a lucid, readable exposition and commentary whose greatest service was to present what Littré believed sound and compelling in Comtism with a persuasive clarity Comte himself never achieved. In 1864 he wrote his famous 'Préface d'un disciple' for the second edition of Comte's *Cours*, and in 1867 founded the *Revue de philosophie positive*. Other works followed, and even during his final, painful illness he could still testify that Comte had given him 'un idéal, la soif du meilleur, la vue de l'histoire et le souci de l'humanité'.[2]

Yet this devotion never blinded him to Comte's defects, and he was as important as the leader of the 'dissident positivists' as in the role of propagandist. He separated from Comte with great regret in 1852. In a tone of sad astonishment he thereafter attacked Comte's deviations from his own original philosophy: notably his religious dogmas, his 'subjective method', his subordination of the mind to the heart, and his erection of ethics as a seventh science. These and other criticisms are summed up in a devastating chapter in the book of 1863 on Comte's 'retour à l'état théologique'. Not

---

[1] Littré, *Comte*, pp. 662–3, 529, and p. ii.
[2] Cited by E. Scherer, *Études sur la littérature contemporaine*, Calmann Lévy, 1863–95, 10 vols., vii. 346.

that Littré was a superficial materialist, unaware of men's religious aspirations: he, like Kant, could marvel at the starry heavens or, like Pascal, feel terror before their silence.[1] But Comte was betraying the scientific and positivist method, in his view, replacing respect for truth and the facts by dogmatic emotionalism.

Littré also defended the strict positivist position (as he saw it) both against its hostile Christian and eclectic critics and, more notably, against those 'esprits mi-positifs et mi-métaphysiques', as he called them, who claimed to be its protagonists but also tried to re-interpret and thus falsified it.[2] Hence he attacked those who claimed positivism's support for materialism: materialists and spiritualists alike make metaphysical statements about the 'unknowable', asserting that all phenomena derive from a material or a mental 'substance' that is never observed. He also criticized Renan and Berthelot on similar grounds.[3] Not only is Renan's sketch of world history largely conjectural but he alleges that God is immanent in the universe, in each of its creatures, gaining greater self-consciousness the more advanced is the creature on the ladder of evolution. This pantheistic notion is extremely improbable in itself, Littré replies, for it defines God as both personal and impersonal, both in the Absolute and in the process of becoming; and, above all, it is purely subjective and quite unverifiable. Berthelot, though less of an Hegelian than Renan, is also divided between positivism and metaphysics, whereas these can never be reconciled, Littré maintains. He also opposed Spencer's famous attempt to unite science and religion by the claim that both meet on the shores of the 'unknowable', this being both the object of religious thought and the last term by which the sciences are confronted. Littré points out that the 'unknowable'—which he acknowledges to be a positivist conception—is only regarded as unknowable by Spencer and the scientists: theologians pretend to know it and erect dogmas about it—and even Spencer slips into describing it. And, lastly, he even took Mill to task, defending

[1] Cf. ibid., vii. 343.

[2] His attack is best developed in his 'Préface d'un disciple' to Comte, *Cours*, t. i, especially pp. xxvi–xliv.

[3] He is commenting on Renan's letter to Berthelot on 'Les Sciences de la nature et les sciences historiques' (*R.D.M.*, 15.10.1863) and Berthelot's reply.

Comte on many points against the criticisms of the English thinker's *Auguste Comte and Positivism* (1865). Positivism is not merely a theory of knowledge as Mill thinks; it is 'une conception du monde' and gives not merely hypotheses but certainties. He also attacks Mill's argument that positivism does not necessarily exclude *belief* in a supernatural order. For Littré it is as meaningless to speak of conjectures about the 'unknowable' as of knowledge about it. We may contemplate the 'unknowable' and be moved by it. 'C'est un océan qui vient battre notre rive, et pour lequel nous n'avons ni barque ni voile, mais dont la claire vision est aussi salutaire que formidable'; 'rien n'élève plus l'âme que cette contemplation'.[1] But we can neither know nor guess at its nature.

Littré here seems to anticipate logical positivism's assertion in the twentieth century that all metaphysical statements, however tentative, are linguistically nonsensical. But his comments on Mill in general reveal—as does his acceptance of certain doctrines in the *Cours*—that he himself deserted positivism at some points. Like Comte he is a 'scientific realist': sense-experience gives us direct knowledge of the world itself, not merely of our mental 'representations' of it. Thus he can add that we *know* that causation is a part of the real world, that 'la notion de cause n'est pas immanente à l'esprit humain'.[2] Hence science gives certainties, positivism is 'a conception of the world', and even belief in a supernatural can be excluded. Littré is here forgetting Descartes's malignant demon, Hume's scepticism, and especially Kant's *Critique of Pure Reason*, and neglecting—like Comte himself and also like their contemporary Karl Marx—all the difficulties of the 'realist' position. He tends, moreover, to fall into the very materialism he has condemned; this is a common charge made by his contemporaries.[3] Thus he can write: 'Le monde est constitué par la matière et par les forces de la matière,' or equate man's 'soul' or 'mind' with the functioning of the nervous system.[4] Although he was to the last—

[1] Littré, *Comte*, pp. 519, 525.

[2] 'La Philosophie positive: Comte et Mill', *R.D.M.*, 15.8.1866, p. 853.

[3] Cf., for example, C. Renouvier, 'De la philosophie du dix-neuvième siècle en France', *L'Année philosophique—Première Année (1867)*, 1868, pp. 36 ff.; and E. Caro, 'Émile Littré', *R.D.M.*, 1.5.1882, pp. 29, 31-32.   [4] 'Préface d'un disciple', op. cit., p. ix.

or at least until his death-bed conversion to Catholicism, if such it was[1]—one of the more consistent positivists of his time, he owed too much to Comte not himself to lapse occasionally from the pure doctrine he defended so staunchly.

5. *Hippolyte Taine*

Although it is often contended that Comte had a widespread influence on nineteenth-century thought, Littré was his only eminent disciple in France prior to Durkheim. Neither Renan (whose disparagement has been noted) nor Taine, who only read the *Cours* about 1860 when his own ideas were already formed, owed more than an isolated notion to him. Yet both thinkers had a positivist starting-point, although they too betrayed it in developing their philosophies.

Renan's ideas will be studied in a later chapter, but he demands at least passing mention here. He offers a further instance of the transition from strict positivism to scientism, and his youthful book on *L'Avenir de la science*, written in 1848 and 1849, a few years after he renounced his Christian faith, is a *locus classicus* of optimistic confidence in science and fervent belief that there are no limits to its scope. Under the influence of Burnouf, the great orientalist, and his earlier teachers, his hopes were centred especially upon *philologie*, by which he understood the history of the human spirit through the ages. It can offer a new, 'scientific' philosophy and save us from the 'shipwreck of scepticism' on moral and metaphysical questions to which the positivist outlook might seem to have condemned us. Science is to replace religion as a guide for mankind, and Renan can declare:

Ce n'est donc pas une exagération de dire que la science renferme l'avenir de l'humanité, qu'elle seule peut lui dire le mot de sa destinée et lui enseigner la manière d'atteindre sa fin.

The mere faith of a religious system will yield to the certainty science can give, for, he assures us, 'il viendra un jour où l'humanité

---

[1] On this question, cf. two articles by P. H. Loyson in *La Grande Revue*, t. 62, 1910, pp. 469–83, and t. 101, 1920, pp. 353–62. Cf. also Baron F. von Hügel's account (although Littré is not named) in *Essays and Addresses on the Philosophy of Religion*, London, Dent, 1931–2, 2 vols., i. 3–4.

ne croira plus, mais . . . où elle saura le monde métaphysique et moral, comme elle sait déjà le monde physique'.[1] He even alleges that science can itself become a religion, offering a new creed as well as a moral law. In often-quoted words he claims:

La science est donc une religion; la science seule fera désormais les symboles; la science seule peut résoudre à l'homme les éternels problèmes dont sa nature exige impérieusement la solution.[2]

In later life he was to descend from these heights into a sometimes trivial scepticism, but in 1860 he could still urge that this religious task was science's 'only worthy aim', and in 1890 reaffirm that he was right to have believed in science and taken it as the goal of his life.[3]

His no less famous contemporary and friend, Hippolyte Taine (1828–93), presents an equally striking case. He achieved repute over a surprisingly broad range of subjects—in literary history with his studies of La Fontaine (1853), Livy (1856), and the *Histoire de la littérature anglaise* (1864) (as well as incisive articles on Stendhal and Balzac); in philosophical polemics with *Les Philosophes classiques du dix-neuvième siècle en France* (1857); in art history, in which he was professor at the École des Beaux-Arts from 1864, with works on Italian, Flemish, and Greek art, collected in *La Philosophie de l'art* (1882); in psychology with *De l'intelligence* (1870); and in history with his great and controversial work on *Les Origines de la France contemporaine* (1875–93). Yet underlying this diversity all his writings have a unity of aim—to explore human psychology, whether directly or as revealed in the minds of literary and artistic creators and of great historical figures like Robespierre and Napoleon. They also manifest a unity of method, a method expounded in the prefaces to the *Essai sur Tite-Live* and the *Essais de critique et d'histoire*, the preface and last two chapters of *Les Philosophes classiques*, the famous *Introduction* and the chapter on Mill in the history of English literature, and the preface and other parts of *De l'intelligence*. They seek to

[1] *L'Avenir de la science—Pensées de 1848*, 23ᵉ éd., Calmann Lévy, 1929, pp. 36, 91.
[2] ibid., pp. 31, 108.
[3] *Dialogues et fragments philosophiques*, 12ᵉ éd., Calmann Lévy, 1925, p. 296, and *L'Avenir de la science*, p. xix.

justify a single, universal method by showing its fruitfulness in all these spheres. It is here that Taine the philosopher is best seen.

Even as a youth he wished to be 'un critique qui essaye de philosopher', and in 1891, shortly before his death, he could still declare: 'J'ai toujours aimé, sinon la métaphysique proprement dite, du moins la philosophie, c'est-à-dire les vues sur l'ensemble et sur le fond des choses.' [1] This last phrase is significant: as a thinker he sought, above all, completeness and certainty of knowledge. An intellectual who rejected every authority except reason and who lost his Christian faith as a youth, he longed for a synthetic view of the whole of life and the universe, for 'l'absolue, l'indubitable, l'éternelle, l'universelle vérité'.[2] Hence he dreamt of a scientific metaphysics, 'la science complète', 'celle qui explique toutes choses par rapport à l'absolu, en montrant qu'elles empruntent leur nécessité de l'absolu',[3] and this in turn determined his reaction to the English and German philosophies of his day. English positivism, he thinks, has achieved clarity and reliability in its method but is too earth-bound and neglectful of metaphysics; German idealism has built magnificent metaphysical systems but on insecure *a priori* foundations. Taine hoped to reconcile the merits of the two schools, to fuse Mill and Hegel.[4]

Taine's exposition of his method for a scientific metaphysics—his main contribution to philosophy—begins from positivism. 'Toute réalité est perçue expérimentalement par l'homme,' he claims, or, again, in the preface to *De l'intelligence*—in words often used as a motto for Naturalism in literature: 'De tout petits faits bien choisis, importants, significatifs, amplement circonstanciés et minutieusement notés, voilà aujourd'hui la matière de toute science. . . .' [5] He satirizes the eclectics from this viewpoint in *Les Philosophes classiques*: not only do they attribute existence to their own abstractions but these are not even extracts from experience—as all 'true abstractions' must be, in Taine's view. To

---

[1] *Essais de critique et d'histoire*, 14ᵉ éd., Hachette, 1923, p. v, and *Hippolyte Taine, sa vi et sa correspondance*, Hachette, 1902-7, 4 vols., iv. 332.   [2] ibid., i. 71.
[3] Cited by A. Chevrillon, *Taine—Formation de sa pensée*, Plon, 1932, p. 92.
[4] Cf. *Histoire de la littérature anglaise*, v. 300, 374, and *Les Philosophes classiques du dix-neuvième siècle en France*, 13ᵉ éd., Hachette, s.d., pp. 20, 370.
[5] *De l'intelligence*, 16ᵉ éd., Hachette, s.d., 2 vols., i. 2; cf. Chevrillon, op. cit., p. 94.

talk as though 'faculties', 'capacities', and even 'substance' and 'the self' really exist is to fall into metaphysical illusion[1]—an illusion into which, ironically enough, Taine himself seems to fall later— in talking of 'facultés maîtresses' for example. Nor is *a priori* knowledge any more acceptable, and in consequence he severely qualifies his youthful admiration for Spinoza (as early as 1849) and Hegel (in 1852). His own 'method of abstraction', in contrast, is to work wholly within the field of observed facts, he alleges, and to eschew false abstraction: it is derived from scientific procedure itself. To gather facts is only 'the starting-point of science'; one must then search for the 'causes' which order and determine these facts. To do this, one proceeds by abstracting what is common to a whole group of facts in order to form an 'hypothesis' as to what is its 'causal fact', after which one tests experimentally to see whether this hypothesis is justified. 'Abstraction, hypothèse, véri- fication, tels sont les trois pas de la méthode. Il n'en faut pas davantage, et il les faut tous.'[2] Thus, for example, he maintains in his *Introduction à l'histoire de la littérature anglaise* that the literary historian, having collected facts and studied the personality of an author, can go on to discern the three great causes of *race, moment*, and *milieu* from which his work stems. In this way, moreover, literary study can make its contribution to the science of psy- chology.

Although this method is that of any scientist, provided only that Taine's 'causes' are equated with science's 'laws', he claimed to be going *beyond* positivism. The explanation of this apparently para- doxical situation is that Taine's interpretation of the results of the method went far beyond the positivist interpretation of science's results: it was here that Taine transgressed his positivist starting- point, and on this transgression rested the superstructure of his method for a scientific metaphysics. For in reality Taine means more by 'causes' than a scientist means by 'laws'. 'Laws' for the sciences are not absolute certainties. From a finite number of observations one cannot induce a law of infinite applicability; no set of observations can be known to be wholly exhaustive and accurate; it *may* be that the 'order' the sciences 'discover' in Nature

---

[1] Cf. *De l'intelligence*, i. 1-2.   [2] *Les Philosophes classiques*, p. 363.

is in fact 'projected' upon it by the human mind; to adopt Kant's distinction, we know phenomena and not 'things in themselves'. Thus scientific laws give a considerable degree of 'practical certainty' and are justified by their predictive utility, but science can never pretend to give certain or comprehensive knowledge of 'reality in itself'. Taine, however, circumvents these limitations, and he does so in virtue of two assumptions taken from Spinoza and Hegel when he was a young man and underlying all his mature thought: first, that a rigorous determinism operates in the world, and secondly, that reality is rational—in Spinoza's words, that 'the order and connexion of ideas is the same as the order and connexion of things'. The former view banishes the possibility of chance and assures us that Nature is a unity, 'une hiérarchie de nécessités', each and every part of it causally related to the rest.[1] The latter belief allows Taine to discount the relativism of Kant and the positivists: the intelligibility of the world inheres in the world itself and is not merely projected upon it by us, and the correlation between reality and our minds vouches for the reliability of our observations; perception reveals the 'things in themselves', it is 'une hallucination vraie'—a curious description in which Taine pays simultaneous homage to both the phenomenalist and the realist positions.[2]

These assumptions pave the way for the full presentation of his method. By abstraction from a group of observed facts we may reach the 'cause' of the group, and for 'cause' we may now substitute terms like 'generating formula', 'explanatory reason', or 'true definition'—for a definition of, say, 'gravity' or 'a sphere' does not merely define a name as Mill thought (i.e. our use of the word), but 'la cause intérieure et primordiale de toutes ses propriétés'.[3] Science, in short, can reach 'true definitions': it need no longer be confined to the 'how' of phenomena but can grasp the 'why' of reality.[4] As Taine triumphantly puts it, 'nous ne sommes plus capables seulement de connaissances relatives et bornées; nous sommes capables aussi de connaissances absolues et sans limites'.[5]

---

[1] ibid., p. 370; cf. *De l'intelligence*, ii. 383–4.   [2] *De l'intelligence*, ii. 10 and *passim*.
[3] *Histoire de la littérature anglaise*, v. 360.   [4] *Essais de critique et d'histoire*, p. viii.
[5] *De l'intelligence*, ii. 383–4.

From groups of these 'causes' or 'definitions' we can now abstract again to uncover *their* 'causes', and so on until eventually we reach the all-inclusive 'cause' or 'definition' of each of the particular sciences. And we may then abstract yet again from even these 'sovereign definitions' and perceive the supreme cause from which everything in Nature derives: 'nous découvrons l'unité de l'univers et nous comprenons ce qui la produit'.[1] We shall have conquered the summit of the pyramid of knowledge and achieved the goal of metaphysics—and all this by a method Taine believes is scientific. Where everywhere in Mill he had found an 'abyss of chance' and an 'abyss of ignorance', he himself has attained a totally certain and comprehensive knowledge.

Taine's vision, yielding to pantheistic exaltation, may be an inspiring one, but this attempted fusion of positivism and idealism is unsatisfactory, from the former's standpoint at least. It rests on *a priori* assumptions, we have seen, that can never in principle be verified. His attitude to 'facts' is also far looser than that of a scientist, especially when he claims that 'causes' are 'facts'—a claim essential to his view that in 'true abstraction' we never move outside the realm of facts. 'Nutrition', 'decomposition', 'gravity'—these are facts for Taine, whereas for science they are names used to summarize a group of phenomena, phenomena alone being regarded as facts.[2] Or again he can equate and claim the same validity for scientific facts and the conclusions of a literary historian, for 'une formation de tissus observés au microscope', 'un chiffre d'équivalent constaté par la balance', *and* 'une concordance de facultés et de sentiments démêlés par la critique'.[3] His usage of 'cause' is equally unscientific—so that, for instance, he regards as 'causes' not only nutrition, decomposition, and gravity, but also the species to which an animal belongs;[4] and he has also been accused of confusing efficient and final causes.[5] Taine's method may be modelled on that of the sciences, but since an

---

[1] *Les Philosophes classiques*, p. 368. On Taine's pantheism, cf. pp. 121-5 below.
[2] ibid., pp. viii, 358.   [3] *Essais de critique et d'histoire*, p. xxi.
[4] *Les Philosophes classiques*, p. 136.
[5] Cf., for example, E. Caro, *L'Idée de Dieu et ses nouveaux critiques*, Hachette, 1864, pp. 222-3; J. Lachelier, cited by V. Giraud, *Essai sur Taine*, 6ᵉ éd., Hachette, s.d., pp. 297-8; and Chevrillon, op. cit., p. 272.

Hegelian meaning is given to 'facts', 'laws', and 'causes', it is certainly not, as he alleges, the scientific method itself.[1]

Taine applied his method to the fields of history, art, literature, and psychology, often to stimulating purpose—a man's work may often be valuable even if ill-based philosophically. But he did not apply it to metaphysics itself, surprisingly enough, or to religion, which for him was only 'une sorte de poème tenu pour vrai',[2] or even to ethics. 'Je n'ai point tant de prétention [he remarks] que d'avoir un système: j'essaye tout au plus de suivre une méthode.'[3] Yet he did believe he had prepared the way for an extension of the scientific method into these fields, and he could assert, having surveyed its past achievements: 'Dans cet emploi de la science et dans cette conception des choses il y a un art, une morale, une politique, une religion nouvelles, et c'est notre affaire aujourd'hui de les chercher.[4] This famous assertion illustrates that the real conclusion of his thought was scientism, scientism resulting from the addition of German idealism and positivism. Like Comte, he urged that science could surmount its own boundaries, and it is thus not surprising that Mill, for instance, was as critical of this aspect of his work as any anti-positivist. Taine has sought to reject 'the inherent limitations of human experience', to reach up to 'an absolute truth, valid for the entire universe, and independent of the limits of experience'.[5] It is small wonder that his metaphysical endeavour, however understandable or impressive, failed.

A similar judgement may fairly be passed upon the whole tradition of thought we have followed from Comte to Taine, and of which many lesser examples could be given—Berthelot, Ernest Havet, and the Zola of *Le Docteur Pascal* and *Le Roman expérimental*, for example. Too much was claimed for science, too much was promised on its behalf. Reality was exclusively equated with what is scientifically knowable: hence the seemingly paradoxical fact that the 'unknowable', in origin a positivist notion that acknowledges the limitations of scientific method, was invoked in the last

---

[1] The best discussion of Taine's 'Hegelianism' is D. D. Rosca, *L'Influence de Hegel sur Taine*, Gamber, 1928.   [2] *Histoire de la littérature anglaise*, t. i, p. xxxiii.
[3] *Essais de critique et d'histoire*, p. xiii.   [4] *Histoire de la littérature anglaise*, iv. 390.
[5] J. S. Mill, *Dissertations and Discussions*, vol. iv, London, Longmans, 1875, pp. 113, 118.

decades of the century by *opponents* of positivism like Bourget and Brunetière. Again, the provisional, working determinism of the sciences was replaced in Taine and others by a form of fatalist determinism: hence Boutroux, for example, pointing to an element of indeterminacy in Nature, would appear to be countering the positivist position itself and not merely, as he was in fact, a perversion of it. Yet again, Taine claimed that science gives knowledge of 'reality in itself'—the same 'scientific realism' we saw in Comte and Littré—with the illogical corollary that reality *is* what science can know and nothing more: hence the further apparent paradox that Henri Poincaré later—a major figure in the true positivist tradition—should have been taken so often for an anti-positivist when he argued that the laws of science are 'useful hypotheses' or that a particular geometrical system is not necessarily 'true to reality' but only 'convenient'. In short, the outcome of these thinkers' work was to confuse positivism properly speaking with scientism, and sometimes with fatalism and materialism as well, and to associate it in men's minds with a narrowing of human interest, an exclusive concentration upon what is accessible to scientific study. In varying degrees they all betrayed the positivist standpoint and replaced it by a new metaphysics, for that is what their exaggerated trust in science involved, a metaphysics, despite all their progressive intentions, that proved to be mentally restrictive and against which the Symbolist poets would understandably react into a cult of the mysterious and immaterial, whilst others like Bourget, Brunetière, and Huysmans would return to Catholicism. Their confusions also necessitated a new critical scrutiny of the methods and assumptions of the sciences. Not all the scientists of their time or all the philosophers sympathetic to science accepted their views, and the final years of the century were to see a notable progress in the philosophy of science, effected by scientists like Claude Bernard, Ribot, and Poincaré, and philosophers like Cournot, Renouvier, and Lachelier. They would greatly qualify their predecessors' well-nigh religious trust in science and wholly reject their pretension that, like a deity, it could be all-powerful and all-knowing.

IV

Social Religions

1. Henri de Saint-Simon

PIERRE TRAHARD comments on the revolutionaries of the 1790's: 'Rares sont ceux qui versent dans l'incroyance totale, l'athéisme ou la libre-pensée.' [1] The same was true of the following generation of social activists. Just as the former subscribed to the Revolutionary cults of Nature, Reason, and the Supreme Being, of 'la Sainte Liberté', 'la Sainte Égalité', and 'la Patrie', so the latter compounded religions of Humanity, Nature, Progress, and Justice, sometimes underrun, moreover, by a glorification of the Revolution itself and of France in the manner of Michelet's *Le Peuple*. This chapter will attempt to make a representative selection amongst the many such creeds which were developed during our period, especially in the years up to 1848.

The primary concern of these thinkers was with social utility, again like their predecessors. Their wider political theories fall outside the scope of this study and can only be rapidly indicated, but at their heart in almost every case—Proudhon is the outstanding exception—there lies a social religion, that is to say a system whose primary, though not necessarily exclusive preoccupation is with religion as uniting and inspiring a whole society and with men as citizens rather than as private individuals. All would have repudiated emphatically A. N. Whitehead's claim that religion is what a man does with his solitariness.

The first of these social prophets to demand attention, and one of the most influential, is Henri de Saint-Simon (1760–1825). We saw earlier the impetus lent to the growth of positivist thought by his ideas about the reorganization of science and its extension to include the study of society in the form of 'la science de l'homme'. Yet even more influential were his political and economic theories, so much so that even Marx and Engels were led to praise him as

[1] *La Sensibilité révolutionnaire (1789–1794)*, Boivin, 1936, p. 156.

65

being 'with Hegel, the most encyclopaedic mind of his age'. He has commonly and rightly been seen as a founder of socialism— even though he denied that there is any necessary clash between the capitalists and the workers. Far from holding that view, indeed, he urged that, whereas previous societies have been dominated by soldiers and the nobility, in the nineteenth century capitalists and workers together—'les industriels', as he termed them—should take over power and plan society and economic production for the physical, mental, and moral well-being of 'la classe la plus nombreuse et la plus pauvre'. He attacked, unlike Marx and many later socialists, not the owners and managers of industry, but solely 'les oisifs'—princes, nobles, soldiers, politicians, and landlords, who live as parasites on society and add nothing to its prosperity. In his ideal community work will be the primary right and duty of all and private property will be allowed only where it is rightly used for the benefit of society as a whole. Not that he wanted a democracy, which he regarded as the rule of ignorance rather than knowledge; economic and social organization should be in the hands of the industrialists, bankers, and scientists.

Yet society requires more than reorganization and the stimulus of industrial and technological expansion. Above all it needs a new, unified philosophical and moral faith to replace the Christian religion, for this, in his view, has become indifferent to social progress because of its concern with the after-life. 'Il faut passer de la morale céleste à la morale terrestre.'[1] The new code to which he aspires is to be spread through universal primary education, but he accepts that reason alone will prove too weak a motive-force: men's emotions must also be aroused. To achieve this will involve the creation of a new 'spiritual power' to supersede the Catholic Church. In his earlier career he believed that a purely scientific and indeed materialistic religion, without a God or a theology, would suffice to impel men to communal service. In his very first book, *Lettres d'un habitant de Genève* (1803), he proposed to base this creed on the law of gravitation, which for several years (in common with Fourier and others) he thought to be the great unifying

[1] *Œuvres de Saint-Simon et d'Enfantin*, Dentu et Leroux, 1865–78, 47 vols., xix. 37.

principle of the universe. He enshrined Newton as his religious prophet, with a 'Council of Newton' to take the place of the Catholic hierarchy and 'temples of Newton' for worship, research, and instruction. A little later he revised this religion and gave it the name of 'physicism', but he was soon forced to recognize that whilst it might satisfy the educated class, only a theistic creed could appeal to 'la classe ignorante'. He therefore came to accept that the notion of God he had earlier thought outworn could at least stand as a useful symbol of the unity of Nature, of the 'One-ness of All', and in his final years he devoted himself to developing the new faith in more detail. The outcome was his 'nouveau christianisme'. 'Pour faire de grandes choses, il faut être passionné . . . [he is said to have declared on his death-bed]; la religion ne peut disparaître du monde: elle ne peut que se transformer.'

The transformation he proposed is found in his last work, entitled *Nouveau Christianisme*, written only two months before his death in May 1825, and first published in the same year. It is subtitled 'Premier Dialogue', but he was never to write the second and third dialogues, which he planned to devote to the theoretical and scientific justification of his religion and to its ethic, worship, and dogma. His central plea is for a return to what he alleges to be 'the true spirit of Christianity', to which Catholics and Protestants alike have been false. The book's title-page bears a significant epigraph from St. Paul's Epistle to the Romans: 'Celui qui aime les autres a accompli la loi. Tout est compris en abrégé dans cette parole: tu aimeras ton prochain comme toi-même.' [1] This indicates at once his own understanding of Christianity's 'true spirit', and he criticizes the existing churches in the light of it. The Roman Church, manipulated since the fifteenth century by power-priests and worldly popes, neglects social morality, remains in quiescent ignorance of modern scientific and industrial knowledge, permits in its own territory of the Papal States the 'most vicious and anti-Christian' administration in Europe, protects the Inquisition and the Jesuits, both wholly contrary to the Christian spirit of gentleness, charity, and honesty, and sides with

[1] ibid., xxiii. 99.

the rich against the poor in order to preserve its own domination over the laity. Saint-Simon can praise Luther for his achievement as a critic of Rome, but when he established a new church he too disregarded the social significance of Christ's teaching and encouraged a meek obedience of the secular powers. Protestants have also been excessively preoccupied with the Bible, he thinks, to the neglect of present-day problems, and their fundamentalism fetters them to long-outdated dogmas and blinds them to all new ideas. Moreover, their ban on the use of art, sculpture, and music in their churches has made worship a less effective incentive to moral action.

These criticisms clearly reveal Saint-Simon's own conviction that religion's essential concern is morality; as he says,

la doctrine de la morale sera considérée par les nouveaux chrétiens comme la plus importante; le culte et le dogme ne seront envisagés par eux que comme des accessoires, ayant pour objet principal de fixer sur la morale l'attention des fidèles de toutes les classes.[1]

He begins his dialogue with an imaginary conservative—who is later 'entirely convinced' and becomes 'a new Christian'—by affirming his belief in God, though whether as symbol or as reality remains in mystery. He then passes with almost suspicious rapidity to the central principle of his creed and, in his eyes, of Christ's own message. 'Dieu a dit: *Les hommes doivent se conduire en frères à l'égard les uns des autres*; ce principe sublime renferme tout ce qu'il y a de divin dans la religion chrétienne.'[2] He deduces from this that religion's primary task in the present age is to direct society towards 'le grand but de l'amélioration la plus rapide possible du sort de la classe la plus pauvre', an obligation that the Christian churches have signally failed to shoulder.[3] Man's purpose lies less in salvation for an after-life (in which Saint-Simon almost certainly did not believe) than in helping to achieve 'le plus haut degré de félicité que [l'espèce humaine] puisse atteindre pendant sa vie terrestre'.[4]

Here is the doctrinal kernel of the new religion, for which, had

---

[1] *Œuvres de Saint-Simon et d'Enfantin*, xxiii. 116–17.
[2] ibid., xxiii. 108.   [3] ibid., xxiii. 117.   [4] ibid., xxiii. 148.

he lived, he intended to provide a form of worship, a creed, a priesthood, and a comprehensive new 'theology' that would synthesize all existing knowledge. His aim, it is clear, is to translate Christianity into this-worldly terms. This life is no longer a mere testing-place for eternity but potentially the setting for paradise itself. The 'golden age' does not lie in the past, in the Garden of Eden, or in a future life in heaven, but in the earthly future, in the perfection of social order. Nor is this his only difference from Christianity. He also rejects the doctrine of the Fall of man and substitutes his own optimistic view of human nature. Men have improved morally through the ages in step with the wider movement of progress, and he ardently believes that it is within their power to establish a perfect society. Nor, finally, can he accept the Christian preoccupation with spiritual perfection to the exclusion of man's physical well-being. Christianity has had too narrow a conception of what is important in human nature; its 'repression of the flesh' must yield to a reinstatement of 'the whole man' and a rehabilitation of life's sensual pleasures. In short, Saint-Simon omits or drastically amends Christianity's doctrines of man, sin, redemption, grace, the future life, and (it would certainly appear) God. His criticisms of the Christian religion are often suggestive and soundly based in historical fact, but his followers might well wonder whether this new creed ought to be called Christianity at all. It is in essence a social gospel of fraternity and of work on behalf of the poor and oppressed, and its whole emphasis is summed up in his final exhortation to the rulers of the world—the conclusion of *Nouveau Christianisme* and the last words he was to write:

PRINCES, Écoutez la voix de Dieu, qui vous parle par ma bouche; redevenez bons chrétiens, cessez de considérer les armées soldées, les nobles, les clergés hérétiques et les juges pervers comme vos soutiens principaux; unis au nom du Christianisme, sachez accomplir tous les devoirs qu'il impose aux puissants; rappelez-vous qu'il leur commande d'employer toutes leurs forces à accroître le plus rapidement possible le bonheur social du pauvre! [1]

But to share these generous-hearted social aims is not to accept

[1] ibid., xxiii. 192.

69

Saint-Simon's claims that they constitute the only essential doctrine of the teaching of Christ.

2. The Saint-Simonians

It was in fact left to his followers, after his death, to expand his religious ideas into an organized creed quite separate from Christianity. Its leading proponents were Prosper Enfantin (1796–1864), an engineer of a mystical turn of mind, educated like so many Saint-Simonians at the École Polytechnique, Olinde Rodrigues (1794–1851), and Saint-Amand Bazard (1791–1832). Theirs was the 'religion of love' that inspired Heine and other 'Young German' poets of the 1830's and 1840's and that in France affected Pierre Leroux and, partly through him, such Romantic writers as George Sand, Hugo, Sainte-Beuve, and Vigny, whilst as a school of social thought the Saint-Simonians were to have an even wider influence—on Mill, Carlyle, Marx, and Engels amongst others.[1] Briefly, they modified their master's economic and political teaching in the direction of state socialism, advocating public ownership of all industry and banking and the abolition of property inheritance. They also inspired the creation of railways and canals and the expansion of industry, and several of them became, indeed, leading engineers, financiers, or industrialists. They have even been called 'the most important single force behind the great economic expansion of the Second Empire', partly by virtue of their own initiative and ability, partly through their former adherent, Louis-Napoléon himself, 'Saint-Simon on horseback', as Sainte-Beuve once dubbed him.[2]

Here, however, their ideas and activities in relation to the industrial revolution, though unquestionably more influential, interest us less than their religious ideas. These were expounded, after the journal *Le Producteur* ceased in 1826, by means of fortnightly public lectures—probably in imitation of Comte, who was

[1] For their influence in Germany and England, cf. the works by Butler, Mueller, and Pankhurst in Bibliography, pp. 225–6 below. For the French writers, cf. D. O. Evans, *Le Socialisme romantique—Pierre Leroux et ses contemporains*, Marcel Rivière, 1948, and also M. Leroy, *La Politique de Sainte-Beuve*, 6e éd., Gallimard, s.d., pp. 29–114.

[2] F. M. H. Markham, 'Introduction' to *Saint-Simon: Selected Writings*, Oxford, Blackwell, 1952, p. xli. Cf. G. Weill, 'Les Saint-Simoniens sous Napoléon III', *Revue des études Napoléoniennes*, iii, 1913, pp. 391–406.

already giving *leçons* at his home. The lectures, usually delivered by Bazard but collectively prepared, ran from December 1828 to 1830, and whilst they dealt with social and economic ideas, they tried especially to justify the new religious formulation of Saint-Simonism, for this was repugnant to certain scientifically minded followers. They stress, first, that the natural sciences do not exclude religion.[1] Science can prove nothing against 'les deux idées fondamentales de toute religion: *Providence* et *destination*'—the existence of God and of a providential plan. On the contrary, science itself derives from an essentially religious idea—that there is order and regularity in the world of phenomena. It will be seen, once the critical scepticism inherited from the eighteenth century has dispersed, as 'le moyen donné à l'esprit humain de *connaître les lois par lesquelles* DIEU *gouverne le monde*; de connaître, en d'autres termes, LE PLAN DE LA PROVIDENCE'. Thus the sciences will in future extend and strengthen 'le *sentiment* religieux, puisque chacune de leurs découvertes . . . devait aussi agrandir, confirmer, fortifier l'AMOUR que l'homme peut concevoir pour la suprême *intelligence* qui le conduit sans cesse à de meilleures destinées . . .' Secondly, the natural sciences deal with a very restricted area of experience, excluding man's moral and social life, and hence they have been unable to give any general explanation of the universe. Thirdly, it is erroneous to imagine that, as progress has advanced, religion has declined. This may be true of the destructive critical period of the seventeenth and eighteenth centuries, but on a far longer view of history we see that man's religions have themselves evolved with the evolution of knowledge, moving (for instance) from fetichism and polytheism to monotheism. Science and religion must develop hand in hand, religion giving up its authoritarian claims to 'absolute truth' and science ridding itself of anti-religious bias, of 'les SOPHISMES implantés dans les esprits par la philosophie critique', 'les PRÉJUGÉS de l'athéisme', 'les HYPOTHÈSES désolantes de l'égoïsme'.[2] Scientific scepticism thus placated, the way was now prepared for the new religion and the organization of the new religious sect.

[1] *Doctrine de Saint-Simon: Exposition—Première Année, 1829*, ed. Bouglé and Halévy, Marcel Rivière, 1924, pp. 486-9. [2] ibid., p. 500.

The history of this sect was one of tragi-comic excess and exceedingly rapid rise and decline. Within four years of Saint-Simon's death they had elaborated a religious doctrine, founded their new Church (in December 1829), complete with a hierarchy of 'fathers' and 'apostles', and organized departmental churches in provincial cities like Dijon, Lyons, Metz, Montpellier, and Toulouse, and they also had centres in Belgium. Hymns and songs were composed, a calendar was drawn up which celebrated a different famous man on each day of the week and each date in the month, and rituals were arranged for such occasions as baptism, marriage, and burial. By late-1831, however, the sect was already afflicted by schism. Largely because of Enfantin's views on divorce and the liberation of women, Bazard, Leroux, and others withdrew after a very stormy 'réunion générale de la Famille' on 19 November—of which, characteristically, the Saint-Simonians published a verbatim account. The majority sided with Rodrigues, however, when he concluded the meeting—despite Leroux's impassioned protests—by saluting 'le Père Enfantin' as 'l'homme le plus MORAL de mon temps, . . . le CHEF SUPRÊME de la RELIGION SAINT-SIMONIENNE'. (*'Bravos et applaudissements prolongés'*, reports the published transcript.)[1] In 1832 the surviving members founded a religious community at Ménilmontant, just outside Paris. Here, under the spell of Enfantin's personality, there lived in a state of celibacy and without servants a group of highly intelligent men—engineers, scientists, doctors, lawyers—whose day, from 5 a.m., was spent in digging, washing up, cooking, and brick-laying, as well as in lectures and religious rites. To this period belong some of the more comic episodes in the fortunes of this creed: the public confessions of mutual love; the cult of beards and of waistcoats buttoning at the back—as a reminder of each man's dependence on his fellows; the unsuccessful search—leading by 1833 to the Near East, with which Enfantin felt a mystic affinity—for the 'Mère suprême' who was to take up priestly office at the side of the 'Père suprême', a role refused in turn by George Sand and (it has been said) Lady Hestor Stan-

---

[1] B. P. Enfantin and É. Barrault, *Religion saint-simonienne: Morale*, Librairie Saint-Simonienne, 1832, p. 58.

hope. Two of the hymns sung at Ménilmontant may perhaps illustrate the sect's characteristic mixture of humanitarian ardour and fatally humourless solemnity. The first, by Barrault, was for after meals, prior to renewed digging.

> Au travail!
> Notre force est réparée;
> Remplis d'une ardeur sacrée
> Marchons!
> Oui, nous rendrons au monde
> Cette vigueur féconde
> Qu'il a mise en nos cœurs.
> Père,
> Nous sommes prêts, marchons!

The second example is the final verse of *L'Homme Nouveau*, to be sung to the air of the *Marseillaise*.

> Ennemis du SAINT-SIMONISME,
> Vainement vous portez vos coups;
> Il détruira le fanatisme:
> DIEU l'inspire et sera pour nous. (*bis*)
> En dépit de la calomnie,
> L'APÔTRE propage sa foi;
> Le bonheur du PEUPLE est sa loi,
> L'UNIVERS voilà sa patrie.
> Enfants du même DIEU, plus de servilité.
> L'HOMME NOUVEAU chérit le Père et sent sa dignité.[1]

It is perhaps not surprising if a trip to Ménilmontant became a favourite week-end outing for many Parisians.

It ended in the trial of Enfantin in 1832 for offending against public morality; official concern had been aroused, especially by his division of humanity into the sexually constant and inconstant and his proposal of easy divorce for the inconstant. He and two 'apostles' were imprisoned and the community was dissolved. By the time he was released his followers had almost all gone, and he too was now obsessed by a new idea, that of a Suez Canal—finally

[1] *Chants*, no publisher or date, p. 9, and *Chansonnier saint-simonien*, no publisher or date, pp. 4–5.

carried out later by Lesseps, a lapsed Saint-Simonian who was also to undertake another of Saint-Simon's schemes, the building of the Panama Canal. After leading an unfortunate expedition to Egypt, Enfantin later became the chief promoter and general secretary of the Paris-Lyon-Méditerranée railway organization, and though he published *La Science de l'homme* in 1858 and *La Vie éternelle* in 1861—both new expositions of his former ideas—when he died in 1864 he was a successful business man and a contented *père de famille* rather than a religious prophet.

Yet it would be superficial to dismiss the Saint-Simonian religion because of Enfantin's excesses and the more absurd details of sacerdotal organization. Its leaders undoubtedly combined alert intelligence with their messianic eccentricity, and its main characteristics set a pattern for later social religions. First, it is essentially a corporate creed which affirms that the principle of individualism or 'antagonism' must yield to the principle of unity or 'association'. Bazard explicitly rejects religion that is merely 'le résultat d'une contemplation intérieure et purement individuelle'. True religion must be '*l'expression de la pensée collective* de l'humanité, la *synthèse* de toutes ses *conceptions*, la *règle* de tous ses *actes*'. Secondly, it is inextricably linked with the future social order, so much so that the lecturer can assert that 'l'institution politique de l'avenir . . . ne doit être qu'une institution religieuse'.[1] Conversely, this religion's primary purpose is to inspire and maintain this secular order, and its central doctrine, as for Saint-Simon, is moral: love of one's fellows and especially of the hitherto underprivileged. 'DIEU m'a donné mission [declared Enfantin in one of numerous similar addresses to his followers] d'*appeler* le PROLÉTAIRE et la FEMME à une destinée nouvelle; de faire entrer dans la SAINTE FAMILLE HUMAINE tous ceux qui jusqu'ici en ont été *exclus*. . . .'[2] Thirdly, this doctrine moves away from the Christian notion of God as separate from His universe and adopts a pantheistic conception in which God and the world are one.[3] Fourthly, it contends that whilst Christianity was an advance on previous

---

[1] *Doctrine de Saint-Simon*, p. 487.
[2] *Religion saint-simonienne: A Tous*, Librairie Saint-Simonienne, 1832, p. 1.
[3] Cf. *Doctrine de Saint-Simon*, pp. 489–90.

religions in its intellectual and moral beliefs, it has grossly neglected and indeed despised the physical realm. The Christian
Church preaches mortification of the flesh, views celibacy as a
higher state than marriage, teaches that work is a curse inherited
from Adam, disregards men's material well-being, and adopts a
reactionary political role; it places the goal of life in another
world, defines God as wholly spiritual, and sees this world as no
more than a vale of tears. In opposition to this deep-rooted attitude the Saint-Simonians, like their master, preach the 'rehabilitation of matter'—and with it of work, marriage, sex, and man's
physical well-being. They claim to be concerned, unlike the
Christians, with all three of the major elements in human life as
they see it: intelligence, represented in the new society by 'les
savants', love, represented by both the new religion and the artists,
and force or matter, represented by 'les industriels'. Body is to be
reconciled with mind, the temporal power with the spiritual, the
State with the Church, and hence Bazard can proclaim:

C'est un nouvel état moral, un nouvel état politique que nous annon-
çons; c'est donc également un état religieux tout nouveau; car, pour
nous, *religion, politique, morale*, ne sont que des appellations diverses
d'un même fait. . . .[1]

Such are the main features of a cult that is to be propounded
theoretically by the savants—its 'theologians'—and in a more con-
crete and moving fashion by its 'priests'—the artists, who are
called by the Saint-Simonians as by Comte, the Marxists, and
others later to devote themselves to work of moral utility that can
inspire high ideals.

It has to be admitted, however, that the Saint-Simonians' religion, in marked contrast to their economic and political thought,
was all but still-born. One of their best historians concludes that it
was a 'very miserable failure'.[2] In part this was due to the temperament and excesses of Enfantin and to the secession of able
thinkers like Bazard and Leroux to which these led, but it was

[1] ibid., p. 486.
[2] S. Charléty, *Histoire du saint-simonisme (1825-1864)*, 2ᵉ éd., Hartmann, 1931, p. 359.

perhaps no less the outcome of the religion's doctrinal short-comings. The basic defect lies in its exceedingly vague concept of 'God'. One may acknowledge the world's 'infinite unity', but why deify it? And when this pantheistic divinity is defined as 'l'amour infini, universel', can that be reconciled with all Nature's cruelties? Even if it can, is not this too vast and amorphous a deity for a limited human mind to *love*? As Carlyle was to remark, Saint-Simonism lacks a symbol of deity—God made tangible as in the Christian Incarnation. Truth to tell, Saint-Simon and his disciples alike were only mildly interested in the existence of God and other similarly extra-terrestrial mysteries. Bazard and Rodrigues, for instance, were at first indifferent to the question of a future life, and in 1829 Enfantin himself dismissed the Creation and death as 'deux inconnues supérieures à l'intelligence humaine'.[1] Bazard refers to 'la *Religion* ou la morale, la *Théologie* ou la science, le *Culte* ou l'industrie', and these equations are characteristic—theology as the study of *Nature*, religion as *morality*, worship trans-formed into business management.[2] Lamartine once commented: 'C'est une religion, moins un Dieu; c'est le christianisme, moins la foi qui en est la vie',[3] and for all practical purposes this is true. Con-sequently, since social utility was placed so far above the love and worship of a deity, mysticism and spirituality were largely absent from this religion, and this fact, as Durkheim perceptively re-marks, affected Saint-Simonism's value even as a regulator of social and economic morality. He points out that Christianity has been able to fulfil its social role because, quite the reverse of Saint-Simonian theology, it set God beyond things.

Mais si Dieu se confond avec le monde, comme nous dominons le monde autant qu'il nous domine, comme le monde par lui-même n'est pas une force morale, nous sommes de niveau avec la divinité, et par conséquent, ce n'est pas de là que peut venir la discipline indis-pensable.[4]

---

[1] Cf. Charléty, op. cit., p. 141.

[2] *Doctrine de Saint-Simon—Deuxième Année, Œuvres de Saint-Simon et d'Enfantin*, xlii. 337.

[3] A. de Lamartine, *Sur la politique rationnelle* (1831), in *Œuvres complètes*, Chez l'auteur, 1860–3, 40 vols., xxxvii. 384.

[4] É. Durkheim, *Le Socialisme*, Alcan, 1928, p. 339.

Gouhier says of Saint-Simon that his was not a religion, but a social philosophy disguised as a religion;[1] despite their good intentions, much the same was true of his disciples. For them religion was above all (in Charléty's words) 'une image pour donner de l'autorité à leurs idées'.[2] Publicity of the wrong sort dispersed the last vestiges of the numinous. This creed inevitably lacked the poetic aura provided by remote origins and an obscure history; the scandal of Enfantin's trial did nothing to compensate.

Yet if the publicity and total absence of mystery that surrounded the *Père suprême's* teaching was a source of its failure, it is only fair to note that Enfantin almost alone amongst the leaders became aware that the supernatural was all too absent from his creed. By 1830, in his 'Lettre à Duveyrier', he was sketching the ideas on eternal life that he expanded much later in *La Vie éternelle*.[3] He puts forward two different notions, though they seem to be confused in his mind. First, since God is all that is (his pantheist premiss), it follows that every soul is eternal like God. Secondly, he argues that each soul persists by virtue of its reincarnation in a succession of individuals. He suggests, for example, that St. Paul, Saint-Simon, and Enfantin himself are three incarnations of the same soul. It has to be remarked, unfortunately, that both notions greatly diminish the reality of the individual. The first denies ultimate independence to even the soul that is reincarnated. God, Enfantin declares, is 'la vie éternelle et universelle: donc toute existence est une manifestation de la sienne'. The second theory holds the consequence that whilst what is for the present 'my' soul may be immortal, my personality (that which is Saint-Simon and not St. Paul, for example) enjoys no future life, except in so far as (a third theory, more lightly sketched) my thoughts and actions may 'live on' in the future. Thus Enfantin's doctrine offers the believer a far more insubstantial immortality than the Christian— and at the same time requires no less of an act of faith in the unprovable, for there is no evidence either for the reincarnation theory or for the belief that Nature, the Saint-Simonian deity, will

---

[1] H. Gouhier, *La Jeunesse d'Auguste Comte et la formation du positivisme*, 1933–41, 3 vols., iii. 231.
[2] Charléty, op. cit., p. 362.   [3] Cf. ibid., pp. 141 ff.

endure eternally. It is also noteworthy that just as the soul's successive 'existences' are all in this world, not in a world to come, so heaven and hell take on a purely terrestrial location.

L'enfer, le purgatoire, le paradis [writes Enfantin], c'est la vie mauvaise, progressive, bonne; . . . c'est la triple phase de peine, d'éducation et de récompense que parcourt toute existence, à travers les siècles et les mondes, dans le sein de Dieu.[1]

The Saint-Simonians made what in retrospect seems a further error. They opted for authoritarianism and against liberalism, and this in an age of widening freedom of thought. Their choice, common to many others of both Right and Left, resulted partly from Enfantin's own personality but more fundamentally from the fact that Catholicism was their model. Even Saint-Simon himself, significantly, praises Bonald for his emphasis upon a 'systematic unity', and he also admired Joseph de Maistre. None the less, at the conclusion of *Nouveau Christianisme* Saint-Simon repudiated the authoritarian methods of the Roman Church and contended that persuasion by argument would suffice to convert others to his creed.[2] But his followers, seeing religion as above all institutional and centred upon the state, and convinced that only a strong religion could canalize the flood waters of a society in a condition of revolutionary change, reverted to the autocratic assumptions of Rome. They became, as Erdan wittily remarks, 'les jésuites du socialisme',[3] and in this regard at least Flaubert's Deslauriers in *L'Éducation sentimentale* is quite right when he refers to the Saint-Simonians as 'un tas de farceurs qui voudraient nous refaire le catholicisme'.[4] Men who had thrown off the intellectual chains of the Papacy despite its claims to supernatural inspiration were unlikely to accept the new fetters of Enfantin's all-too-human dogmatics. Hence this religion not only failed to establish itself, but

---

[1] Cited by Charléty, op. cit., p. 323.

[2] *Œuvres de Saint-Simon et d'Enfantin*, xxiii. 178–9.

[3] A. Erdan, *La France mystique*, Coulon-Pineau, s.d., 2 vols., ii. 514. For an extended discussion of this union of social 'messianism' and authoritarianism, cf. J. L. Talmon's two volumes, *The Origins of Totalitarian Democracy* and *Political Messianism: The Romantic Phase*, London, Secker & Warburg, 1952 and 1960. On the Saint-Simonians, cf. the latter volume, pp. 35–124.

[4] G. Flaubert, *L'Éducation sentimentale*, in *Œuvres*, Gallimard, 1946–52, 2 vols., ii. 169.

the disrepute into which it fell did disservice to the wiser social theories of its founders. Charléty even concludes that the attempt to create a religion was their 'fundamental error'.[1]

3. *Charles Fourier and Pierre Leroux*

Schism swiftly afflicted the Saint-Simonian sect, as we saw, but those who broke with it often preserved both a marked religious concern and elements of the creed they had rejected. They renounced Enfantin but not Saint-Simon. Some, like Philippe Buchez, turned to a Catholic socialism and argued that Saint-Simon's political and industrial plans could be fulfilled only if the Christian ideas of charity, equality, and fraternity were fully applied to social affairs. Constantin Pecqueur, after rejecting Saint-Simonism on account of its authoritarian tendencies, also adopted an approach that was at least semi-Christian. In some ways not unlike Marx, he refused, however, to accept class-warfare as a means of changing society and based his advocacy of collective ownership of the means of production upon the principles of divine justice. It is true that by 1844 when he published *De la république de Dieu* he seems to have diverged from Christianity; he now preaches a progressivist 'religion of fraternity' whose adherents he calls 'philadelphes'. But its doctrines and ethics are still close to the basic Christian teachings.[2] Yet another lapsed Saint-Simonian who turned to Christianity was Jean Reynaud. Whilst assisting Leroux with his *Encyclopédie nouvelle*, he developed strong illuminist interests, derived mainly from Ballanche. He was concerned as much with the private individual as with humanity as a whole and was unconvinced that either Saint-Simon's or Fourier's social schemes could remedy the evils of earthly life. His best-known work, *Terre et ciel* (1854), a collection of his articles in the *Encyclopédie nouvelle*, advocates a somewhat eccentric religion which he nevertheless claims, quoting the Bible, St. Augustine, and St. Thomas Aquinas in his support, to be consistent with orthodox Christianity. He firmly rejects pantheism, arguing that the evil and

---

[1] Charléty, op. cit., p. 362.
[2] Cf. G. Isambert, *Les Idées socialistes en France de 1815 à 1848*, Alcan, 1905, pp. 284 ff.

suffering in the world cannot be regarded as part of God, but one critic has none the less aptly referred to 'le caractère astronomique de sa théologie et de sa philosophie'.[1] His basic belief is in the indefinite progress of humanity, but he fuses it with a theory of the transmigration of souls from planet to planet. The universe, in which God is ceaselessly creating, is infinite in both extent and duration, and men have before them an endless series of existences on different planets, during which they will be progressively purified and improved. We are thus not only immortal but, in the very long run, perfectible. Étienne Cabet offers a final example of a social reformer who claimed to invoke Christianity. He is best known as a utopian communist who preached complete socialization and founded a model community, Icaria, first in Texas, then, after a disastrous failure, in Illinois. His theories rested upon a religious basis, however. He not only believed in the existence of God, but in *Le Vrai Christianisme* (1846) he advocated a return to the 'communism', as he argues, of Christ's own teaching and of early Christian practice—a practice which still persisted, he thinks, in the 'social radicalism' of the Middle Ages. He also claims to have shown in this lengthy book that Christ, the apostles, and the Church Fathers all promised 'paradise on earth'. 'Toute la Doctrine de Jésus-Christ se résume en ces mots [he concludes]: *Règne ou Royaume de Dieu sur la Terre*', and this he defines—very comprehensively, if rather abstractly—as 'le Règne de la *Perfection*, de la *Toute-Puissance*, de la *Justice*, de la *Bonté*, de l'*Amour paternel*, et, par suite, de la *Fraternité*, de l'*Égalité*, de la *Liberté*, de l'*Unité*, de la *Communauté*'.[2] Such is true communism—'l'intérêt général, social, commun substitué à l'intérêt individuel, personnel, égoïste et exclusif'—and on the basis of this definition he does not hesitate to conclude that Christianity is communism. 'Oui [he exclaims], JÉSUS-CHRIST est COMMUNISTE!!!'[3]

Other and perhaps more important reformers held, however, that Christianity was beyond renovation—a view reinforced by the Papal condemnation of Lamennais's *Paroles d'un croyant*. They

[1] Erdan, op. cit., ii. 545.
[2] É. Cabet, *Le Vrai Christianisme suivant Jésus-Christ*, Au Bureau du 'Populaire', 1846, pp. 627, 618, 619.   [3] ibid., pp. 619, 620.

often proposed, therefore, at least a partial substitute for it, commonly compounded of social utopianism and illuminism. Such was the case of Charles Fourier (1772–1837). Fourier was never a Saint-Simonian and referred contemptuously to 'these sacerdotal playactors'. Yet he was far from irreligious. He thought of himself as a 'servant of God', as 'the social Augustine'. 'Quelle est la cause de cet aveuglement dont les peuples civilisés sont frappés? [he asks] C'est qu'ils n'ont ni foi ni espérance en Dieu.' [1] He believed that God has so created man that all human desires and passions, if properly directed and sublimated, can be harmonized in the good life. Even the most unpleasant tasks appeal to somebody at some time; to take a famous example, children positively enjoy activities involving dirt and will therefore be honoured above all others in the new community for the scavenging work they will do. Men are naturally good; it is a wrong environment which has made them bad. What is required is a social organization in which their natural liking for change can be satisfied by constant variety of work and by allowing each person to do what, at any moment, he wants to do. These and Fourier's other aims can best be achieved, he thinks, by founding small, self-supporting, voluntary communities, *phalanstères*, of which a number were in fact to be established in North America after his death through the initiative of Albert Brisbane and other disciples. [2] Each group will inhabit a large communal building, complete with ballrooms, library, church, dining hall, school, sanatorium, and meeting rooms, and surrounded by fields, gardens, and orchards. The members of these rural utopias will live in social amity and mutual co-operation and (to quote the Articles of Association adopted at Brook Farm, the group made famous by Nathaniel Hawthorne) will conform to 'the principles of justice and love . . . in accordance with the laws of Divine Providence'. Fourier claimed, indeed, that a law of harmony, of 'passional attraction', operates in the human

---

[1] C. Fourier, *Le Nouveau Monde industriel*, Bruxelles, Librairie Belge-Française, 1840, 2 vols., ii. 196. Cf. H. Louvancour, *De Henri de Saint-Simon à Charles Fourier*, Chartres, Durand, 1913, p. 413 and ch. xv, *passim*.

[2] An interesting account of the Fourierist and also the Icarian groups in America is given by M. Holloway, *Heavens on Earth: Utopian Communities in America, 1680–1880*, London, Turnstile Press, 1951, ch. viii, xi.

and planetary spheres alike, a law established by God but ignored by the rigid, joyless moral codes of most past and present societies. 'Le devoir vient des hommes [he asserts], l'attraction vient de Dieu.' It is ironic that even the most successful of the Fourierist communities, the North American Phalanx in New Jersey, should have lasted only twelve years, and that several of the others ended through the quarrels of their members. As to life after death, Fourier holds a theory that mingles fantasy and an absurd precision. He believes that the dead inhabit the higher levels of the atmosphere and are endowed with acuter powers of enjoyment than the living. And at the same time he believes in reincarnation. We all have alternately earthly and 'superior' existences, and Fourier calculates that we shall have 400 earthly lives totalling 27,000 years interspersed with 54,000 years in the 'superior' realm. Finally, when our planet ends, we shall all pass to a new world— where the same alternation will recommence.

Yet, although he once claimed to be 'le Messie de la raison', he did not want to create a new religious sect. His conviction was that personal freedom alone would lead to social harmony without any need for an organized 'spiritual power'. His thought was predominantly social, and religious only by virtue of his trust in a semi-deified Nature and the rather indistinct God who created it. It was rather his followers who linked Fourierism and religion— Eugène Pelletan, who developed a pantheistic 'religion progressive'; Victor Considérant—founder of the journals, *La Phalange* and *La Démocratie pacifique*, for which Leconte de Lisle wrote his early poems—who contended that Protestantism, Catholicism, and the Fourierist philosophy would shortly be united in a new creed; Hippolyte de La Morvonnais, Abel Transon, and several others, who claimed that Fourierism and Catholic teaching were already compatible.[1]

Of all these social religions one of the most influential, excepting only Saint-Simonism, Comtism, and the lyrical Christian socialism of Lamennais, was that of Pierre Leroux—probably the

[1] On the Catholic Fourierists, cf. J. B. Duroselle, *Les Débuts du catholicisme social en France (1822–1870)*, P.U.F., 1951, pp. 120 53.

first to use the term 'religion of humanity' (in *De l'égalité* in 1838). Leroux (1797–1871) was perhaps the most widely revered social thinker of his day. 'Ce profond philosophe, ce hardi théoricien . . .; toujours grand, même dans ses erreurs, ennoblies par sa bonne foi'—thus declared Balzac, portraying him as Léon Giraud in *Illusions perdues*. George Sand, a devoted friend from 1835 until his death, proclaimed herself 'un disciple muet et ravi devant sa parole', and her socialist novels, especially *Spiridion* (1839)—its hero Alexis is a fusion of Lamennais and Leroux—*Consuelo* (1842–1843), and *La Comtesse de Rudolstadt* (1843–5), often reflect his thought.[1] Other writers respected him hardly less, notably Baudelaire, Sainte-Beuve, Hugo, Vigny, Heine, Renan, and—in England—Charles Kingsley; his influence extended even to Walt Whitman.[2] A printer by trade and as regards philosophy largely self-educated, he joined the Saint-Simonians in 1830 and helped to make *Le Globe* into their propaganda organ. By the end of 1831, however, he had broken with Enfantin, and during the following years he devoted himself to spreading Saint-Simon's and his own social ideas through the *Encyclopédie nouvelle*, the *Revue encyclopédique*, the *Revue indépendante*, and the *Revue sociale*. His first book, *De l'égalité*, appeared in 1838, followed by his two best-known works, *Réfutation de l'éclectisme* in 1839 and *De l'humanité* in 1840. He was driven into exile in 1851 and only returned to Paris in 1869, where he died two years later, almost forgotten.

Yet if he is unknown today to all but scholars, his thought is not without historical and even intrinsic interest. He perhaps came closest to expressing in systematic fashion the humanitarian, progressivist, and partly pantheist 'religion' that was embraced—with individual variations—by some at least of the leading members of the Romantic literary movement—as their affection and admiration for him help to confirm.[3] Leroux follows the Saint-Simonians in stressing that every stable society must be built upon

[1] H. de Balzac, *Illusions perdues*, Calmann Lévy, 1892, 3 vols., i. 271; G. Sand, *Correspondance*, Calmann Lévy, 1882–4, 6 vols., ii. 293.
[2] For evidence of his reputation and influence, cf. Evans, op. cit., and also H. Roddier, 'P. Leroux, G. Sand et W. Whitman ou l'éveil d'un poète', *R.L.C.*, xxi, 1957, pp. 5–33.
[3] Such at least is the view of A. L. Guérard, *French Prophets of Yesterday*, London, Fisher Unwin, 1913, p. 128, confirmed to some extent by Evans, op. cit.

a religious foundation. 'La société sans la religion, c'est une pure abstraction que vous faites. . . .' [1] But Christianity is no longer adequate to the times. 'La révélation est successive [he roundly asserts], et le christianisme n'a pas tout révélé.' Its basic fault he regards, like the Saint-Simonians again, as lying in a false dualism of spirit and matter. Hence it has concentrated on men's spiritual salvation to the neglect of their physical well-being and has divorced religion from social life—whereas Leroux wants to insist that 'la pensée humaine est une, et elle est à la fois sociale et religieuse'.[2] Its tendency to gnosticism has also led it to think more of God than of man, to make love of one's fellows subsidiary to love of God, to make the idolatrous claim that Christ is the only true son of God, and to condemn and repress man's natural desires—what he refers to as 'l'égoïsme nécessaire et saint'.[3] The same underlying scorn for man, he adds, has led the Church to vest authoritarian control in a priestly caste.

It is thus not surprising if man today is in a state of religious uncertainty; 'le doute insensé parcourt et sillonne la terre en tous sens'. Yet he is also expectant; suffering from inequality, injustice, and material want, he is ready for a new creed, anxious for 'le signal de son départ pour chercher un nouveau ciel et une nouvelle terre'.[4] Leroux believes he can meet this need and provide 'une nouvelle synthèse générale de la connaissance'. This should draw on Christian teaching, just as Christianity borrowed from Greek and Hebrew thought. We must not break the chain of tradition, for all religions have the same eternal basis and express 'des formes passagères et progressives d'une vérité éternelle'.[5] Despite this eclectic principle, however, Christianity must now be surpassed. 'Il y a quelque chose de plus grand que le christianisme: c'est l'Humanité.' [6] In *De l'humanité*, in the words of its sub-title, he offers 'la vraie définition de la religion'. 'Une intuition s'empara de nous [he tells us elsewhere]. Nous eûmes foi en Dieu présent

---

[1] 'Aux philosophes', *Revue encyclopédique*, li, 1831, pp. 499–516, as reprinted in Evans, op. cit., p. 215.

[2] ibid., p. 215.

[3] *De l'humanité*, Perrotin, 1840, 2 vols., i. 203.

[4] 'Aux philosophes', op. cit., pp. 216, 222.　　　[5] Cited by Evans, op. cit., pp. 56, 61.

[6] *De l'humanité*, i. 197.

dans l'humanité.' [1] Attacking the excessive individualism, as he thinks, of the eclectic philosophers and earlier rationalists, he argues that the individual exists chiefly by virtue of his relationship to his society and, beyond even that, to mankind as a whole. Humanity is an organic, developing entity, linked throughout the ages, *'une chaîne indéfinie dont chaque génération et chaque homme en particulier n'est qu'un anneau'*.[2] From this he deduces that man's true moral law lies in 'solidarity' and 'harmony' with his fellows, past, present, and future, and in devotion to the progress of mankind. He even claims that progress is the eternal truth behind all religions, 'le Verbe des antiques religions', and he flourishes 'la sainte bannière de la perfectibilité' as confidently as do the Saint-Simonians or Comte.[3] Unlike them, however, he did not deny the reality of the individual, and he remained an ardent democrat and defender of personal rights. He concedes that 'l'humanité n'est pas un être véritable'. Each man is 'un être réel dans lequel vit, à l'état virtuel, l'être idéal appelé humanité', and though he stresses that the individual is but a fragment of the greater whole, he does not deny the fragment's reality.[4]

'Dieu est toujours notre base,' he says in the preface to *De l'humanité*.[5] Yet his notion of God is not entirely clear. He attempts to avoid both anthropomorphism and pantheism. God is in man —the belief on which he founds his moral imperative: 'Aimez Dieu en vous et dans les autres.' [6] We are all 'sons of God', not Christ alone, although he admits that some men manifest their 'divinity' more clearly than others.[7] He even argues that God's immanence in man is a central idea of Mosaic religion, an idea stifled by Christianity in order to elevate Christ the more. This view also leads him to contend that, far from religion requiring a separate priestly caste, as found in most world-religions and in the Saint-Simonian cult, all men are priests. Yet he claims at the same time that God is omnipresent in Nature. The world appears to us under three aspects—as 'totalité', 'force', and 'cause'—and these are God's

---

[1] *Réfutation de l'éclectisme*, Gosselin, 1839, p. 203.   [2] ibid., p. 4.
[3] ibid., pp. 201, 203.   [4] *De l'humanité*, i. 251, 256.
[5] ibid., t. i, p. xvii.   [6] ibid., i. 209.
[7] ibid., ii. 330.

three 'facultés ou natures différentes indivisiblement unies'.[1] It is thus hard to deny that Leroux's deity is both somewhat incoherent and probably pantheistic.

He also developed a theory of immortality. In contrast to Christianity he believes there is no future life, no paradise or hell 'hors du monde, hors de la nature, hors de la vie'. 'Le ciel, le véritable ciel [he rather ambiguously says], c'est la vie, c'est la projection infinie de notre vie.' We are immortal by virtue of belonging to humanity, and beyond that, to Nature. 'Vous *êtes*, donc vous *serez*. Car, étant, vous participez de l'*être*, c'est-à-dire de l'être éternel et infini.'[2] 'Vous embrassez l'éternité sous l'aspect de l'humanité. Vous êtes Dieu-Homme.'[3] Moreover, we live on in future generations, and Leroux adds a new interpretation of this belief which renders the life-to-come less shadowy and metaphorical than it might otherwise seem. Like Enfantin and others, he accepts the theory of metempsychosis. Although my body dies and decays, and also my memories of my past life, yet my soul is reincarnated in a succession of future bodies, and thus he can declare: 'Nous sommes non seulement les fils et la postérité de ceux qui ont déjà vécu, mais au fond et réellement ces générations antérieures elles-mêmes.'[4] This is undoubtedly—given the fact of metempsychosis—to lend a new reality to his picture of immortality and a fresh impetus to our work for the humanity of the future.

Lastly, Leroux comes to believe the time has come for a new 'national religion' to be instituted, free of the theocratic despotism of Rome.[5] He regrets 'the state's complete indifference' to religion; the distinction between the civil and religious spheres—another consequence of Christian dualism—is 'absurd and unworkable'. Religion is 'necessary' and 'in fact inevitable' in every society: hence the need for it to be controlled by the state, not left in the hands of priests.[6] He envisages a great democratic Council to decide upon the dogmas, rites, and prayers of the new cult.

---

[1] For another formulation of this doctrine of a divine Trinity, cf. *De l'humanité*, i. 120.
[2] ibid., i. 228, 244.   [3] ibid., i. 997.   [4] ibid., i. 270.
[5] Cf. his book, *D'une religion nationale, ou du culte*, nouv. éd., Boussac, 1846.
[6] ibid., pp. 78, 47.

Thereafter, although adults will be allowed freedom 'to think and believe' (speech is not mentioned), education of the young will be strictly in accord with the national religion, the prescribed ceremonies in regard to birth, marriage, and death will (it would seem) be compulsory for all, and there will be a 'citizen' in every town to give the people moral instruction.[1] Leroux also submits that freedom for other religions can only be temporary. Tolerance springs from indifference; 'le principe . . . de la liberté des cultes . . . est incompatible avec un État bien organisé'.[2] Yet, rather like Rousseau, he believes that this 'civil religion' reconciles authority and liberty, for the individual will be 'free religiously' since he helps to create the religion and can ensure that personal rights are safeguarded.[3] 'Nous sommes tous prêtres [he affirms], au même titre que nous sommes tous citoyens.' Leroux was entirely sincere in his democratic professions; if he came perilously close to a new intolerance, this was because religion was socially so all-important in his eyes that it could not be entrusted to either Catholic conservatism or private whim. A similar conviction was, in this same decade, leading the most famous social prophet of the age, Auguste Comte, to an explicitly authoritarian position.

4. Auguste Comte

Comte separated from Saint-Simon in 1824, in part if not largely, because of the increasingly religious trend in his master's thought. Ironically, after completing his *Cours de philosophie positive*, Comte himself moved even more emphatically in the same direction. Partly under the influence of his love-affair with Clotilde de Vaux, 'his incomparable angel', a relationship lasting from 1844 to her death in 1846, partly out of the same need as Saint-Simon recognized to strengthen his social ethic by an appeal to men's emotions, Comte erected a religion of humanity side by side with his 'positive' philosophy and political theory: the three formed a trilogy that would 'direct the spiritual reorganization of the West'. He enters now what he called his second career: in the first, a new Aristotle, he had transformed science into philosophy, in the second, a new St. Paul, he would transform philosophy into

[1] ibid., pp. 117-18, 126, 128.   [2] ibid., p. 130.   [3] ibid., p. 115.

religion. Short works sketched his ideas—the sixth chapter of his *Discours sur l'ensemble du positivisme* (1848), *Le Calendrier positiviste* (1849), *Le Catéchisme positiviste* (1852); they were definitively expressed in his *Système de politique positive* (1851–4), whose subtitle is 'Traité de sociologie instituant la religion de l'humanité', and in the *Synthèse subjective* (1856). Yet, though he speaks of his two careers, he also stresses the unity of his work: throughout he has thought of 'the goal of positive science' as being 'a sound philosophy' capable of supplying 'the foundation of true religion'. Earlier his aim was to show the *intellectual* superiority of positivism 'over all forms of theology'. That achieved, 'feeling takes the first place' that rightly belongs to it.

Le nouveau sacerdoce occidental ne pouvait dignement terminer la fatale insurrection de l'intelligence contre le sentiment qu'en procurant d'abord à la raison moderne une pleine satisfaction normale. Mais, d'après ce préambule nécessaire, les besoins moraux devaient ensuite reprendre directement leur juste prépondérance, pour construire une synthèse vraiment complète, où l'amour constitue naturellement le seul principe universel.[1]

The elaborate and somewhat artificial systematization of the new religion can easily hide its essentials. He devised a hierarchy of priests, their stipends rising by a neat mathematical progression. He planned to convert first Europe, then Russia, the Mohammedans, the Hindus, and the Africans. He established a cult of 'sociolatry', with a logically ordered list of festivals celebrating the 'fundamental social relations' (humanity, marriage, the paternal, filial and fraternal relations and that of master and servant), the 'preparatory states' of man's religious development (fetichism, including festivals of the animals, fire, the sun and iron, polytheism and monotheism), and the 'normal functions' (women, the priesthood, the 'patriciate'—the capitalists—and the proletariat), with even a 'General Festival of Holy Women' carefully provided for the extra day in leap years. He introduced a new calendar with months named after great men like Aristotle and Archimedes and starting from 1788. He prescribed the 'social

[1] A. Comte, *Système de politique positive*, Mathias, Carilian-Gœury et Dalmont, 1851-4, 4 vols., i. 3-4.

sacraments' of presentation, initiation, admission, destination, marriage (not before twenty-eight for men and twenty-one for women), maturity, retirement, transformation, and (seven years after death, so all-inclusive are Comte's provisions) incorporation. All these are symptoms of Comte's mania for detailed arrangement but remain subsidiary to the simple doctrinal kernel of his creed.

First, wishing to replace 'revealed religion' by 'proven religion', he substitutes for the supernatural God of Christianity a new deity, 'Humanity', now renamed 'le Grand Être'. Instead of worshipping an imaginary god, separate from the world and human activity, men will devote themselves to a deity that unquestionably exists and that demands no less reverence and service than the gods of the past—demands, indeed, even more, for its very 'preservation and development' will rely on our love for it. Positivist religion thus satisfies the intellect in that its object is real, not illusory, and, unlike Saint-Simonism, it provides a tangible deity who can be symbolized in the guise of great men of the past. And if anyone protests that humanity is merely a collective term for individual men, Comte's answer is clear: 'l'homme, proprement dit, n'existe que dans le cerveau trop abstrait de nos métaphysiciens. Il n'y a, au fond, de réel que l'humanité. . . .' The individual, as he had claimed in the *Cours*, is 'a pure abstraction'.[1] Moreover, this cult harmonizes everyday life and the religious life, whereas earlier cults divided them and encouraged private contemplation and asceticism. As Comtians our thoughts will be centred on knowledge of humanity, our affections on love of her, our actions on her service; science, poetry and morality will be devoted to 'the study, the praise and the love of Humanity', and life will become 'a continuous and intense act of worship'.[2]

Secondly, love is enshrined as the principle of all moral action. Positivism has now occupied the field of moral truth, henceforth 'its principal domain'. Our selfish instincts are naturally stronger than the unselfish, but Comte is convinced that under the impact of the new worship, led by the priests and by women, the original

---

[1] ibid., i. 334, and *Cours de philosophie positive*, 2e éd., Baillière, 1864, 6 vols., vi. 590.
[2] *Système*, i. 330, 332.

source of all moral influence, altruism will gain the ascendancy— a development assisted in particular by the working class, of whom Comte, characteristically, declares:

. . . Dégagés de toute grave responsabilité pratique, les prolétaires s'associent naturellement au pouvoir théorique, d'après la disponibilité d'esprit et l'insouciance personnelle qui les disposent mieux que leurs chefs temporels aux vues d'ensemble et aux sentiments généreux.[1]

Thus what the Greeks and Romans never attempted and what the medievals tried but never achieved, owing to their military and aristocratic society, namely the subordination of politics to morals, will be established in the new era. And what is the source of love and hence of moral action? Comte's reply is unambiguous: the feelings, the 'heart'. He admits that 'the victory of social feeling over our innate self-love' is rendered possible only by 'a slow and difficult training of the heart', in which the intellect—'placé irrévocablement au service du cœur'—must co-operate. But to this end will work 'the mutual love of man and woman', in a marriage that is henceforth to be indissoluble, 'with all the other family affections that precede and follow it', a rejuvenated didactic art and literature, and above all a political 'substitution of duties for rights'.[2] 'Dans l'état positif, qui n'admet plus de titres célestes, l'idée de *droit* disparaît irrévocablement'; 'nul ne possède plus d'autre droit que celui de toujours faire son devoir'; 'dans toute société régulière, chaque citoyen fut-il toujours érigé en un fonctionnaire public'.[3] Comte stresses the point, for—significantly —'the ultimate object of Positive religion' lies not in 'the act of contemplating and adoring Humanity' but in its active service. And as we become aware of the 'continuity' linking us with our ancestors and descendants and of our 'solidarity' with all our

---

[1] *Système*, i. 323–6.   [2] ibid., i. 356, 349, 361.
[3] ibid., i. 361, 363. Comte's constitutional proposals reflect the same attitude. A popular dictatorship of three rulers will be established with power to convene and dissolve a representative assembly, whose only duty will be to vote the budget and audit accounts. 'Perfect freedom of speech and discussion' will be allowed—and are essential before any governmental measure is carried out—but 'such discussion should not bind the government legally' (ibid., i. 381–2). Significantly, Comte remarks that whereas the motto of the Revolution was 'liberty and equality', and that of the 1830–48 period was 'liberty and order', the new slogan will be 'order and progress' (ibid., i. 378–80).

fellows of whatever century, we shall give ourselves to that 'social co-operation', inspired by love, which alone can lead us to Comte's social utopia.[1]

As to immortality, Comte was quite free of the occultist notions of metempsychosis, interstellar migration, and the like. Man lives on only in those who follow him, by virtue of his thoughts and actions.[2] Our 'objective' bodily life is followed by a 'subjective' existence in the 'hearts and minds of others', and Comte especially stressed the commemoration of the dead in his provision of festivals. One can also note that what Comte refers to as this 'noble immortality' is confined to the 'true servants of humanity', what his followers termed 'the *holy* dead'. That is to say, the future life for Comte is conditional as well as 'subjective'. George Eliot's positivist hymn on this theme is famous:

> O may I join the choir invisible
> Of those immortal dead who live again
> In minds made better by their presence; live
> In pulses stirred to generosity,
> In deeds of daring rectitude. . . .

Comte believed that such aspiration could provide a powerful stimulus to moral action.

For Mill 'an irresistible air of ridicule' surrounds Comte's religion; 'others may laugh, but we could far rather weep at this melancholy decadence of a great intellect'.[3] He, Littré, and others rejected this creed, and even Pierre Laffitte, Comte's successor as leader of the French positivists, was lukewarm about it. But for a considerable period the Church of Humanity prospered—in France, with 'priests' like Lagarrigue, in Scandinavia and North America, and in Brazil, where positivism to this day greatly influences educational practice.[4] In England, too, Comtism thrived, winning the interest of academics in London and Oxford

---

[1] ibid., i. 362.

[2] Cf. especially his *Catéchisme positiviste*, Carilian-Gœury, 1852, pp. 32–33.

[3] J. S. Mill, *Auguste Comte and Positivism*, 2nd ed., London, Trübner, 1866, pp. 153, 199.

[4] For its influence and fortunes in the Americas, cf. the works by Hawkins in the Bibliography, p. 225 below, and P. Arbousse-Bastide, *La Doctrine de l'éducation universelle dans la philosophie d'A. Comte*, P.U.F., 1957, 2 vols. (for influence in Brazil).

—at Wadham College, in particular—and of other intellectuals like Harriet Martineau, G. H. Lewes (both translators of Comte), John Morley, and George Eliot.[1] Not all of these were adherents of the Church itself. Some, like Harriet Martineau, joined the Unitarians. Others like Frederic Harrison, leader of the London Positivist Society at Newton Hall, J. H. Bridges and E. S. Beesly, followed Laffitte in emphasizing Comte's social and ethical teaching at the expense of his religion. But others, led by Richard Congreve, were to found churches in London (Chapel Street), Liverpool, Newcastle, Sunderland, Leicester, and elsewhere. In their hands, despite schism and the eccentricities of isolated leaders—the Romanizing tendencies of Malcolm Quin in our own century, for instance—positivism took on something at least of the dignity and emotional appeal we normally associate with Christianity, as emerges even now as one reads their books of services, hymns, and anthems.[2] Indeed, some Christian hymns were taken over as they stood: for example, Newman's 'Lead, kindly Light', 'Come, O! thou traveller unknown', and 'These things shall be! a loftier race'. Many others were adapted, as when 'Now thank we all our God' became:

> Now, come with joyful heart
> To sing aloud in chorus,
> The tale of all that Love
> Hath won and suffered for us. . . .

Yet others were newly written—an 'Ave Clotilde', for instance, or a hymn 'To Auguste Comte' ('Great prophet and revealer, | First of the holy Dead . . .'). As to the Comtist services, a single prayer used in Liverpool—that just preceding the benediction—must serve as illustration of the language employed and of the emotional values that can be given to Comte's dogmas. After the sermon and final hymn, the congregation prays:

[1] For its influence and fortunes in England, cf. the works by McGee, Mueller, and Quin in the Bibliography, pp. 225–6 below, and also B. Willey, *Nineteenth-Century Studies* and *More Nineteenth-Century Studies*, London, Chatto & Windus, 1949 and 1956.

[2] The following quotations are from books used in the Liverpool Temple of Humanity, and I am indebted to my colleague, Dr. C. Baier, for allowing me to consult the copies in his possession.

Praising thee, Holy Humanity, as is most meet, for all the blessings thy past has accumulated for us; for the rich treasures of knowledge, beauty, and wisdom it has handed down; for its long roll of great exemplars, our cloud of witnesses, which ministers comfort, support, and guidance in our need, and in particular for Auguste Comte, who, under the inspiration of Clotilde, has interpreted thy past, taught us to use its treasures, rightly to honour its examples; lastly, as we are here in England more especially bound to do, for the full liberty to speak and act which we enjoy: we pray that we may not be found unworthy of such benefits, but that day by day, in all humility and singleness of purpose, with all boldness and yet tenderness for others, we may magnify thee, and attain for ourselves, and help others to attain the great blessings communion with thee will give: Union, Unity, Continuity. *Amen.*

The temple at which this prayer was used was the last English positivist church, closed as recently as the end of the Second World War.

For a present-day reader, however, the Comtian faith is of interest less for its direct influence—which was comparatively slight—than as an embodiment of a widespread nineteenth-century ambition: to satisfy religious aspiration by deifying man-kind, to redirect the hopes and devotion hitherto turned away from this world towards the creation of a happier and more moral society on earth. Here is a far from ignoble ideal: it is the quin-tessence of much that was best in nineteenth-century secular thought. Yet mankind has feet of clay ill-becoming for divinity. Comte claims that humanity is 'un . . . Grand-Être, éminemment réel, accessible, et sympathique, en tant que composé de ses propres adorateurs, quoique évidemment supérieur à chacun d'eux'.[1] But quantity is not quality, and to think of humanity's past and present follies and crimes is to doubt whether it can qualify as a fitting object of religious worship. Comte would have been undisturbed by this. *Le Grand Être* is to be identified in particular with the best part of mankind (though, strictly, it is *l'ensemble* des êtres humains'). And, secondly, he is in reality less interested in worship of a *perfect* deity than in practical service. Yet

[1] *Système*, i. 394.

this fact makes it the more evident that his 'God' is enshrined at the cost of suppressing what for many Christians is the essence of religion—the sense of the holy, awe and wonderment before the infinitely perfect. In contrast, Comte declares that 'la nouvelle religion, toujours caractérisée par la réalité et l'utilité, ne comportera aucune dégénération ascétique ni quiétiste'.[1]

What, in the second place, of Comte's moral principle of love? One can note at once that his claim to have founded a scientific ethics cannot—in principle—be justified: it is impossible to *prove* that we ought to 'love others' or to pursue any other moral end-in-itself. Here, then, his pretension to have passed from 'revealed religion' to 'proven religion' falls to the ground. But cannot a Christian applaud the erection of love as Comte's 'ultimate principle'? He may to some degree, but he must also feel that Comte's 'love' is a rather dulled reflection of Christian 'charity'. First, for Comte love is not its own justification; the motto of his religion reads: 'L'amour pour principe; l'ordre pour base, et le progrès pour but.' He seeks to utilize love (some may think to exploit it) in order to achieve social progress. Whilst the Christian has a parallel hope of 'progress in the spiritual life', for him love is not just a means but a good in itself. Secondly, love for Comte springs from the feelings; it is emotional, not spiritual, in essence. Comte would of course deny that the spiritual is anything other than emotional, but the deepest difference lies in the conceptions of human nature implicit here. For the Christian, 'charity' presupposes divine grace at work in sinful man. Comte, though he sees that man's 'self-love' normally outweighs his altruism, can yet speak of 'la morale spontanée', of 'the spontaneous morality of the emotions', as his English translator puts it.[2] Dig deep enough, he is suggesting, below the superstitions, prejudices, and vices fostered by society, educate men out of their socially undesirable feelings, and you will uncover an innate and uncorrupted goodness. This important contention, deriving from the later *philosophes*, Rousseau and Romanticism, can never be wholly dis-

---

[1] *Système*, i. 394.
[2] ibid., i. 394; cf. *System of Positive Polity*, transl. Bridges, London, Longmans, 1875, p. 317.

proved, despite the apparent evidence to the contrary, for it is always possible to submit that this sadistic or selfish impulse, that feeling of pride or contempt are remnants of a corrupt society's impact on the individual, and one can also point out how much different communities do in fact condition different moral attitudes in their citizens. Hence, we saw, Comte shares the trust of Rousseau in the innate goodness of the working classes. Yet it is perhaps no coincidence that both thinkers end by legislating for some kind of 'civil religion', by wishing to *force* men to be good.

V

Metaphysical Religions

1. Natural Religion: Victor Cousin

THE creeds studied in the previous chapter were first and foremost concerned with external life in society; the individual's inner development was valued primarily for its consequences in the world of action. Other thinkers looked for a more genuinely inward and spiritual alternative to Christianity. The distinction between 'social' and 'metaphysical' religions is by no means a clear one. The deities of Saint-Simon and Comte, for instance, were metaphysical concepts at bottom, and conversely a metaphysician like Cousin valued religion for its social consequences as well as for the personal enrichment and sense of direction it might bring. Yet there were differences of emphasis, of attitude, of presentation, that make this division real enough to be convenient. Whereas Saint-Simon, Comte, Leroux, were primarily social thinkers, the writers to whom we now turn were above all philosophers and their doctrines were all patently the products of speculative reason.

Pascal, in a famous contrast, distinguished between 'the God of Abraham, Isaac, and Jacob'—the personal God of Christianity, known by individuals as their Lord and friend—and 'the God of the philosophers'—a metaphysical construct, a first cause, an ultimate principle, a deity that may be intellectually satisfying but seems remote and abstract to the non-philosophical worshipper. Such was the God of Descartes, the 'divine clockmaker' of Voltaire and other eighteenth-century deists, the divinity whose existence is allegedly demonstrated by the scholastic 'proofs'. The mind, as Comte's famous law relates, abandons the theological for the metaphysical state and tries to replace Christian supernaturalism by an intellectual equivalent more readily acceptable to sophisticated, rational minds. We have already seen something of the nineteenth-century criticisms of such systems: they are rejected as bones without flesh, powerless to convert or inspire any save the philosophers themselves. Yet the tendency to devise such 'metaphysical religions' persisted in the nineteenth century, albeit gradually weakening in its later years. Jouffroy, for example, after losing his Christian faith, can declare:

Mon intelligence, excitée par les besoins et élargie par les enseignements du christianisme, avait prêté à la philosophie le grand objet, les vastes cadres, la sublime portée de la religion.[1]

The attempts that were made were even original to some extent, for most of them did not offer a rationalized form of Christianity, as had Descartes or the deists, but an alternative to it. The theodicy of Renan, Vacherot, or the pantheists, did not even purport to be Christian, and the same was true of the Hegelian notion of the Absolute and of the 'natural religion' of the eclectics—the first creed that calls for attention in this chapter.

Posterity has been harsh in its judgement of the leader of the eclectic group, Victor Cousin (1792–1867). Scherer, for instance, asserts: 'il ne manquait pas seulement du grand génie spéculatif, il manquait même de la vraie notion de la science', whilst Ravaisson dismisses him as a mere orator.[2] Yet these verdicts apply, if at all justly, to the later administrative half of his career rather than his earlier years. Cousin lectured at the Sorbonne from 1815 to 1820, at which date his course was suspended under suspicion of liberalism, and again from 1828 to 1830. This was a period of distinctive philosophical achievement: he read with remarkable catholicity, gathering an extensive knowledge of the history of philosophy; he contacted contemporary German thinkers, above all Hegel—with most significant results for some of his pupils; he developed his own ideas on a wide variety of subjects—theory of knowledge, ethics, philosophy of history, metaphysics, amongst others—and gave them, in his vigorous, fluent lectures, a deeply influential expression. Sainte-Beuve declares that the earlier

---

[1] T. Jouffroy, *Nouveaux mélanges philosophiques*, 3e éd., Hachette, 1872, pp. 85–86.

[2] E. Scherer, *Études sur la littérature contemporaine*, Calmann Lévy, 1863–95, 10 vols., iv. 79, and F. Ravaisson, *Rapport sur la philosophie en France au dix-neuvième siècle*, 5e éd., Hachette, 1904, pp. 33–34. Cf., amongst others, C. Secrétan, *La Philosophie de la liberté*, 2e éd., Durand, 1866, p. vii.

courses left 'an almost legendary memory' and 'created a revolution in French philosophy'. Scherer tells us that in 1828 as many as 2,000 people attended his lectures, and Jules Simon says of this audience:

Ils retrouvaient leur maître et leur idole, et le retrouvaient grandi par la persécution. La leçon fut très belle, l'enthousiasme de l'auditoire fut sans bornes. . . . Il était le représentant, le chef, l'inspirateur [de la jeunesse].[1]

And another of his successors, Paul Janet, can praise him as '[le] principal maître de la culture philosophique de notre siècle'.[2] We shall never understand the expectant enthusiasm of his young listeners and the influence he exerted on philosophers like Jouffroy, Simon, Janet, Quinet, and others, unless we appreciate the ambitious range of what he was attempting. He sought a creed that preserved the best in Christian faith but was certainly not to be equated with it: a middle way between what seemed to many of his day the shallow, desolating scepticism of eighteenth-century *philosophie*, on the one hand, and the obscurantism and dogmatism of the Catholic hierarchy and the traditionalists on the other; a constructive *summum* comprising a minimum of essential tenets—tenets, he believed, which most rational minds could readily accept. Whilst he was more respectful to Christianity in his later years, Cousin had earlier affirmed that his task was to lift religious belief from the 'half-light' of the Christian faith into the 'clear light of pure thought'.[3] Even in 1853, when he was striving to make his thought acceptable to the Catholics, his true view still intruded—as when he remarked:

Une vraie théodicée emprunte en quelque sorte à toutes les croyances religieuses leur commun principe, et elle le leur rend entouré de lumière, élevé au-dessus de toute incertitude, placé à l'abri de toute attaque.[4]

[1] Sainte-Beuve, 'V. Cousin', in *Les Grands Écrivains Français: XIXe siècle: Philosophes et Essayistes*, Garnier, 1930, 3 vols., ii. 134, 170; Scherer, op. cit., iv. 76; and J. Simon, *Victor Cousin*, 5e éd., Hachette, 1921, pp. 23–24.

[2] Paul Janet, *Victor Cousin et son œuvre*, 3e éd., Alcan, 1893, p. 398.

[3] *Cours de l'histoire de la philosophie moderne: 2e série*, t. i, nouv. éd., Didier et Ladrange, 1847, p. 19.   [4] *Du vrai, du beau et du bien*, 2e éd., Didier, 1854, p. 452.

Philosophy is even now seen as the superior of theology, and whilst we may feel after the event that his venture was unsuccessful, we cannot deny its magnitude or its independence of Catholic orthodoxy. He would never have been so bitterly attacked by Catholics, condemned as a pantheist, a fatalist, an anti-Christian corrupter of the young, if he had only been trying (as some of his critics imply) to whitewash established religion.[1] His disciples shared his attitude: Jouffroy, recounting his loss of belief in pages which scandalized the Christians of 1843, or penning his deeply anti-ecclesiastical article, 'Comment les dogmes finissent'; Bouillier, translating, with an admiring preface, Kant's *Religion within the Limits of Reason*; Bersot, engaging in open controversy with Lacordaire; Simon, publishing his *Religion naturelle*.

Cousin's starting-point is the principle of eclecticism. The philosophies of the past (which fall into four principal groups, he thinks—sensualism, idealism, scepticism, and mysticism) each have their share of truth as well as of error. We must draw from all of them, borrowing 'ce qu'elles ont de commun et de vrai', rejecting 'ce qu'elles ont d'opposé et de faux', and thereby reach a kind of philosophical highest common factor. Moreover, we possess a faculty of 'rational intuition' which allows us to apprehend as self-evident certain 'eternal' and 'absolute' truths. From these sources we can derive a philosophy suited to serve as the foundation for a unified society, to which all men of good will can assent, and which is 'l'alliée naturelle de toutes les bonnes causes'.

His ideas were most fully expressed in his best-known book, *Du vrai, du beau et du bien*, based on lectures given in 1818,[2] and in the preface to his *Fragments philosophiques* (1826). Cousin begins by rejecting materialism and determinism. Man is a duality of soul

---

[1] For a discussion of the criticisms of Cousin, cf. Janet, op. cit., ch. xii and xv; cf. also J. Pommier, *Deux études sur Jouffroy et son temps*, Alcan, 1930.

[2] The first version of the work is the 1836 edition, edited by A. Garnier; the later editions from 1840 to 1853 suffer from a number of suppressions which Cousin then felt it politic to effect. Since only the last of these editions is generally available, I have quoted from it here, even though the treatment of 'the true' is more limited than in the original.

and body, and his soul will survive physical death. He also possesses free-will and is thus morally accountable for his actions. He then turns to the question of the existence of God. If we examine any example of human thought, Cousin argues, and especially scientific thought, we shall find that it assumes certain 'universal and necessary principles', such as the reality of causal connexions in the world and the reality of time. Without these assumptions we end in Hume's solipsism or, at best, Kant's 'scepticism', uncertain whether the 'categories' of cause, time, and so on, may not merely be projected by our own mind on to the 'world in itself'. Cousin claims to refute both Kant and also the view that general principles are no more than inductions from particular instances. Further, just as there are (according to this argument) universal and necessary truths, so too, 'above real beauty there is a beauty of another order, ideal beauty', and above our moral feelings and judgements there is an ideal good.[1] Now, we cannot feel the 'eternity' of these values of truth, beauty, and goodness without going on to postulate an eternal mind who created them and who sustains them by his contemplation. As Cousin puts it, 'la vérité suppose un être en qui elle réside, et les vérités absolues supposent un être absolu comme elles, où elles ont leur dernier fondement'. This 'being' is, of course, God: 'le vrai et absolu idéal n'est autre que Dieu même'; 'Dieu est la substance, la raison, la cause suprême, l'unité de toutes ces vérités [absolues]'.[2] It is noteworthy that, in Cousin's view, we cannot know God directly. Lacking a mystical temperament, he seems to deny the reality of any personal encounter with God and asserts that we know Him only through the intermediaries of knowledge, art, and virtue. His outlook derives from Plato rather than Christ. Although he says that 'love' must be added to intellectual affirmation, he remarks that his way to God is 'the way of metaphysics'.[3] And to listen to his description of God is certainly to feel that we are a long way from the personal 'God of Abraham, Isaac, and Jacob':

[1] *Du vrai, du beau et du bien*, pp. 167 and 403 ff.
[2] ibid., pp. 168, 104.
[3] ibid., p. 72, note 1; cf. Janet, op. cit., pp. 83–85.

[Dieu] est tout ensemble unité absolue et unité multipliée, infini et vivant, immuable et principe du mouvement, suprême intelligence et suprême vérité, souveraine justice et souveraine bonté, devant lequel le monde et l'homme sont comme le néant, et qui pourtant se complaît dans le monde et dans l'homme, substance éternelle et cause inépuisable, impénétrable et partout sensible, qu'il faut tour à tour rechercher dans la vérité, admirer dans la beauté, imiter, même à une distance infinie, dans la bonté et dans la justice, vénérer et aimer, étudier sans cesse avec un zèle infatigable et adorer en silence! [1]

Not surprisingly, Christians accused him of excessive rationalism and of ignoring the relevance of faith and mystical experience in religious commitment. Their principal objection, however—much invoked by Catholics in their attack on eclectic control over university philosophy in the 1840's—was that his system was pantheistic. The passage just cited is more orthodox than most—though even here he refers to God as 'unité absolue et unité multipliée'. Elsewhere he describes his deity as 'infini et fini tout ensemble, triple enfin, c'est-à-dire à la fois Dieu, nature et humanité'; or, again, he remarks: 'si Dieu n'est pas dans tout, il n'est dans rien'.[2] Even a disciple like Simon admitted that 'it is difficult not to say' that the charge of pantheism was justified.[3]

His discussion of moral obligation was no less marked by intellectualism. Indeed, it borrowed much more from Kant than from Christianity: to introduce Kantian ideas into France was one of his greatest services to ethical thought. Reason tells us that there is moral good and evil, and we at once feel an obligation to do good and avoid evil. Duty is thus 'la vérité devenue obligatoire', and if truth is known only by reason, it follows that to obey the law of duty is to obey reason.[4] 'Obey reason' is too vague a maxim for practical action, however; Cousin therefore seeks to clarify its implications. The characteristic of reason is its universality, and hence we may say that any action is rational and good if it can be universalized without contradiction. (If all men were persistent thieves, for example, theft would become both pointless

[1] *Du vrai, du beau et du bien*, pp. 459–60.
[2] *Fragments philosophiques*, 4ᵉ éd., Ladrange et Didier, 1847, 4 vols., *Préface de la 1ᵉʳᵉ éd.* (1826), iv. 34.
[3] Simon, op. cit., p. 40.   [4] *Du vrai, du beau et du bien*, p. 371.

and, since the very concept of personal property would soon disappear, logically impossible.) One knows an act to be right by this test—'que le motif de cette action étant généralisé vous paraisse une maxime de législation universelle que la raison impose à tous les êtres intelligents et libres'. Thus Cousin can conclude:

Obéir à la raison, tel est le devoir en soi, devoir supérieur à tous les autres, les fondant tous et n'étant fondé lui-même que sur le rapport essentiel de la liberté et de la raison. On peut dire qu'il n'y a qu'un seul devoir, celui de rester raisonnable.[1]

Is this analysis adequate to the full range of men's actual moral judgements, in particular to their approval of the most self-denying forms of devotion and personal sacrifice? And is it possible, for most of us, to 'love' so intransigently metaphysical a deity as Cousin's? And even if we could, is not this deity so imprecisely and vaguely described that we should not know what we loved? Can any save metaphysicians worship what too often seems little more than a collection of abstract nouns? Cousin can rightly point out that his system teaches, as well as the existence of God, 'la spiritualité de l'âme, la liberté et la responsabilité des actions humaines, l'obligation morale, la vertu désintéressée, la dignité de la justice, la beauté de la charité'. Yet, despite his high-minded sincerity, a truly religious spirit somehow fails to animate these rationalist bones. It is hard not to agree with Vigny's percipient note in his *Journal* in 1829:

L'éclectisme est une lumière sans doute, mais une lumière comme celle de la lune, qui éclaire sans échauffer. On peut distinguer les objets à sa clarté, mais toute sa force ne produirait pas la plus légère étincelle.[2]

Some at least of Cousin's younger disciples were conscious of this defect. Caro's *L'Idée de Dieu et ses nouveaux critiques* (1864) attacks alike the God of 'naturalism'—a mere 'geometric law or blind force'; the Hegelian deity—'qui ne serait que l'Être indéterminé, origine et commencement des choses, ou l'Esprit absolu,

---

[1] *Du vrai, du beau et du bien*, p. 372.

[2] Cousin, ibid., p. iv, and A. de Vigny, *Journal d'un poète*, nouv. éd., London, Scholartis Press, 1928, p. 23.

résultat et produit du monde'; and the idealism of Vacherot—which 'to save God's divinity denies His reality'. Caro himself believes in 'le Dieu vivant, le Dieu intelligent', a loving deity hardly separable from the Christian God, whilst on the doctrine of immortality he concludes like an orthodox believer: 'restons inébranlablement attachés à cette croyance en la vie future qui seule fait que ce soit la peine de vivre'.[1] A few years later Paul Janet was to go a step further and urge the claims of 'natural Christianity'.[2] This is almost the same in content as 'natural religion', he points out, but whereas the latter is 'une création *a priori*, sans racines dans les habitudes des hommes', Christianity is 'un fait historique dans lequel presque tous nous avons été élevés'. As illustrations of the creed he envisages he instances Locke's 'reasonable Christianity', Kant's 'religion within the limits of reason', and Lessing's 'progressive Christianity'. He concedes that it has little chance of success in France, divided as she is between Catholics and atheists. But he hopes that in other, more Protestant countries the old churches may be taken over by '[une] grande Église philosophique'—even though he admits in conclusion that for the present this may be too utopian a hope.

His fellow-eclectic, Jules Simon (1814–96), was less sanguine and less willing to compromise with Christianity. Simon began his career as a university teacher and an editor of Descartes, Malebranche, Bossuet, and Arnauld. Later he became a *député*, a *sénateur*, and a Minister in successive governments after 1870, and was also a distinguished political and educational theorist. In 1856 he published *La Religion naturelle*, a book that well exemplifies the religious ambitions of the eclectics and which went rapidly into several editions and was at once translated into English. Unlike Cousin in his final years, Simon makes no attempt to conciliate Catholic thought. He is firm in his 'respect for the Christian religion', but he rejects its intolerance, its rites and priesthood, and its theology. He is in fact inquiring whether man must unavoidably choose between revelation on the Catholic model and

---

[1] E. Caro, *L'Idée de Dieu et ses nouveaux critiques*, Hachette, 1864, p. 453.
[2] Paul Janet, 'Le Problème religieux', in *Les Problèmes du dix-neuvième siècle*, 2e éd., Michel Lévy, 1873, pp. 482–99.

scepticism, whether there may not be a rational 'middle way'. His answer is his natural religion, a simple creed consisting, he claims, of no more than 'deux ou trois dogmes aussi simples que sublimes, légués au sens commun par la science de tous les siècles'.[1]

The first two Parts of the book deal with God and His nature and are largely a repetition of Cousin. If they are also somewhat vague, this is not surprising, for Simon follows his master in postulating that God cannot be known 'in His essence' by our imperfect intelligence. God exists but is incomprehensible, and to 'humanize' Him is to move towards pantheism. We can only affirm that He is all-good and all-powerful. Rather strikingly for a rationalist, Simon thinks that the established 'proofs' of God's existence are of little use, for the unusual reason that, as he claims, very few men can really deny God. To be led to Him, it is enough to look at the world, to follow one's feelings, or to think—'car notre raison, en se développant, s'élève vers Dieu comme par une force invincible'.[2] From this starting-point he goes on, in the third Part, to expound his belief in an objective moral law and also in immortality, declaring that the dogma of rewards and punishments in a future world is one of the strongest props of virtue and 'a necessary part of natural religion'.[3] Only in the final lengthy Part on 'le Culte' does he go significantly beyond Cousin; it is now that he seeks to endow this rationalist creed with a richer spiritual and emotional appeal.

Since God is 'le vrai, le beau et le bien par essence' (though if God cannot be known 'in His essence', it is hard to see how this can be said), since He is 'notre bienfaiteur, notre soutien et notre espérance', we should love and worship Him. We do this best by accomplishing our duty. 'Faire le bien, c'est adorer. Aimer, travailler, se dévouer, c'est adorer, c'est prier.'[4] Simon has most to say about prayer, for he thinks it the essential element in the 'cult' of any religion, rites and ceremonies being no more than 'a discipline to regularize and direct prayer'. He rejects intercessory prayer: God is immutable and will not change events and interfere with natural laws for the sake of mere man. But other,

---

[1] J. Simon, *La Religion naturelle*, 4e éd., Hachette, 1857, pp. xvi, xxvi.
[2] ibid., pp. xxvi–xxvii. [3] ibid., p. 369. [4] ibid., pp. xxx, 317, 319.

more important aspects of prayer remain as 'a duty and a need'. 'Prier, c'est d'abord et avant tout adorer'—to think of God, His glory, goodness, and perfection. We can also 'ask for strength, resignation and virtue'; to do so is not in fact to expect God to intervene, for such a prayer 'n'est au fond qu'un ferme propos de faire le bien et qu'une aspiration vers Dieu'—an interpretation which might not be accepted by most praying believers but at least preserves Simon's principle of God's immutability.[1] We should pray at regular times, he urges, both in private and publicly —in the family circle, for example. 'Le matin, on demandera du courage; on formera la résolution de bien faire. Le soir, on se recueillera dans le silence pour se juger soi-même sous l'œil de Dieu.'[2] As well as the pursuit of duty and the practice of prayer the 'cult' of the natural religion includes 'expiation', a notion that is vaguely defined but seems to involve feeling penitence for one's wrong-doings and accepting punishment for them as rightfully inflicted.

Further than this Simon refused to go. He excluded all idea of a church, priests, or imposed rites, and his religion required no form of initiation and no kind of submission to dogma or authority. He equally rejected any notion of a state religion, and he added that it would give a misleading and dishonest impression to join in Christian services.[3]

Simon would admit that this creed is vague and rather abstract and that its God may appear remote and dissociated from human life; these features, he remarks, reflect the limits of human thought.[4] But he would argue that at least it 'rests always on reason' and not on a blindly accepted 'revelation', and if it lacks organized external expression, this means that, unlike all 'positive religions', it is tolerant.[5] It also consecrates our moral actions—for 'tout ce qu'on fait de bien en pensant à Dieu est un acte de religion'—and (its supreme advantage) all men can unite in lending allegiance to it.[6] 'Le seul précepte de la religion naturelle

---

[1] ibid., pp. 373–4, 329–35.   [2] ibid., p. 376.   [3] ibid., pp. 382–3, 398.
[4] ibid., p. 370.
[5] ibid., pp. 362, 341. He asserts of 'positive religions', strikingly in one so sympathetic to the 'religious sentiment': 'Si, par impossible, une religion cessait d'être intolérante, elle ne serait plus une religion' (p. 341).   [6] ibid., pp. 378, 383.

est d'être honnête et d'adorer Dieu': these were Simon's sole demands—exactly the same, one can note, as those of Voltaire's deism a century before. Yet Simon had attempted at the same time to inspire this rudimentary philosophy with a religious content and a spiritual earnestness that it lacked in the writings of the *philosophe*.

This is not to imply that the natural religion developed by Cousin and Simon is likely to appeal to any save abstract philosophers: its deity and its cultus are alike too insubstantial. Nor would most unbelievers be converted by its arguments for the existence of God, and, if they were, there remains a wide gap between Cousin's 'vrai et absolu idéal' and the loving, heavenly Father of the Christian faith. Not surprisingly, therefore, other metaphysical thinkers of the age looked in different directions for their deity.

2. Ernest Renan

The eclectics' religion may stem from intellect rather than spirituality. Ernest Renan certainly did not intend to fall into the same error. His later dilettantism has led to accusations against him of mere 'religiosity'; 'il donne aux hommes de sa génération ce qu'ils désirent, des bonbons qui sentent l'infini', remarked one contemporary.[1] But in reality he sought a creed that whilst excluding the supernatural should provide as complete a replacement for the Catholic faith as he could attain. The deism of the eighteenth century was a mere intellectual husk in his view, 'sorte de théologie mesquine, sans poésie, sans action sur l'humanité'.[2] The devout Breton home in which he was reared and the education he received in his Catholic seminaries both deepened his religious temperament and encouraged his proclivity for contemplation and introspection. It would be wholly erroneous to think that, in rejecting Catholicism in 1845, he was also rejecting religion. His continuing preoccupation with religion, and even with Christianity, clearly underlies his work as a *philologue* from the *Études d'histoire religieuse* (1857) to the *Histoire des origines du*

---

[1] X. Doudan, *Mélanges et lettres*, Calmann Lévy, 1876–7, 4 vols., iv. 143.
[2] *L'Avenir de la science—Pensées de 1848*, 23e éd., Calmann Lévy, 1929, p. 473.

christianisme (1863–81) and the *Histoire du peuple d'Israël* (1887–93), and whilst there may be pride in his youthful separation from Catholicism, there is also regret. Looking wistfully at German Protestant scholars, he longs for the same 'conciliation d'un esprit hautement religieux avec l'esprit critique', and he asserts later that he wished to abandon no more of Christianity than was demanded by his rejection of the idea of the supernatural.[1]

For some twenty years or more he seems to have believed that he could successfully integrate the scientific outlook with what is indispensable in religion. In his progress from *L'Avenir de la science* (written in 1848–9) through the *Essais de morale et de critique* (1859) and articles like 'La Métaphysique et son avenir' (1860) and the 'Lettre à Berthelot' (1863) to the *Dialogues philosophiques* (written in 1871) he was developing a new religious creed for a positivistic age—something, moreover, that was intended to be far more genuine than 'des bonbons qui sentent l'infini'.

A little has already been noted of the exaltation with which he embraced science, and especially *philologie*, and the religious hopes he projected upon it.[2] Science can 'become' a religion and give us, at last, metaphysical and ethical knowledge, 'résoudre l'énigme, . . . dire définitivement à l'homme le mot des choses, . . . l'expliquer à lui-même, . . . lui donner le symbole que les religions lui donnaient tout fait et qu'il ne peut plus accepter'.[3] Having rejected both supernaturalism and traditional metaphysics in the name of a positivist theory of knowledge, Renan sometimes described philosophy as no more than the sum of men's speculations and 'dreams' about the universe and human life. But on other occasions he put forward a rather different conception—philosophy can be built up from the facts given by the established sciences, starting, that is to say, from an *a posteriori* basis, not *a priori* as in previous metaphysical systems. In the dedicatory letter to *L'Avenir de la science* he declared that Burnouf had realized his own hope—of '*la science devenant la philosophie*', and later he pictured each science bringing its results 'en tribut à la science universelle'.[4]

[1] *Souvenirs d'enfance et de jeunesse*, éd. 'Collection nouvelle', Calmann Lévy, s.d., pp. 256, 302. [2] See pp. 57–58 above. [3] *L'Avenir de la science*, p. 23.
[4] ibid., p. 4, my italics, and *Essais de morale et de critique*, 10ᵉ éd., Calmann Lévy, 1928, p. 81.

This 'science du tout' is sometimes represented as purely conjectural, a personal gloss upon the established sciences, a mere metaphysical reverie. But at other times he can even say: 'philosopher, c'est connaître l'univers',[1] and he so often describes philosophy as a 'science' that he seems—at least with one half of his mind—to believe that it makes a genuinely scientific addition to our knowledge. *Philologie,* the 'science' of the history of the human spirit, is the most fruitful starting-point for the new philosophy, he thinks, and from it will develop a 'science of man' that can at the same time be religious.[2] Man is essentially a changing being, and what philological study of his development from primitive times reveals is that he has ceaselessly evolved towards the goal of 'la conscience', ever greater self-awareness and self-control. 'Le progrès vers la conscience est la loi la plus générale du monde'—of the world as well as of man, for the physical sciences show everywhere in Nature a constant *devenir*, driven by an impulse comparable to Bergson's *élan vital*, by 'un secret ressort qui pousse le possible à exister'; 'le monde est en travail de quelque chose'.[3] Upon this interpretation of progress he founds his 'scientific religion'. He equates the moral good with the direction in which man is actually moving (as he believes) and he names as God the 'Ideal' of consciousness and perfection that will ultimately be reached; the goal of the world-process that Hegel called 'the Absolute' Renan reinterprets as God. Thus 'l'œuvre divine du progrès' is to bring God into existence.[4]

Here are the elements of his religion—a view of God and an ultimate moral purpose—that must be sketched in more detail. God is the final goal of progress—complete consciousness, 'l'absolu de la raison', what he sometimes calls 'the Ideal'. And this goal is also the first cause of the universe, 'le principe de l'évolution déifique, . . . le créateur par excellence, le but et le premier moteur de l'univers'.[5] He had in mind the analogy of plant germination. Just as the bud is predetermined by the particular flower it is to grow into, so God already exists as a potentiality or 'ideal' in the

---

[1] *Dialogues et fragments philosophiques*, 12ᵉ éd., Calmann Lévy, 1923, p. 292.
[2] *L'Avenir de la science*, p. 308.   [3] *Dialogues*, pp. 181, 22–23.
[4] *L'Avenir de la science*, p. 222.   [5] *Dialogues*, pp. 67, 54.

growing consciousness of men and animals. 'L'idéal existe; il est éternel; mais il n'est pas encore matériellement réalisé; il le sera un jour'; 'en tant que réalité, Dieu sera; en tant qu'idéal, il est.' [1] And thus Renan sometimes comes close to pantheism: 'Dieu n'est pas seulement au ciel, il est près de chacun de nous; il est dans la fleur que vous foulez sous vos pieds, . . . dans cette petite vie qui bourdonne et murmure de toutes parts, dans votre cœur surtout.' [2] At other times he goes even further—and wanders very close to the notion of an immutable God existing from eternity to eternity.

Dieu est plus que la totale existence; il est en même temps l'absolu; . . . il est le lieu de l'idéal, le principe vivant du bien, du beau et du vrai. Envisagé de la sorte, Dieu est pleinement et sans réserve; il est éternel et immuable, sans progrès ni *devenir*. [3]

As Renan himself points out, we are back here almost to the eternal I AM of the Old Testament. God may not be personified but He is active in our life, and Renan can claim that 'une volonté supérieure se sert de nous, et fait quelque chose par l'humanité', a Will by whose side 'la nature n'est qu'une apparence; l'homme n'est qu'un phénomène'. [4]

Renan also finds a moral sanction to replace the supernatural Christian ethic. Where the *philosophes* urged us to 'follow Nature' and to pursue happiness as our supreme end, Renan reinterprets their injunction to read: 'follow the direction of evolution'— evolution towards consciousness and the 'realization' of 'God'. Significantly, whilst this end may be reached by 'quelque chose d'analogue à l'humanité', it lies beyond man's grasp, he comes to think; [5] man's reward will be in 'the memory of God', and he will rightly be surpassed and sacrificed in the upward struggle. In *L'Avenir de la science* man had been Renan's central concern, and his religion was described as 'le pur *humanisme*, c'est-à-dire le culte

[1] ibid., pp. 78, 145.
[2] *L'Avenir de la science*, p. 85; cf. *Dialogues*, p. 187.
[3] *Dialogues*, pp. 184-5.
[4] ibid., pp. 49, 252. Earlier in the same *dialogue* the speaker had agreed that there is in the observable universe 'aucune trace de l'action d'êtres déterminés, supérieurs à l'homme et procédant par des volontés particulières' (p. 10). Renan fails to reconcile the two views.
[5] ibid., p. 67.

de tout ce qui est de l'homme'.[1] But later it turned into a super-humanism, in which man was only a means and whose political counterpart was Renan's *aristocratisme*. Thus, unlike Christianity, this creed set God beyond the reach of man. Why, however, should we 'follow evolution'? Renan contends, first, that the evolutionary process is good. To discount the idea of a supernatural he has first argued that 'la nature est d'une *insensibilité* absolue, d'une *immoralité* transcendante'. But some thirty pages later, in the first *Dialogue philosophique*, in order to establish his new ethic he affirms: 'Le mal, c'est de se révolter contre la nature. . . . Son but est bon; veuillons ce qu'elle veut.'[2] True human obedience to Nature lies in virtuous action—even though he admits that man usually has 'un intérêt actuel à ne pas être vertueux'! He concedes that Nature employs deceitful means to trick us into collaborating in her 'divine work'—means such as religion, love, our liking for goodness and truth—but, attacking Schopenhauer, he declares revolt against Nature to be 'le crime par excellence, le seul crime à vrai dire qu'il y ait': 'le grand homme doit collaborer à la fraude qui est la base de l'univers'.[3] This rather strident tone cannot hide the contradiction in this notion of Nature, nor can it redeem the naturalistic fallacy on which his whole ethic rests—the illegitimate jump from 'this is' to 'this is good'. Nor is his position improved when he goes on to say, secondly, that man cannot but follow evolution whether he wishes to or not. Nature will always triumph over us: 'la moralité se réduit ainsi à la soumission'.[4] But if we must obey, the injunction that we ought to obey loses its meaning.

Yet Renan's ethic—though ill-founded—is in practice not without its appeal. His concept of consciousness includes the pursuit of beauty and moral good as much as of truth and intellectual advance. The contemplation of beauty, moral living, the search for truth, are all acts of true religion for him, and the perfect man will be a poet, a philosopher, a savant and a virtuous person at the same time.[5] His notion of 'intellectual culture' is thus very wide,

[1] *L'Avenir de la science*, p. 101.   [2] *Dialogues*, pp. 13, 46, my italics.
[3] ibid., pp. 38, 43, 45.   [4] ibid., p. 43.
[5] *L'Avenir de la science*, pp. 318, 11, and *Dialogues*, p. 309.

and it is worthy of attentive respect, even from those for whom the 'order of charity' is far higher than the intellectual and aesthetic orders.

'God' and 'moral purpose' established, the way was open for him to re-introduce in newly interpreted forms the concepts and practices of Catholicism. There may be no immortal life in a supernatural hereafter, but we live eternally by virtue of the small contribution we make to progress: 'c'est dans le souvenir de Dieu que les hommes sont immortels'.[1] Paradise loses its heavenly location, but can be brought down to earth and will be established here 'quand tous auront part à la lumière, à la perfection, à la beauté, et *par là* au bonheur'.[2] Nor is mystery banished, 'ce mystère infini que nous entrevoyons dans un nuage', for God has willed that man should never possess more than 'des lambeaux de vérité'.[3] This religion, like the Christian, seeks to embrace the infinite: the experimental method has revealed 'cet infini réel, que jamais [l'homme] n'atteint dans les plus hardies excursions de sa fantaisie'. Worship is directed now to its true object, for 'la vraie façon d'adorer Dieu, c'est de connaître et d'aimer ce qui est'.[4] Prayer remains 'comme hymne mystique' and as a means of self-examination, having been freed of its superstitious and self-centred elements.[5] Love of God is re-expressed but not discarded: 'aimer Dieu, connaître Dieu, c'est aimer ce qui est beau et bon, connaître ce qui est vrai', and in his reverence the Renanian believer will feel all the humility and submissiveness of the Christian before God.[6] A kind of sanctification of life—'par la pureté de l'âme et l'élévation du cœur'; a sense of communion with one's fellow believers; even a half-hope of a resurrection—'[qui] se fera par la science, soit de l'homme, soit de tout autre être intelligent'; a doctrine of good and evil and a belief in the moral conscience and '[les] instincts divins du cœur de l'homme': these too find a place in his system.[7] Hence Renan can assure us that his is 'une religion tout aussi suave, tout aussi riche en délices, que les cultes

[1] *Dialogues*, pp. 52, 139.   [2] *L'Avenir de la science*, p. 330.
[3] *Dialogues*, p. 332.   [4] *L'Avenir de la science*, pp. 96, 126.
[5] *Dialogues*, p. 14.   [6] ibid., p. 326, and *L'Avenir de la science*, p. 474.
[7] *L'Avenir de la science*, pp. 473, 475, and *Dialogues*, pp. 44, 190.

les plus vénérables'.[1] It will also have a priesthood, composed of philosophers, scholars, artists, and poets (once again this class is invited to fulfil a religious function). They will revive 'le sacerdoce poétique des premiers civilisateurs' and be guardians of 'la vraie *théologie'*—'la science du monde et de l'humanité'—whilst the churches of the religion will be the reformed schools, the *scholae*, of the future.[2]

It is worth while to dwell on Renan's system for it was one of the fullest-developed fusions of various nineteenth-century tendencies —at once claiming to be a religion of science, of progress and of the metaphysical ideal. And after the authoritarian social creeds of Comte and the Saint-Simonians it brings a breath of genuine spirituality. Despising the *esprit de système* of a Comte, he rejected any religion that was primarily turned outwards or that had little place for the wonderment, humility, and growth in sanctification of the individual believer. In him intellect, imagination, and feeling combined in search of religion as an end, not as a means, as a free and sincere personal experience and not as an imposed or propaganda-induced 'civil religion'.

But is it an acceptable creed that he offers? We have noted the weakness of his ethical position. His conception of 'God' is hardly better founded. First, as Littré noted, it is a mixture of contradictory elements—God as both personal and impersonal, both in the Absolute and in the process of becoming.[3] Secondly, his linking of 'God' with the growth of consciousness depends upon his subjective interpretation of a personally selected part of the evidence. Thus in a conjectured history of the universe in seven periods he alleges that even in the four epochs before plants and animals appeared 'progress towards consciousness' was present and forms 'the most general law of the world'—a view that is doubtfully true, to say the least.[4] Again, his equation of the 'science of man' with *philologie*—which concentrates on the history of human consciousness—prejudges what he claims to be

---

[1] *L'Avenir de la science*, p. 318.
[2] *Dialogues*, p. 312, my italics, and *L'Avenir de la science*, p. 165.
[3] É. Littré, 'Préface d'un disciple', in A. Comte, *Cours de philosophie positive*, 2ᵉ éd., Baillière, 1864, 6 vols., t. i, p. xxxii.
[4] Cf. Renan's 'Lettre à Berthelot', *Dialogues*, pp. 175–7, 181.

his conclusion, for he has excluded from his survey all other aspects of human nature save that of man's mental development. However inspiring, this religion is not scientific. Both here and in his interesting discussion of the methods of *philologie* (to include intuition and the *esprit de finesse* of the literary critic[1]) he was far closer to Bergson than to the positivist theory of knowledge in whose name he abandoned Christianity. In reality he vividly illustrated the 'metaphysical' stage described by Comte in which 'les agents surnaturels sont remplacés par des forces abstraites, véritables entités (abstractions personnifiées) inhérentes aux divers êtres du monde, et conçues comme capables d'engendrer par elles-mêmes tous les phénomènes observés'.[2] Renan's 'God', 'the Ideal', is exactly summed up here—and equally applicable is Comte's comment that this is little more than a modification of the 'theological' stage.

It is thus small wonder perhaps that after 1871 Renan should have moved towards his final ironic scepticism. He still spoke on occasion in tones of priestly elevation, but more and more he came to believe that philosophy is an idle game and that, outside the few certainties of a strict positivism, all values and criteria of judgement are personal.[3] And indeed his religion is best regarded not as the scientific creed he often held it to be but as a system of 'as if' 'fictions', as his personal metaphysical 'reverie'.[4] As such it may still stimulate our own thinking.

3. Étienne Vacherot

A less influential—perhaps because less thoroughly developed— 'religion', based upon a metaphysical concept of the 'Ideal', was offered by Étienne Vacherot (1809–97). As well as writing on the history of neo-platonism and on political questions, Vacherot was one of the few explicitly metaphysical philosophers of the Second Empire period. Though always independent in his thought, he was allied in his general outlook with the later eclectics and was

---

[1] *L'Avenir de la science*, pp. 149–53 and *passim*.
[2] *Cours de philosophie positive*, i. 9.
[3] *Feuilles détachées*, 17e éd., Calmann Lévy, 1922, p. 17.
[4] This approach is interestingly developed by C. Smith, 'The Fictionalist Element in Renan's Thought', *French Studies*, ix, 1955, pp. 30–41.

sharply critical of contemporary positivism. Despite this fact, however, Taine took from him the elements of his method of abstraction; he is portrayed as M. Paul in *Les Philosophes classiques du dix-neuvième siècle*.

Vacherot wished in reality to establish a middle way between positivism and its opponents, to reconcile science and metaphysics, and the sub-title of his most original work, *La Métaphysique et la science* (1858), is 'Principes de métaphysique positive'. Although appreciative of the scientific methods in their own fields, he stresses that they can only generalize from the observed facts; they cannot 'explain' them in any final sense. Thus they can never satisfy the mind's desire for a synthetic view of the universe. In this situation some turn to religious faith, but this, he asserts, is to fall into unnecessary scepticism about the possibility of metaphysical knowledge; hence his epigrammatic comment: 'grattez le croyant, vous reconnaîtrez bien vite le sceptique'.[1] Others claim —wrongly in his view—that the 'heart' is a source of knowledge. 'Le cœur n'est qu'un écho [he protests]. Il ne fait que rendre en accents passionnés la parole de vérité tombée de l'intelligence.'[2] Only reason is trustworthy, and although existing metaphysical systems—materialism, idealism, and eclecticism, for example—are one-sided, this is because they have not been based upon a critical reassessment of our various faculties. Vacherot undertakes this task and proceeds to rebut Kantian scepticism in regard to both science and metaphysics. Science does give knowledge of the real world, he argues: although science 'se fait avec l'esprit, elle ne se fait pas de l'esprit'.[3] He makes the same claim, more boldly, for the first of two kinds of metaphysics, what he calls 'positive metaphysics'. It works from the knowledge given by the sciences to a synthetic view of the world as a whole, and although its conclusions are never susceptible of empirical verification, they are as reliable and as closely related to the real world as those of geometry—to which he explicitly likens it: 'métaphysique et géométrie ont pour origine l'analyse des données concrètes et pour critère le principe de contradiction'.[4] And this approach, he says,

---

[1] *La Métaphysique et la science*, 2ᵉ éd., Chamerot, 1863, 3 vols., i. 297.
[2] ibid., i. 110.   [3] ibid., ii. 367.   [4] ibid., ii. 222.

will lead us to see the world as a unity, as 'l'Être infini, absolu, universel, principe, substance et fin de toutes choses'. Here is the doctrine of the unity of all substance which aroused Christian disapproval of his first work, on the *Histoire de l'école d'Alexandrie* (1846–51).

But Vacherot rejects pantheism, first because he believes in human free-will and secondly because the world contains much that is evil, and to call the world God, as pantheism does, is to misapply a term that has always been linked with the idea of moral perfection. 'Il n'y a que Spinoza et son école qui ose faire [du monde] un Dieu, contre le cri de toute conscience vraiment religieuse.' [1] Later he will even accuse pantheists of 'pure atheism'. He also rejects monotheism, because of the same evil in the world, which he thinks incompatible with the existence of a morally perfect Creator—and also because he believes that perfection and existence are mutually exclusive in principle. Far from accepting the scholastic argument that what is perfect must exist (or it would not be perfect), he holds that what is perfect must be non-existent—as a reality, that is to say. For, he continues, the perfect can certainly exist as an *ideal*, and alongside 'positive metaphysics' he now places 'ideal metaphysics'. The former studies reality, the latter studies the ideal or perfect, an abstraction created by man by means of extrapolation from the imperfect. It is this concept which religions and philosophers have wrongly personified in the past as God. Opposing them, he declares: 'Un Dieu parfait ou un Dieu réel, il faut que la théologie choisisse.' [2] Vacherot chooses the former and urges that 'ideal metaphysics' can be the theology of the future, the study of God as the Ideal, and that it can preserve our notion of perfection (for him the essence of all religions) amidst the 'shipwreck of the idols of the old theology'.[3]

Le Parfait, c'est le Dieu de la pensée pure, en dehors du temps, de l'espace, du mouvement, de la vie, de toutes les conditions de la réalité; . . . le Dieu dont l'activité est sans mouvement, la pensée sans développement, la volonté sans choix, l'éternité sans durée, l'immensité sans étendue: ce Dieu-là n'a pas d'autre trône que l'esprit.[4]

[1] ibid., iii. 236.   [2] ibid., iii. 247.
[3] ibid., iii. 266.   [4] ibid., iii. 218.

Nor does Vacherot regard this as a demotion of God or as a regrettable compromise with the scientific outlook. Religion in the past has violated human freedom and tried to make men saints; philosophy, he claims, 'with a less violent but more healthy and more assured action, makes of us men'.[1] To those who object that his God is only an abstraction he replies that it both answers the needs of our 'religious sentiment' and provides a stimulus to virtuous action. Nor is this religion lacking in emotional force in his eyes:

Abstraction vaine pour les sens ou l'imagination, tu es la souveraine vérité pour l'Intelligence qui pense et pour l'âme qui aime. L'imagination seule est idolâtre, la sensation seule est athée. . . . Idéal! Idéal! Tu es bien le Dieu que je cherche. Ta lumière est la seule qui puisse faire évanouir à jamais les deux fantômes de l'idolâtrie et de l'athéisme.[2]

But he allows—both in 1858 and in *La Religion* (1869)—that for those in whom imagination is predominant, religious symbolism and the personification of the Ideal may be helpful, provided only that they never forget that 'nulle réalité ne peut être Dieu'.[3]

The ethic linked with this metaphysical theology is obvious: virtue lies in striving towards the perfection which we have made God. Not that the ethic depends on the metaphysics, for Vacherot insists that the source of morality is in self-sufficient 'facts of conscience'. Whether the world is governed by a good God or a Devil, by fatality or chance, is irrelevant. He affirms—increasingly so in his later work, written under the influence of Maine de Biran—that 'l'homme n'en a pas moins sa nature propre, sa fin, sa loi, son droit et son devoir, tous points qu'il appartient à la psychologie et à la morale seules de fixer'.[4] And consequently, in *La Science et la conscience* (1870), he defends the 'rights of conscience' against the excesses of the scientific spirit.

Vacherot's creed is certainly less open to philosophical objection than Renan's, especially if one isolates it—as is easily done—from his views on 'positive metaphysics'. His argument that per-

[1] Cited, from a private letter, by D. Parodi in his most helpful article, 'La Philosophie d'É. Vacherot', *Du positivisme à l'idéalisme—Philosophies d'hier*, Vrin, 1930, p. 40, note 2.
[2] *La Métaphysique et la science*, iii. 282.   [3] ibid., iii. 284.
[4] Cited by Parodi, op. cit., p. 87.

fection and reality must be mutually exclusive is no more justified than its converse, but otherwise he was defending so limited a line as to be unassailable. He affirmed his personal beliefs and no more. The only questions one can justly pose are whether these beliefs are adequate, either intellectually or emotionally, if they claim to replace supernatural religion, and whether, for a self-confessed metaphysician, Vacherot did not leave many questions unanswered. Did he himself come to feel the force of these points? He may have done so, for in one of his last books, *Le Nouveau Spiritualisme* (1884), he seems to be moving closer to the spiritualist philosophers and even to Christianity. He now tentatively characterizes God as 'cause première et fin dernière [du monde]', although he still wants to insist—now less defensibly—that God is wholly immanent and exists only as an ideal in our minds.

4. Pantheism

One of the most frequent accusations made against most of the 'substitute-creeds' we have surveyed in this and the preceding chapter was that of pantheism. Reviewing French philosophy in the nineteenth century up to 1867, Renouvier concluded: 'Son esprit, son caractère consistent en une espèce de panthéisme et de fatalisme.'[1] And Christian and neo-criticist attacks upon it, growing in vigour as the century advanced, faithfully reflected its widening appeal. Abbé Maret's *Essai sur le panthéisme* (1840)—which especially strengthened Catholic opposition—even argued that *all* rationalism ends in pantheism. Poitou, in 1864, contended that 'the idea of God is in peril': 'en continuant de parler de Dieu, on conteste sa réalité; on nie à tout le moins sa personnalité, ce qui équivaut à le détruire'.[2] So sensitive was he to this danger that he even discerned pantheistic traces in Lamennais. Caro's *L'Idée de Dieu et ses nouveaux critiques*, in the same year, had a similar, if less exclusive, preoccupation, whilst much of Renouvier's discussion of contemporary ideas aimed to refute the fatalism endemic in pantheism.

[1] C. Renouvier, 'De la philosophie du dix-neuvième siècle en France', *L'Année philosophique—Première Année* (1867), 1868, p. 100.

[2] E. Poitou, *Les Philosophes français contemporains et leurs systèmes religieux*, Charpentier, 1864, pp. vii–viii.

The concern of these and other writers was well founded. The Romantics' concept of 'Dieu en nous' and their attitude to Nature both tended in the direction of pantheism. Lasserre can claim that this is the very synthesis of Romanticism, whilst even Henri Girard, defending Romantic religious thought against Catholic and classicist attacks, agrees that they are 'tout pénétrés d'une sorte de panthéisme mystique'.[1] Lamartine, after his earlier attempt to adumbrate a rational religion, moved towards a deification of Nature, which he describes as God's 'eternal witness', God's 'voice' speaking to us; in *La Chute d'un ange* God is made to declare:

> Mes ouvrages et moi nous ne sommes pas deux.
> Formes, substance, esprit, qu'est-ce qui n'est pas moi?

Hugo made a similar passage from deism to the outlook expressed in *Pan* (*Les Feuilles d'automne*):

> C'est Dieu qui remplit tout. Le monde, c'est son temple.
> Œuvre vivante, où tout l'écoute et le contemple!

Later, under occultist influences, his pantheism is even less ambiguous, as when he writes in *William Shakespeare* (1864):

> Par Dieu . . . nous entendons l'infini vivant.
> Le moi latent de l'infini patent, voilà Dieu.
> Dieu est l'invisible évident.
> Le monde dense, c'est Dieu. Dieu dilaté, c'est le monde.[2]

'Ô nature! ô mère éternelle!' exclaims Gérard de Nerval, linking Nature-worship with the cult of Isis.[3] Saint-Simon and his disciples offered still clearer examples. Enfantin speaks of 'notre formule du dogme panthéistique trinaire', and a favourite Saint-Simonian hymn proclaimed:

> Dieu est tout ce qui est;
> Tout est en lui, tout est par lui,

---

[1] P. Lasserre, *Le Romantisme français*, Mercure de France, 1907, p. 527; H. Girard, 'La Pensée religieuse des romantiques', *Revue de l'histoire des religions*, t. 89, 1924, p. 151.

[2] *William Shakespeare*, Charpentier et Fasquelle, s.d., p. 33.

[3] *Les Filles du feu*, Champion, 1931, 2 vols., i. 290–1.

Nul de nous n'est hors de lui,
Mais aucun de nous n'est lui . . .[1]

'[Dieu] est tout ce qui est', reaffirmed Enfantin at the very end of his career,[2] and the master's own 'new Christianity' and Leroux's 'religion of humanity' likewise divinized Nature.

The influence of German thought, especially of Hegel and to some extent of Goethe, encouraged a similar tendency, and the same was true, we saw, of the teaching of Cousin, one of Hegel's leading interpreters.[3] Many of the eclectics' opponents were hardly less pantheistic: Renan, most obviously; Taine, as we shall see; even, in Renouvier's judgement, Littré, by virtue of his belief in 'laws immanent in the world which govern everything';[4] and a variety of minor writers—such, for example, as Eugène Pelletan.[5] Nor were the Germans the only philosophical influence of importance here. The fortunes of Spinozism also are indicative of pantheism's growing appeal.[6] In seventeenth-century France Spinoza had been an object of horror to the orthodox and of curiosity to occasional free-thinkers. In the eighteenth century he was seen as a materialist and an anti-Christian. Voltaire was typical in regarding him as a rather barren atheist,

Esprit subtil et creux, moins lu que célébré,
Caché sous le manteau de Descartes, son maître . . .;

and even in the 1800's the Idéologues and others retained this view.[7] It was primarily through the mediation of Cousin and his

[1] B. P. Enfantin and É. Barrault, *Religion saint-simonienne: Morale*, Librairie Saint-Simonienne, 1832, pp. 70, 141.
[2] Cited from *La Vie éternelle* (1861) by S. Charléty, *Histoire du saint-simonisme (1825–1864)*, 2ᵉ éd., Hartmann, 1931, p. 323.
[3] Another eclectic university teacher favouring pantheism was Lerminier; cf. A. Nettement, *Histoire de la littérature française sous le gouvernement de juillet*, 2ᵉ éd., Lecoffre, 1859, 2 vols., i. 492.
[4] Renouvier, 'De la philosophie', loc. cit., p. 39.
[5] Cf. E. Pelletan, *Profession de foi du dix-neuvième siècle*, Pagnerre, 1852, pp. 14, 25, 26, 411, and *passim*.
[6] For a brief sketch, cf. Paul Janet, 'French Thought and Spinozism', *The Contemporary Review*, xxix, 1877, pp. 1072 ff., and 'Le Spinozisme en France', *Rev. Philos.*, xiii, 1882, pp. 109 ff.; and V. Delbos, *Le Problème moral dans la philosophie de Spinoza et dans l'histoire du spinozisme*, Alcan, 1893, pp. 489–528.
[7] Voltaire, *Satires: Les Systèmes*. On Spinoza in eighteenth-century France, cf. P. Vernière, *Spinoza et la pensée française avant la Révolution*, P.U.F., 1954, 2 vols, t. ii, and, for a

school that the reassessment of his thought achieved by Lessing, Schleiermacher, Goethe, and other German writers entered French philosophy. For the first time the religious aspect of Spinozism was stressed, and pantheism was emphatically distinguished from atheism. Only now did Spinoza take on his role as 'the patron saint of unbelievers', as in England for Shelley, Froude, Lewes, Arnold, George Eliot, and 'Mark Rutherford'.[1] Cousin even claimed that he was a theist and saw his work as 'un hymne mystique, un élan et un soupir de l'âme vers celui qui, seul, peut dire légitimement: *Je suis celui qui suis*'.[2] Indeed, for eclectics such as Jouffroy, who gave the first detailed exposition of his metaphysics, Saisset, translator of Spinoza's works in 1842, and Damiron, author of a *Mémoire sur Spinoza et sa doctrine* (1843), his fault was to be, in Cousin's words, 'so filled with the sentiment of God that he loses therein the sentiment of man' and ends in what Vacherot —himself markedly affected by Spinozism—called a 'monstrous fatalism'.[3] Later admirers included idealists like Adolphe Franck and Paul Janet, Renan, who paid him eloquent tribute in a lecture on the bicentenary of his death in 1877,[4] and above all Taine.[5] The committee formed in 1877 to collect subscriptions for his statue comprised thinkers of such diverse outlooks as Littré, Taine, Claude Bernard, and Berthelot, Renan, Jules Simon, Janet, and Adolphe Franck:[6] only the Christians and the neo-criticists remained intransigently antagonistic.

The pantheist assertion that all is God and that God is all may take two forms—the theistic, which begins from a religious belief in God and concludes that the world is illusory compared with the

---

briefer discussion, Hassan El Nouty, 'Le Panthéisme dans les lettres françaises au 18ᵉ siècle', *Revue des sciences humaines*, fasc. 100, 1960, pp. 435–57.

[1] On his impact in England, cf. W. H. Stone, *Religion and Art of William Hale White*, Stanford U.P. and London, O.U.P., 1954, pp. 101–21. Stone notes that 'Spinoza brought [them] a religious rather than an academic message' (p. 102).

[2] V. Cousin, *Fragments philosophiques*, 4ᵉ éd., Ladrange et Didier, 1847, 4 vols., iii. 58.

[3] Cousin cited by Janet, 'French Thought and Spinozism', loc. cit., p. 1087; Vacherot, *La Métaphysique et la science*, i. 267–8.

[4] Cf. E. Renan, 'Spinoza', *Nouvelles études d'histoire religieuse*, Calmann Lévy, s.d., pp. 499–533.

[5] On Taine's debt to Spinoza, cf. Delbos, op. cit., pp. 498–520.

[6] Cf. Janet, 'French Thought and Spinozism', loc. cit., p. 1091 note.

divine reality; the atheistic, which begins from the scientific belief in the unity of the world and proceeds to deify this unity. In either case, whereas deism stresses the transcendence of God, and monotheism both His transcendence and His immanence, pantheism stresses solely His immanence—God in the world, God as the world, the world as God. The emphasis upon divine immanence was marked even in Christian circles in the nineteenth century: the Creation was often thought of as less a series of acts at the beginning of time than a gradual evolution, still incomplete, in which God is at work. It was even more evident in non-Christian thinkers, whether they began from the Romantic belief in the goodness of Nature; or, secondly, from the occultist and Oriental belief in Nature's unity; or, thirdly, from the metaphysical concepts of Spinoza and Hegel; or, lastly, from the scientific belief in the determined interrelation and unity of the universe, man included. From these different starting-points, Romantics, occultists, eclectics, and *scientistes* like Renan and Taine all converged on the pantheist position, even where—as is not uncommon—they stoutly denied the fact.

Most of these varying types of pantheism have already been illustrated. The case of Taine may suffice as sole example here—a particularly interesting case, since his pantheism sprang primarily from scientific and philosophical sources. We saw earlier that Taine's method for a 'scientific metaphysics' claims to lead us to the all-inclusive 'causes'—the 'supreme cause', indeed—of Nature.[1] 'Nous découvrons l'unité de l'univers et nous comprenons ce qui la produit'; we survey 'ces créatrices immortelles, seules stables à travers l'infinité du temps qui déploie et détruit leurs œuvres, seules indivisibles à travers l'infinité de l'étendue qui disperse et multiplie leurs effets'.[2] The pantheistic passages which conclude *Les Philosophes classiques* are well known, but a fuller statement of his feelings is found in his famous article on 'Sainte-Odile et Iphigénie en Tauride' (1868).

Taine begins by admitting to the same need for religious

---

[1] Cf. pp. 58–63 above.
[2] *Les Philosophes classiques du dix-neuvième siècle en France*, 13ᵉ éd., Hachette, s.d., p. 368.

devotion as 'Buddhist or Christian pilgrims', what he interprets as '[le besoin] d'oublier les choses momentanées et changeantes, de contempler les êtres fixes, éternellement jeunes, les puissances primitives, la grande source dont notre petite vie n'est qu'un flot'. The sole difference, he says, is that for him 'les dieux anciens' are 'délivrés de leur enveloppe légendaire': they are 'plus beaux, puisqu'ils sont plus purs'.[1] As we contemplate the forests and landscape surrounding the monastery at Sainte-Odile, we feel that 'les choses sont divines', we experience 'la sublimité et l'éternité des choses'; 'nous sentons flotter en nous [the references are, significantly, non-Christian] les rêves du Véda, d'Hésiode; nous murmurons quelqu'un de ces vers d'Eschyle . . .'[2] He finds the same awareness in Goethe's *Iphigenia*: such works as this are 'les vrais bréviaires qu'il convient de lire, lorsque nous entrons dans un des grands temples naturels'. These religious terms and comparisons are far from fortuitous: they witness to Taine's attempt to identify himself with the pantheist cult. Iphigenia's worship, he continues, springs from 'la faculté de comprendre les dieux intérieurs qui vivent dans les choses, et dont les choses ne sont que les dehors'; 'le divin est sur la terre', 'regarder c'est prier'. Unlike Christianity she does not introduce any separation between God and Nature, nor does she limit her idea of the gods by dogma or reasoning.[3] Hers is a 'healthy' religion, not sick and sad as Taine believes Christianity to be. The contrast is an extensive one, as he reveals when he describes Iphigenia:

Elle est une sainte, comme les plus chastes vierges du moyen âge.— Mais elle n'a point subi les angoisses maladives, les langueurs mystiques, les extases énervantes du cloître. Son âme est saine et n'a jamais défailli sous l'obsession du rêve; elle n'a point été exaltée ni brisée; elle n'a eu rien à retrancher ni à violenter dans son intelligence ni dans ses instincts. Aucune doctrine, aucune discipline, aucune crise intérieure, aucune contrainte extérieure n'ont altéré l'équilibre de sa vie. Elle n'est point fille de la grâce, mais de la nature; elle a crû, comme une belle plante dans un bon sol, droite et haute, et c'est d'elle-même qu'elle se tourne vers la lumière.[4]

---

[1] *Derniers essais de critique et d'histoire*, 6ᵉ éd., Hachette, 1923, p. 72.
[2] ibid., pp. 77–78.   [3] ibid., pp. 79–81.   [4] ibid., p. 85.

Unfortunately, Christianity—'une tourmente de quinze siècles'—
replaced this ancient cult and fostered a division within man which
is still manifested today in a variety of unhappy ways. Modern
man has learnt to contrast the physical and the spiritual, the
natural and the supernatural; consequently, 'il a cessé de considérer
la vertu comme un fruit de l'instinct libre, et d'allier les délicatesses
de l'âme à la santé du corps'. Since the Renaissance only Goethe has
re-attained a full harmony.[1] Yet men's age-long dream of an
'ideal world' persists, Taine concludes, impossible to attain completely, but none the less valuable and noble. To think of it, as we
gaze at Nature, is man's greatest privilege.

This elevated essay disappoints chiefly in the abstract vagueness
of this conclusion after what has preceded. We ask especially what
ethic follows from this pantheist religion. Taine had given an
answer, however, as early as 1856—in an essay on Marcus Aurelius,
'the noblest soul who has ever lived', of whose moral beliefs he
remarks: 'nous n'avons rien découvert en morale qui atteigne à la
hauteur et à la vérité de cette doctrine'.[2] And it is noteworthy that
Taine claims that this outlook stems from Aurelius's pantheism.
First, since he is assured of the unity and harmony of the world, he
possesses a serene confidence. 'Tout est bien et tout est beau. . . .
Cette nature unique et créatrice, qui pourrait lui nuire, puisqu'il
n'y a rien en dehors d'elle?' Secondly, the individual's sense of his
own transitoriness should make him less preoccupied with himself
and more ready to devote his energy to the ends of '[ce] Dieu
universel dont je suis un des membres'. 'Ce n'est pas moi qu'il
aime, mais l'ensemble; ce n'est donc pas moi que j'aimerai, mais
l'ensemble.' The pantheist will live to serve mankind, and that not
to be praised, loved, or rewarded but because 'nous sommes nés
pour nous entr'aider'. Moreover, the belief in universal determinism carries the corollary that every act has its 'infinite' and un-
avoidable chain of consequences and thus transcends the agent in
its effects. Thirdly, his trust in Nature gives him fortitude and resignation in bearing his own sufferings: 'Je ne puis m'affliger de
mon mal, dès que je vois qu'il m'a été imposé par une nature bonne

[1] ibid., p. 88.
[2] *Nouveaux essais de critique et d'histoire*, 6ᵉ éd., Hachette, 1897, pp. 95, 108.

et qu'il contribue à la santé du monde.' Thus, summing up this ethic, Taine declares:

Il n'y a qu'un être parfait, la Nature; il n'y a qu'une idée parfaite, celle de la Nature; il n'y a qu'une vie parfaite, celle où la volonté de la Nature devient notre volonté.[1]

This position closely parallels that of the Christian religion: to adopt as ours the will of a morally perfect deity. It differs sharply, on the other hand, in that the deity is impersonal (although we saw that Taine tells us that 'the universal God . . . loves the whole').

This age-old doctrine is not lightly to be dismissed; something of its awe before Nature's vastness and beauty, something of its sense of man's ephemerality compared with the celestial galaxies can be shared by most of us. Yet unless Nature is in fact morally perfect, pantheism deifies merely what is biggest—and Taine fails to give evidence of this perfection. If Darwin and his precursors created intellectual difficulties on the moral plane for the Christian, they posed no fewer problems for the pantheist, and one is astonished that Taine should end his essay on Aurelius's philosophy with the assertion that 'sauf des différences de langage, c'est à cette vue d'ensemble que notre science positive aboutit'.[2] Science may be thought to show the unity of Nature, but it is simply untrue to allege that it shows its moral goodness. Likewise, if we think of human nature, we may sympathize with the dream, entertained by minds as different as Taine and D. H. Lawrence, of a 'natural life', without vice or frustration, with virtue become 'un fruit de l'instinct libre', and a harmony of body and spirit flowering in conditions of freedom and sunshine. This dream, indeed, was shared by many nineteenth-century utopian reformers; moreover, if all are united in God, as pantheism claims, the principle of fraternity they cherished is founded in the very nature of things. Yet the utopian communities quickly broke down, and to recall human hatred, sadism, spite, egotism, and pride is to doubt any claim that men are by nature predominantly good.

Pantheism brought many nineteenth-century thinkers an emo-

[1] *Nouveaux essais de critique et d'histoire*, 6e éd., Hachette, 1897, pp. 103–5.
[2] ibid., p. 108.

tional solace, a softening of unbelief and pessimism, but Vigny and Leconte de Lisle, for example, were more realistic when they noted the harsh neutrality of Nature. And in so far as several of the religious systems we have surveyed rest upon faith in Nature's goodness—and this is true of Fourier, the Saint-Simonians, Renan, Taine, and others—it must be said that they impose a greater strain on credulity than the Christian position they sought to replace. Pantheism also fails to account for the first creation of the world, one may notice, but its opponents at this time, and especially Renouvier, were less concerned with this than with the 'fatalism' they discerned at its centre. They contend that its doctrine of determinism denies the individual's freedom and thus, ultimately, his moral responsibility. In a way analogous to the subordination of the individual to the Absolute by Hegel, to Humanity by Comte, pantheism denies the reality and value of human personality, preaches self-effacement in Nature and refuses man all hope of personal immortality. This does not affect its truth or falsity, but it does explain why Renouvier and others cannot believe it to be a morally finer creed than Christianity, which, in contrast, looks to the self-fulfilment of each person, both here and in a life to come, and posits a God who loves and is accessible to every individual.

VI

Occult and Neo-Pagan Religions

1. Occultism

THE social and metaphysical creeds that have been examined were intellectually the most important substitutes for Christianity propounded during our period. But some thinkers, dissatisfied by both alike, repelled by the authoritarian tendencies and the spiritual poverty of the former and by the intellectual abstractness of the latter, sought a faith elsewhere. Inspired by the intensive study of the history of religions during the previous half-century, they turned to the non-Christian religions of past and present. As we shall see, some admired a single one of these creeds, in particular Buddhism, whilst others, religious syncretists, tried to reconcile them in a common belief.

Yet they were certainly not alone in pursuing a religious wisdom that has a far longer history than the Christian Church, and it is time to note, however briefly, the astonishing resurgence of occultism, illuminism, theosophy, freemasonry, and even diabolism that accompanied the decline of Christian belief during the eighteenth and nineteenth centuries—more than time, in fact, for occultism not only ante-dated the substitute doctrines we have considered but strongly influenced some at least amongst them. Its popularity is one of the most arresting illustrations of the religious revival during these years.[1]

'Comment se fait-il', asks Benjamin Constant in De la religion, 'que toutes les fois que les religions positives sont entièrement décréditées, l'homme se précipite dans les superstitions les plus effroyables?'[2] He was speaking of the blood religions of earlier ages, yet it is salutary to realize that the era which prided itself on

---

[1] Like all other students of the subject, I am greatly indebted to the works of Auguste Viatte; cf. Bibliography, p. 229 below.

[2] B. Constant, Œuvres, Gallimard, 1957, p. 1423.

its scientific enlightenment also saw what has been justly called 'une renaissance de l'irrationnel'—as if to justify his contention that man's religious sentiment is so powerful that, when denied an orthodox and disciplined fulfilment, it will express itself in darker, more instinctive, and far more fantastic fashions. From the Renaissance onwards Christian unbelief has all too often gone with what have been nicely called 'wild forms of cosmic speculation, more rebellious against the limitations of common sense, the less certain [men] grew of the infallibility of Christian dogma'.[1] In France, seventeenth-century *libertins*—Cyrano de Bergerac, for example—flirted with doctrines even more strange and unscientific than they claimed Christianity to be. The eighteenth century, still more, witnessed not only the spread of freemasonry, swiftly expanding throughout Western Europe and North America, but also a marked enthusiasm for astrology, mesmerism, and theosophy in all its varied forms. The *philosophes* might weaken the authority of Catholicism, but they also provoked a reaction against their own sceptical and naturalistic outlook; they diverted but could not check the currents of religious feeling in less intellectual men than themselves. Recent scholarship has made evident just how forceful was the impact of occultist ideas in France from about 1760 onwards. As one historian comments, 'ce "siècle des lumières" est aussi celui des illuminés'.[2]

Occultism, 'the doctrines, practices, and rites of things hidden and mysterious', claims to derive its insights into the nature and purposes of the Creation from one or more divine revelations. Some occultists believe in an original revelation made to primitive man and transmitted to the present day by a succession of privileged initiates. Others hold that a number of revelations have been vouchsafed by various prophets of the past. Yet others rely upon personal revelation achieved through mystic submission (quietism), through initiation into a religious sect laying claim to receive divine illumination (illuminism), or through a delicate interpretation of the symbolic meanings of the natural world. All allege that they have attained to the essential truths of which

[1] H. J. Hunt, *The Epic in Nineteenth-Century France*, Oxford, Blackwell, 1941, p. 7.
[2] R. Jasinski, *Histoire de la littérature française*, Boivin, 1947, 2 vols., ii. 124.

historical religions are the incomplete expressions: that is to say, they tend towards syncretism, though they may also argue that one particular religion has reached a fuller insight into occult truth than any other.

To generalize from a host of differing groups and teachers— neo-platonists, gnostics, cabbalists, German mystics like Boehme and Meister Eckhart, Rosicrucians, and many others—occultists hold that the universe was originally perfect and united in God. By a process of emanation from the deity emerged successively angels, men, and animals. Some angels and all men revolted against God: hence their fall and degeneration and the existence of evil and imperfection—and linked with these is our materiality which blunts and even destroys our spiritual faculties. Yet the occultist is ultimately optimistic, like the Christian. By way of suffering, punishment, expiation, our rehabilitation is possible— is, indeed, certain; eventually, men, the fallen angels, Satan himself, will be redeemed. This process may require a long series of reincarnations, here or on other stars and planets. But in due course (at a time which many occultists seek to foretell by consulting sacred texts, signs, or stars) the great end of history, the millennial year, will come, and all will be reabsorbed into perfect harmony.

Although occultism has distinct leanings towards both pantheism and syncretism and always departs from Catholic orthodoxy to a greater or lesser extent, similarities to Christianity are obvious, particularly in the doctrines of man's Fall and future redemption. Many occultists are basically Christian (and some even claim, as did Joseph de Maistre and Ballanche, for instance, to be defenders of Catholicism). This was true of three illuminists of the later-eighteenth century who were particularly influential in nineteenth-century France—Swedenborg, Martinès de Pasqually, and Saint-Martin. Swedenborg (1688–1772), best known as author of *Heaven and Hell*, especially emphasized in his cosmology the notion of correspondences between the spiritual and material realms. The objects of our world are symbols of the unknown and, rightly understood, can lead us to metaphysical knowledge. 'The natural world exists and subsists from the spiritual world', he asserts, and reflects it 'not only in general but also in particular'; he even undertakes to 'treat of the correspondence of the whole of heaven with every part of man'.[1] Although he was a Swede, his teaching spread in France from about 1770, and Swedenborgian groups were formed in Avignon and elsewhere. Martinès (died 1774) stressed that man's miseries are an expiation of his hubristic crime in separating himself from God, with whom he can be reconciled only by means of a strict discipline compounded of magical and masonic rites and by establishing occult relations with higher spirits closer to the Creator. Active in Montpellier from 1754 and later in Bordeaux as the founder of lodges on the masonic model, he became the Grand Master of a tightly regulated illuminist cult. Saint-Martin (1743-1803), a disciple of Martinès, reformed this cult after his master's death and particularly stressed inner mystical experience.

These were the leaders of a broadly Christian form of occultism, and the same was true of Lavater (1741-1801), a Swiss pastor who was particularly famed for reading an individual's character and future from his face. Best-known of non-Christians was the German Mesmer (1733-1815). Believing in 'universal attraction' and arguing that the stars influence both men and animals, he became famous for his studies of 'animal magnetism' and the medical cures he effected by use of hypnosis. Yet others were mere charlatans exploiting the interest aroused by the illuminists—and themselves thereby helping to diffuse their ideas: amongst them Casanova, who utilized the magical to further his amorous successes; Saint-Germain, friend of Madame Pompadour and Louis XV, prophet, political intriguer, and one of the earlier inventors of 'miraculous beauty creams'; and Cagliostro, Italian alchemist, magical healer, freemason, and Rosicrucian.

In the nineteenth century the ideas of these and other theosophists markedly affected both literature and philosophy—and even art, as witness Delacroix, Boulanger, and the book-illustrator Tony Johannot, and music, as in such works as Weber's *Freischütz* and Berlioz's *Symphonie fantastique*. In literature the genres of the *roman noir*, the *conte fantastique* and epic poetry

[1] E. Swedenborg, *Heaven and its Wonders, and Hell*, London, Dent, 1909, p. 39.

all drew inspiration from occultism,[1] as did numerous individuals from Nodier, Senancour, Madame de Staël, Gautier, and Mérimée to Lautréamont, Maupassant, Villiers de l'Isle-Adam, and Huysmans. The religious ideas of the Romantics, most notably of Victor Hugo; the three novels of Balzac's *Livre mystique*, deeply impregnated with Swedenborgian, Mesmerian, and Martinist notions; Nerval's *Les Illuminés*; much in Baudelaire's religious and poetic ideas, not to mention such poems as *Réversibilité* and *L'Héautontimorouménos*; Rimbaud's theory of the poet as a seer —all these also were indebted to occultist thought. Thinkers were no less influenced—Ballanche and Joseph de Maistre, whose illuminist borrowings led Baudelaire to praise him as 'le grand génie de notre temps—un voyant'; Sainte-Beuve, strongly attracted by Saint-Martin in the 1830's (as the hero of *Volupté* illustrates); Saint-Simonians like Enfantin and Olinde Rodrigues; and many other social reformers—Fourier, Leroux, Jean Reynaud, all of whom linked their utopian socialism with theories of metempsychosis, interstellar migration, progress towards universal harmony, and the like—and even, in the case of Reynaud, with druidism.

Nor was it only Catholic traditionalists and agnostic socialists who decorated their systems with occultist theories. A large number of illuminist cults thrived in France throughout the century, increasingly so after about 1830, too minor and too lunatic to call for detailed study here but deserving mention as symptoms of the religious searchings of the age. 'Il pleut des magnétiseurs, à chaque coin de rue,' Viatte drily comments,[2] and with them went Mesmerian societies, led by such 'prophets' as Cahagnet, Baron Du Potet, Henri Delaage, and Madame d'Eldir, founder of 'l'ordre moral asiatique universel', some of them purporting to be orthodox Christians and claiming Christ as 'un magnétiseur divin'. The twenties and thirties also saw a resurgence in the popularity of Swedenborg, whose complete works were first trans-

---

[1] Cf. A. M. Killen, *Le Roman 'terrifiant' ou roman 'noir' de Walpole à Anne Radcliffe*, Crès, 1915; P. G. Castex, *Le Conte fantastique en France de Nodier à Maupassant*, Corti, 1951; and Hunt, op. cit.

[2] A. Viatte, *Victor Hugo et les illuminés de son temps*, 2ᵉ éd., Montréal, Éditions de l'Arbre, 1943, p. 22.

lated into French in 1820.[1] Even a canon of Notre-Dame was con-verted—his task had been to convert the Swedenborgians—and churches in Nantes, Aix, Toulouse, and elsewhere as well as Paris were established to announce the imminence of a new and earthly Jerusalem. Le Boys des Guays proclaims, typically of all these religious revivalists:

Les temps sont enfin accomplis! Le sceau qui avait été mis par Dieu sur les Livres Saints est levé, et la Vérité peut désormais apparaître aux yeux de quiconque désirera de bonne foi la connaître.[2]

Other illuminist groups abounded—and multiplied, for schism was almost a rule with them. There were Right-wing theocratic illuminists like the Polish mystics Hoëné Wronski, Mickiewicz, and Towianski.[3] There were Left-wing progressivist illuminists like Charles Richard, Eugène Pelletan, and Alphonse Esquiros.

The 1830's and 1840's also saw the foundation of several 'Christian Churches' of greater or lesser heterodoxy—the Église Chrétienne Primitive (1834), opened by the Order of the Templars, itself created in 1804, and complete with sacred book, the *Lévitikon* (1831), and a catechism drawn up by a synod in 1836; the Abbé Roch's Église Constitutionnelle Française, closed by the police in 1832; Père Alexandre's Église Catholique Primitive d'Orient, which followed the Greek Orthodox rite; and—best-known of these minor cults—the Abbé Châtel's Église Catholique Fran-çaise, which mingled illuminism and natural religion.[4] Châtel (1795–1857) concluded from the Revolution of 1830, like many others, that Catholicism was in its final decline, and in 1831 he opened his first chapel in Paris. His creed, summarized in a *Caté-chisme* (1833) and his *Code de l'humanité* (1838), taught that God is pure spirit and, denying the doctrine of the Trinity, that Christ was a prophet. He rejected the Christian notions of original sin, virgin

[1] Cf. Viatte, 'Les Swedenborgiens en France de 1820 à 1830', *R.L.C.*, xi, 1931, pp. 416–50.
[2] Cited by Viatte, *Hugo*, p. 50.
[3] On these thinkers, cf. A. Erdan, *La France mystique*, Coulon-Pineau, s.d., 2 vols., and F. Strowski, 'Le Romantisme humanitaire et philosophique', *R.C.C.*, xxi, 1912–13, pp. 209–23. Hugo was an admirer of Wronski.
[4] The best account of these churches is given by J. Vinson, *Les Religions actuelles*, Dela-haye et Lecrosnier, 1888, pp. 528 ff.

birth, transubstantiation, and miracles, and reinterpreted baptism as a mere initiation, the mass as a commemoration, confession as a consultation. He likewise denounced the obligation to fast and the celibacy of the priesthood, and used French in his services in place of Latin—utilizing for the purpose some of Racine's translations of the Psalms. He also stressed the rehabilitation of matter and religion's social applications; his catechism bore the motto: 'Liberté, égalité, humanité'. Yet his humanitarian pantheism—for this is the upshot of his teaching—also included the notions that our soul is an emanation from the divine essence and after death returns to it, and later in life he turned to mesmerism and *spiritisme*. Having had himself dubbed *le primat des Gaules* by the Grand Master of the Templars, he ordained priests and opened further churches, but later his cult was banned by the government, and though he restarted it in 1848 he met with no success.

Other illuminists went even further and claimed messianic status for themselves—notably Louis de Tourreil and Ganneau. Tourreil, writing from about 1845, can allege of himself: 'Et maintenant voici venir un dernier et suprême Messie, qui réunira tous les hommes en un seul troupeau, pour qu'ils n'aient plus désormais qu'un seul pasteur, Dieu.' His doctrine of 'fusionisme' marks 'la dernière évolution religieuse', and he proclaims 1845 as Year I of a new era. God, he preaches, is a trinity of male, female, and love: 'son nom sacré et véritable est mèramourpère'. Below God he postulates a kind of demiurge, 'le grand Evadam' (Ève—Adam), and he also contends that the stars too are all alive—and procreating. As to mankind, Tourreil teaches that we form a 'universal chain', interpenetrating each other, and evolving towards God by means of individual reincarnations. And, since we are dependent on one another, we ought to subordinate ourselves to the whole: hence his guiding ethical principle:

Tout ce que nous faisons, mus par un sentiment général, est bon. Tout ce que nous faisons, mus par un sentiment personnel, est mauvais.[1]

This 'religion fusionienne' is also provided with rites, prayers, and even symbolic gestures (the 'symbole sacramentel' replacing the

[1] Tourreil, cited by Viatte, *Hugo*, pp. 83–85.

sign of the Cross, for instance), and celibacy and indissoluble marriage are alike to be forbidden in Tourreil's dream theocracy: even procreation will not be allowed without permission. Another messiah was Ganneau—'a good and too poetic nature', according to Lévi—who proclaimed himself as 'le Mapah' (mater—pater).[1] Mankind has fallen but can be redeemed by woman, a view which won him the support of the socialist Flora Tristan. Closer to Saint-Simonism than Tourreil's, his system is a protest against the religious, political, and social order of his day, which he sees as 'the monstrous expression of the absorption of woman by man, the poor by the rich, and the weak by the strong'. As his disciple Caillaux declares, 'God is the people', and thus it is not surprising that he should have inspired Alphonse Esquiros's *L'Évangile du peuple* and the Abbé Constant's *Le Testament de la liberté*—as well as interesting Romantics such as Dumas, Nerval, Pétrus Borel, and O'Neddy.

It was the Abbé Constant (1810–75) who, under the name of Éliphas Lévi, popularized another aspect of this occultist movement—the cult of magic—in books, which proved Second Empire best-sellers, like *Dogme et rituel de la haute magie* (1856) and *Histoire de la magie, avec une exposition claire et précise de ses procédés, de ses rites et de ses mystères* (1860). And about the same time *spiritisme* began rapidly to oust magnetism in popularity, principally through the enterprise of Allan Kardec (1804–69), founder of the *Revue spirite*, author of widely read books like *Le Livre des esprits* (1857), and director of flourishing spiritualistic groups. Table-turning, automatic writing, and séances, indulged in, most famously, by Hugo during his exile in the Channel Islands, were so popular that one finds Baudelaire linking the first with gas and steam as a characteristic of the corrupt modern age. A minority even turned to black magic—Eugène Vintras, self-styled 'Organe du Très-Haut', for example, and the Abbé Boullan, portrayed in his friend Huysmans's novel *Là-Bas* as Dr. Johannès.[2] And

---

[1] For a brief account and one of Ganneau's pamphlets, cf. E. Starkie, *Petrus Borel the Lycanthrope*, London, Faber, 1954, pp. 50–55 and 205–8; and É. Lévi, *Histoire de la magie*, liv. vii, ch. 5.

[2] On Huysmans and Boullan, cf. R. Baldick, *The Life of J. K. Huysmans*, Oxford, Clarendon Press, 1955, pp. 154 ff. and *passim*.

later in the century one encounters in Paris a group of *Palla-distes*, followers of the Anti-Pope Lemmi, who deified Satan and sought the complete dechristianization of the world.

This list mentions only some of the many exotic cults that gained greater or lesser support in nineteenth-century France. Even so brief a study as Jules Bois offers of *Les Petites Religions de Paris* (1894) deals with Swedenborgians, Buddhists, theosophists, a 'cult of light' devoted to attacking black magic, satanists, Com-tians, gnostics, followers of Isis, and Essenians—claiming Christ to be an Essene (and Joan of Arc as a second Messiah) half a century before the discovery of the Dead Sea Scrolls. One could go on adding other groups—Moravians, Mormons, Russian illuminists, and freemasons, estimated by one contemporary at about 20,000 in France in 1888.[1]

This astonishing phenomenon springs no doubt from per-manent features of human nature—the fascination of the myster-ious and magical; religious 'enthusiasm';[2] the taste for hermetic exclusiveness; the yearning for the utopian and millennarian and for emotional rebirth; the desire to take religion seriously and to rejuvenate its appeal, to cleanse it from the conventional and habitual. That this is so is evidenced by the persistence of many of these cults today—theosophy, spiritualism, freemasonry, the Swedenborgian Church, amongst others. Astrology retains a column in our popular magazines, the Rosicrucians advertise in our more respectable newspapers, and, to take another minor example, the English translation of Lévi's *Histoire de la magie* re-quired re-printing three times between 1947 and 1951 alone.[3] Yet at the same time occultism had much that could appeal to the nine-teenth century as such. It linked and lent a persuasive, emotional force to concerns that were dear to the age's heart. The trust in progress and in the perfectibility of man; the wish to believe that *all* will be saved; humanitarian idealism; the egalitarian advocacy of a higher status for women, not to add a certain decadent sexu-

[1] Cf. Vinson, op. cit., p. 585.
[2] Many similarities are evident to the varieties of Christian 'enthusiasm' studied by R. A. Knox, *Enthusiasm*, Oxford, Clarendon Press, 1950.
[3] *The History of Magic*, transl. A. E. Waite, London, Rider, 1951.

ality;[1] the syncretist wish to find a unifying faith drawn from all the world-religions; the pantheist tendency noted earlier—all these are expressed in occultist teachings. Some nineteenth-century occultists even managed to pay their respects to the scientific attitude. Joseph de Maistre's *Soirées de Saint-Pétersbourg* (1821) looked forward to a new union of science and religion, 'je ne sais quelle grande unité vers laquelle nous marchons à grands pas'.[2] Mesmer had claimed medical respectability for his discoveries of hypnosis and telepathy, and his followers drew analogies between electric current and the 'telepathic fluid'. Allan Kardec argued that *spiritisme* is a science. Éliphas Lévi asserted that he was a positivist, 'a man of science, not a man of deception', and that both God and science were on his side, and he ended the *Histoire de la magie* with the hope that religion and science, reunited in the future, would 'give help and show love to one another, like two sisters, for theirs has been one cradle'.[3] Balzac, amongst others, illustrates this same point. Louis Lambert interprets man's occult faculties as material products, and his creator earnestly tried to unite science and illuminism.

How interesting, how amazing to watch [writes a recent Balzac scholar] is the conflict fought out in his mind, throughout his whole life, between an irresistible inclination to believe in the occult, in thaumaturgy, mesmerism, somnabulism, cheiromancy, cartomancy, and a persistent desire to explain it away scientifically![4]

Religious aspiration mingled with reverence for science—here is one of the mainsprings of the age's thought, manifested in Balzac and some at least of the occultists as much as in more abstract and perhaps saner thinkers.

2. *The Development of* Philologie *and Religious Syncretism*

Some of these latter were no less interested in the world's non-Christian religions, but they derived their knowledge for the

[1] Compare the recurrent emphases on androgynism, easier divorce, and sexual freedom in these cults with similar themes in literature, as studied by A. E. Carter, *The Idea of Decadence in French Literature, 1830–1900*, Univ. of Toronto Press, 1958.

[2] *Les Soirées de Saint-Pétersbourg*, 8e éd., Lyon and Paris, Pélagaud, 1862, 2 vols., ii. 278, 285.   [3] Cf. Castex, op. cit., pp. 94, 102.

[4] H. J. Hunt, *Balzac's 'Comédie Humaine'*, London, Athlone Press, 1959, p. 57.

most part not from theosophical sources so much as from the very striking developments in *philologie* that must now be sketched. By *philologie* is meant not the primarily linguistic study to which the term refers today, but a far wider 'science' of the history of the human spirit through the ages, and in particular the history of man's religions. Its growth, towards the end of the eighteenth century, was prompted by many motives.[1] Historical relativism and a consequent interest in the rise and fall of earlier civilizations; Romantic *mal du siècle* and hatred of the present, leading to a vogue for *exotisme*, especially in medieval or primitive guise; the occultist belief in the value of mythologies as guardians of metaphysical truth; a wish in some to denigrate Christianity by comparing it with other religions, either to show that all share the same superstitions or that earlier ethics are superior to the Christian ethic; a longing in certain 'honest doubters' to uncover an alternative creed; a pessimistic and even cynical flight to ages that are now dead and thus illustrate with salutary vividness the mortality of human civilizations: these and other causes, varying from scholar to scholar, encouraged this movement. With new standards of scholarly accuracy and evidence historians scrutinized the civilizations of Greece, Rome, India, Scandinavia, China, Egypt, Babylonia, and elsewhere. Rudimentary in Lessing and Herder, reinforced by German enthusiasm for Celtic, Romance, and Nordic folklore, this vast study was already well established on a serious, historical basis in Germany by the start of the nineteenth century. And, by and large, it was from Germany that it entered France through intermediaries like Madame de Staël and above all through two great works on comparative mythology, Creuzer's *Symbolik und Mythologie der alten Völker* (1810–12, translated into French 1825–51), popularized by Constant's *De la religion* (1824–31), and Görres's *Mythengeschichte der asiatischen Welt* (1810, translated into French 1819). In 1795, moreover, the École des Langues Orientales Vivantes had been founded in Paris: this too gave a strong impetus to philological work, as did the

---

[1] Cf. works by Canat, Desonay, and Schwab in Bibliography, p. 229 below, and on the relevant German background F. E. Manuel, *The Eighteenth Century Confronts the Gods*, Cambridge, Mass., Harvard U.P., 1959, ch. vi.

personal contacts with Germany of men like Quinet, who studied at Heidelberg under Creuzer and Görres. As early as 1829, in his preface to *Les Orientales*, Hugo can declare: 'L'Orient, soit comme image, soit comme pensée, est devenu . . . une sorte de préoccupation générale . . . '; 'les études orientales n'ont jamais été poussées si avant'.[1] With studies and translations of ancient texts by orientalists like Burnouf, Langlois, and Fauche and hellenists like Ménard, Thalès Bernard, and Maury, *philologie* became an accredited 'science' and inspired both thought and literature.[2] Its invasion of poetry in the works of Maurice de Guérin, Quinet, Ponsard, Laprade, Bouilhet, Ménard, and Leconte de Lisle is only one example of an influence that extended from the Romantics— as in the 'Hinduism' of Lamartine or Vigny's *Daphné*, for instance —and the Saint-Simonians at one end of the century to Heredia and the *école symboliste* at the other.

Generalization about so many writers is difficult, but four points are relevant and valid enough to demand mention. First, most *philologues* were agreed that each civilization's religion is its central, even determining, feature. Thus Quinet can introduce *Le Génie des religions* (1842) by saying he proposes to 'deduce the political and secular society from the religion'; political institutions, the arts, poetry, philosophy, and, to some extent, events themselves all follow from religion 'comme autant de conséquences nécessaires'.[3] Constant, Ménard, and Renan, amongst others, thought the same. Whereas the *philosophes* had constantly implied that religion is socially reactionary and born of fear and credulity, these thinkers claimed it to be an essential element in human society. For they held, secondly, that men are naturally religious; the 'religious sentiment' (we saw earlier[4]) is 'une loi fondamentale de notre nature' for Constant, Madame de Staël, and many of their successors, and religion is 'la langue universelle de la nature, exprimée par différents signes, différents symboles et rites'. And it was but a step from this rehabilitation of religion after

---

[1] *Les Orientales*, Didier, 1952, pp. 10-11.

[2] By 1864 Émile Burnouf, for example, is writing—'pour la première fois peut-être'— of 'La Science des religions: sa méthode et ses limites'. (*R.D.M.*, 1.12.1864, p. 521.)

[3] E. Quinet, *Le Génie des religions*, *Œuvres complètes*, Pagnerre, 1857-60, 12 vols., i. 7, 12.   [4] Cf. pp. 28-33 above.

the scornful attacks of the *philosophes* to the hope that in these ancient mythologies one might discover a religious belief acceptable
to a nineteenth-century mind. Quinet himself continues with a
classic expression of this attitude:

Dans ce pèlerinage à travers les cultes du passé, errants d'autel en autel,
nous n'irons pas, infatués de la supériorité moderne, nous railler de la
misère des dieux abandonnés; au contraire, nous demanderons aux
vides sanctuaires s'ils n'ont pas renfermé un écho de la parole de vie;
nous chercherons dans cette poussière divine s'il ne reste pas quelque
débris de vérité, de révélation universelle. . . .[1]

Moreover, many of these writers believed in the reality of progress and contended that it operates in the religious as much as the
social realm, that man must therefore inevitably move through a
long succession of creeds, enduring the doubt that comes with the
shedding of each faith, in the confidence that a higher religion
will emerge from his heart-searchings. They were the more encouraged in their search since many of them believed, thirdly, that
primitive mythology enshrined a mystical 'revelation'. Derived in
part, no doubt, from the Christian and Rousseauist ideas of man's
state of innocence before his fall into sin, and also from illuminist
sources, the idea spread that myths express divine truths to which
our corrupted, 'civilized' minds are closed. This view was held by
German and French *philologues* alike, although there were divisions of opinion as to whether the revelation was given to the
priests alone or to the people as a whole and whether its truths
were consciously allegorized or were actually apprehended in
symbolical form.[2] The consequence most often drawn from this
belief is not far to seek: the *essence* of any religion, however over-
laid by dogma and superstition, is *true*—true (some added) for the
present as well as for the past. This was Ménard's conclusion,
whilst even Leconte de Lisle, though he thought religions were
only 'true' for as long as men believed in them, could say in 1852
that art in the past (conceived as in essence religious) was 'la

---

[1] *Le Génie des religions, Œuvres*, i. 13.
[2] For a short account of these differences, cf. H. Peyre, *Louis Ménard (1822–1901)*, New
Haven, Yale U.P., 1932, pp. 213 ff.

révélation primitive de l'idéal contenu dans la nature extérieure'.[1] Renan excluded the notion of a 'revelation', but he too held that mythologies must be thought of not as absurd fables but as 'de grands poèmes divins où les nations primitives ont déposé leurs rêves sur le monde suprasensible'. He also praised the rich, spontaneous intuitions about life achieved by primitive man and hoped that we could pass from our present state of rationalistic analysis to a new stage of synthesis where these insights would again be available to us.[2] But these intuitions, the *philologues* agreed, are embodied in a symbolical form that is unacceptable to the modern mind. Their own task must thus be to reveal the 'meaning' of the myths and symbols by way of a sensitive re-interpretation in which the flair of the literary critic will be as needful as the scientist's method. We must 'demythologize' (to use a present-day term), but in doing so, they stressed, we shall lose nothing essential. As Ménard remarked,

Ce n'est pas blasphémer les Dieux que de les élever dans la sphère idéale, au-dessus des formes fugitives, des incarnations passagères de leur éternelle pensée.[3]

Such were some of the considerations underlying the expansion of *philologie*, an expansion which, in regard to its study of Oriental creeds, was regarded by Leroux, we saw, and also by Quinet as a second Renaissance, 'la Renaissance orientale'. Even orthodox Christians were influenced by it, so that, for instance, we find Lamennais arguing in his *Essai sur l'indifférence* that the intuitions of other religions confirm the truths of Christianity. But non-Christians were naturally more affected, as witness the enthusiasm for Eastern religions of the Saint-Simonians, or of Michelet, who was finally to compile a *Bible de l'humanité* drawn chiefly from the sacred writings of 'les peuples de la lumière', of India, Persia, and Greece, as witness too the succession of epic poems—such as

[1] L. Ménard, *Rêveries d'un païen mystique*, Crès, 1911, p. 83, and Leconte de Lisle, 'Préface des Poèmes antiques', *Derniers poèmes*, Lemerre, 1926, p. 222.

[2] E. Renan, *L'Avenir de la science—Pensées de 1848*, 23e éd., Calmann Lévy, 1929, pp. 266, 259–61, 308–12.

[3] L. Ménard, *Poèmes et rêveries d'un païen mystique*, Librairie de l'Art indépendant, 1895, p. 265.

Quinet's *Prométhée*, Laprade's *Psyché*, Ménard's *Euphorion*, Hugo's *Dieu*—in which the hero searches through the religions of the past for an ideal.[1] Nor should we regard such surveys through the despairing eyes of the Leconte de Lisle of *La Paix des Dieux* and imagine that others shared his belief that all these creeds were irrevocably dead. A very popular idea with orientalists from about 1830, Schwab remarks, was that Christianity could be replaced by a more comprehensive faith, by a syncretist creed derived from the age-long consensus of man's religious insights.[2]

Religious syncretism has a history at least as old as Plutarch, and throughout its early centuries Christianity itself was drawing from other religions, even though formally opposed to syncretism. In later Christian ages, however, syncretists have more often tried to reconcile divergent groups within Christendom, although some have also, especially during the Renaissance period, sought to reconcile the best of Greco-Roman thought with orthodox doctrine—for example, Christian Platonists like Marguerite de Navarre. Aspiration towards a wider reunion of religions remained equally rare during the age of the Enlightenment. For the *philosophes* all religions fell under the same condemnation; the more eclectic spirit of Pope's *Universal Prayer* can grow only where anti-clericalism is weaker. But in the nineteenth century the greater knowledge of other creeds brought by both the *philologues* and the occultists, the intellectual searching prompted by loss of Christian faith, and the rehabilitation of the 'religious sentiment', all conspired to encourage the growth of syncretism in the full sense. Men's different religions came to be considered the transitory and progressive forms of a single eternal truth. This widespread belief was perhaps first held by the illuminists. Fabre d'Olivet, for instance, even devised a syncretist prayer invoking Isis, Cypris, and Minerva, and Ballanche claimed that man's religious systems '[sont] tous venus d'une source commune, tous émanés de l'éternelle vérité'.[3] And it also left its mark on philoso-

---

[1] Cf. Hunt, *The Epic in Nineteenth-Century France.*
[2] R. Schwab, *La Renaissance orientale*, Payot, 1950, pp. 259–60.
[3] Cited by P. Moreau, 'Romantisme français et syncrétisme religieux', *Symposium,*

phers and literary writers, and on the Romantics in particular. Lamartine's *La Chute d'un ange* affirms that each creed has its share of truth and that all religions will gradually be subsumed in a common mysticism, whilst in *Les Recueillements poétiques* (*Utopie*) he identifies this universal belief with his own deism and proclaims:

> Un seul culte enchaîne le monde
> Que vivifie un seul amour . . .

Musset's *L'Espoir en Dieu* expresses the same conviction:

> De quelque façon qu'on t'appelle,
> Brahma, Jupiter ou Jésus,
> Vérité, justice éternelle,
> Vers toi tous les bras sont tendus.

Vigny toys in *L'Almeh* (1831) with the notion of 'une sorte de petit culte, . . . une sorte de moyenne proportionnclle trouvée entre la religion catholique et celle de Mahomet'. Sainte-Beuve urges the readers of *Le Globe*: 'Ouvrez les yeux devant les Védas, les Évangiles, le Coran, les Pères et les Docteurs . . . tous les grands livres de la destinée humaine.' Yet again, Nerval's *Isis* submits that there may well have been, 'dans tous les cultes intelligents, une certaine part de révélation divine'; and, less guardedly, he tells us in *Aurélia*:

Mon rôle me semblait être de rétablir l'harmonie universelle par l'art cabalistique et de chercher une solution en évoquant les forces occultes des diverses religions.[1]

Thinkers later in the century shared a similar ambition, notably the inheritors of Cousin's eclecticism, itself a manifestation of the trend towards syncretism. Michelet would hopefully declare in

---

viii, 1954, pp. 2–3. The Lyons illuminist Roux likewise dreams of 'une religion éclectique, une sorte de théosophie chrétienne', whilst the young Ozanam seeks '[cette] vérité religieuse . . . qui, répandue sur toute la terre, s'est retrouvée chez toutes les nations' (ibid., pp. 4, 6–8). Cf. also L. Cellier, *Fabre d'Olivet*, Nizet, 1953.

[1] Sainte-Beuve, cited by M. Leroy, *La Pensée de Sainte-Beuve*, Gallimard, 1940, p. 244; Nerval, *Les Filles du feu*, Champion, 1931, 2 vols., i. 294, and *Aurélia*, ii, 6, in *Œuvres*, Garnier, 1958, 2 vols., i. 808–9.

La Bible de l'humanité: 'On a vu le parfait accord de l'Asie avec l'Europe . . . . On a vu que l'homme en tout temps pensa, sentit, aima de même.' [1] Pécaut, attempting to found a new 'church' of 'Christian theism', proposed to introduce Zoroastrian prayers and Platonic meditations, whilst his rationalist contemporary Huet hoped for 'la combinaison supérieure des religions et des philosophies du passé, revivifiées, agrandies par le concours fécond de toutes les sciences'![2] Ravaisson concluded his *Rapport* of 1867 with the assertion that Christianity and the highest of 'ancient wisdom' can be summed up in the belief that 'l'amour seul est et l'auteur et le maître de tout'. Boutroux attempted to fuse the best in Greek and Christian morality. Brunetière, still later, though before his own return to Catholicism, supported the notion of a 'Congrès des religions' (a Congress that was finally held in Chicago in 1893) and maintained that all religions have as their essence a belief in human inadequacy and sin.[3] Yet another and unusually sensitive syncretist was Louis Ménard, Parnassian poet, Greek scholar, and neo-criticist thinker.[4] The 'poetic', symbolical language of religions may seem scientifically absurd, but when 'demythologized' it reveals inviolate truths which even the modern free-thinker can accept; the discerning *philologue* can transform 'les fables les plus absurdes en graves paraboles, d'un sens profond et d'une haute moralité'.[5] Moreover, re-interpretation of the myths of past religions—Egyptian, Greek, Hebrew, Christian, and others—uncovers close analogies between them and the persistence of certain central metaphors—of an Eden, of a Calvary, for example. Ménard claims that they preserve a common moral understanding, a 'primitive revelation', in which we today can find 'the secret of our destiny', re-discover the reality of

---

[1] *La Bible de l'humanité*, Flammarion, s.d., p. 20.

[2] F. Pécaut, *De l'avenir du théisme chrétien comme religion*, Cherbuliez, 1864; F. Huet, *La Révolution religieuse au dix-neuvième siècle*, Michel Lévy, 1868, p. 308.

[3] Cf. J. Clark, *La Pensée de F. Brunetière*, Nizet, 1954, pp. 45 ff.

[4] Fuller accounts of Ménard's religious ideas are found in Peyre, op. cit., A. L. Sells, 'Louis Ménard and the Religious Problem', in *A Miscellany of Studies . . . presented to L. E. Kastner*, Cambridge, Heffer, 1932, pp. 459–73, and my own essay on 'The "mystical paganism" of Louis Ménard', in *Studies in Modern French Literature presented to P. Mansell Jones*, Manchester U.P., 1961, pp. 40–60.

[5] *Rêveries d'un païen mystique*, p. 89.

an objective ethical law and our own free-will, and grasp afresh that 'redemption' comes through self-sacrifice. This is the basis of his syncretist creed of 'mystical paganism', well developed in his best-known work, *Les Rêveries d'un païen mystique* (1875). Rightly viewed, all the gods man has ever worshipped can be united in the same pantheon:

> Le temple idéal où vont mes prières
> Renferme tous les Dieux que le monde a connus.
> Évoqués à la fois de tous les sanctuaires,
> Anciens et nouveaux, tous ils sont venus.[1]

One may well respect such aspirations, and they have justly helped to encourage the study of comparative religion over the past hundred years. It is certainly arguable that Christianity has for too long claimed a near-monopoly of religious wisdom. Yet these syncretist attempts confront severe obstacles and may even seem, in their nineteenth-century context, to possess a certain unreality. First, even the few examples cited here point to the difficulty of agreeing as to the 'common truths' of the world-religions. Ravaisson picks out love, Brunetière the doctrine of sin, Ménard the notion of redemption through self-sacrifice. Are there common truths, and if so, what are they? These are harder questions than at least some nineteenth-century enthusiasts seem to have perceived. Again, if one believes (as many of them did) that religious insights and doctrines have been progressively refined over the ages, why should one seek at all to fuse the more ancient with the more developed? Thirdly, and perhaps above all, a majority of the nineteenth-century syncretists—excepting only the occultists —doubted the reality of the supernatural. Had they not, they might well have remained Christians, even if not Catholics. Yet their syncretist explorations do not restore their faith in the supernatural; for the most part they discover an ethic and no more, and even this ethic (one may fairly suggest) is more often than not a projection of their own pre-existing philosophy. In short, their search for a religion is fated to fail by the very metaphysical doubts that inspire it. Ménard is typical: he descries ethical truths

[1] *Panthéon*, ibid., p. 206.

which leave his scepticism about God and immortality untouched. True, he himself argued that religion is in essence ethical; what is not ethical, namely the supernatural element, is *metaphorical*. To the end he was faithful to his 'mystical paganism', later renamed *la religion des morts*. But his readers may well doubt whether he has really achieved the 'alliance de la religion et de la philosophie' that he proclaims. To take only one example, in seeking to reconcile Protestantism and free-thought he offers a new interpretation of the Lord's Prayer.[1] Prayer itself is described as a 'meditation', 'le dialogue de l'homme avec la loi intérieure, qu'il appelle son Dieu', and the free-thinker should understand 'Our Father' as an invocation to this moral law within—which also dwells, Ménard tells us, 'au-dessus des réalités changeantes, en dehors du temps et de l'espace, dans les profondeurs idéales que les religions appellent le ciel'. 'Thy Kingdom come' is referred to '[la] sainte Justice', 'Thy Will be done' to '[la] loi d'universelle harmonie', and it is from 'l'éternelle Justice' that we ask for 'our daily bread'. Can we at all accept that this kind of 'translation' leaves us with more than a finely idealistic but non-religious humanism?

3. Indian Religions: Buddhism

Other *philologues* of the age were interested more in a single ancient faith than in a synthesis of them all. Even Ménard laid his primary emphasis on Greek polytheism. He was distinctly isolated in this, however; interest in Indian religion was far more widespread.

Detailed study of Eastern religion had begun in the eighteenth century, with scholars like Anquetil-Duperron and Bailly in France and William Jones, Warren Hastings, and Charles Wilkins in England, and it was fostered further by the foundation of the École des Langues Orientales Vivantes and of Asiatic Societies in Calcutta, London, and Paris.[2] The nineteenth century saw a grow-

---

[1] 'Commentaire d'un républicain sur l'Oraison dominicale', ibid., pp. 159–66.

[2] Cf. also the studies of German scholars like the Schlegels and Wilhelm von Humboldt —for example, Friedrich Schlegel's much admired *The Language and Wisdom of the Indians*, 1808.

ing number of orientalists at work—Chézy, Langlois, Fauche, and others, and above all Eugène Burnouf (1801–52), teacher of Littré, Renan, J.-J. Ampère, Barthélemy-Saint Hilaire, and many other *philologues*. Side by side with Burnouf's influential *Introduction à l'histoire du bouddhisme* (1844) and other surveys like Saint Hilaire's *Le Bouddha et sa religion* (1858–60), there appeared translations of the Indian sacred books—the *Sacountala* (1830, by Chézy), the *Bhagavata Purana* (1840–7, by Burnouf), the *Rig Veda* (1849–51, by Langlois), the *Bhagavad Gita* (1861, by Burnouf), the *Ramayana* (1853, by Parisot, and 1854–8, by Fauche, in nine volumes, paid for by himself). Whereas Senancour had read the *Bhagavad Gita* in an English translation,[1] and Cousin had omitted Buddhism from his lectures of 1829 explicitly because Colebrooke's study of it had not then appeared, later writers found ample documentation in their native tongue. Interest in Indian ideas gradually became as much an intellectual and literary fashion as a scholarly preserve. It was already evident in the early decades of the century in occultists like Fabre d'Olivet, Saint-Martin, and Ballanche and in the Saint-Simonians, and by 1829 Cousin was declaring: 'L'Orient est le berceau de la civilisation et de la philosophie.'[2] 1838 found Lamartine writing in a letter to a friend: 'la philosophie indienne m'éclipse toutes les autres: c'est l'Océan, nous ne sommes que ses nuages'; and later he was to devote a substantial part of his *Cours familier de littérature* (1856) to the thought and literature of the East.[3] By the 1850's too Leconte de Lisle and his fellow-Parnassians were publishing *poèmes hindous*, in part inspired, no doubt, by the *exotisme* of India —as witness also Gautier—but hardly less by the novel mythology and rich intellectual content of the Indian religions. Still later, one finds Amiel noting '[une] affinité chez moi avec le génie hindou, imaginatif, immense, aimant, rêveur, spéculatif, mais dépourvu de personnalité ambitieuse et de volonté', and approving the fact that

---

[1] Cf. J. Merlant, *Senancour*, Fischbacher, 1907, p. 103. For a discussion of Buddhism's impact on him, cf. ibid., pp. 101–6.

[2] *Histoire de la philosophie au 18ᵉ siècle, Cours de l'histoire de la philosophie moderne*, 2ᵉ série, t. ii, Didier et Ladrange, 1847, p. 111.

[3] On Lamartine and Indian thought, cf. M. Citoleux, *La Poésie philosophique au dix-neuvième siècle—Lamartine*, Plon-Nourrit, 1905, pp. 61–76.

'au milieu des activités dévorantes du monde occidental quelques âmes brahmanisent un peu'.[1]

It may seem surprising at first sight that men who had for the most part rejected Christianity should turn with an almost fascinated curiosity to still more ancient and primitive religions, but the central philosophical reason for this phenomenon is not far to seek: the Indian creeds were peculiarly well adapted to minds that were drawn to religion and yet doubtful of the existence of the supernatural. This fact is well illustrated by the description of the Hindu view of religion given by a leading twentieth-century Indian scholar, S. Radhakrishnan:

Hinduism [he writes] adopts a rationalist attitude in the matter of religion . . . [For it religion] is more a transforming experience than a notion of God. Real religion can exist without a definite conception of the deity . . . *Bodhi*, or enlightenment, which Buddha attained and his followers aim at, is an experience. . . . Belief and conduct, rites and ceremonies, authorities and dogmas, are assigned a place subordinate to the art of conscious self-discovery and contact with the divine. . . . Our longing for perfection, our sense of lack, our striving to attain consciousness of infinity, our urge to the ideal, are the sources of divine revelation.[2]

Hinduism also has a strong mystical bent, as he reveals later, but these isolated extracts indicate how well this religion could meet the desires of thinkers of a scientific and rationalist cast of mind, antagonistic to the ecclesiastical hierarchy, the dogmas, rites, and proscriptions, the authoritarianism of the Catholic Church, who were agnostic as to the existence of God but nevertheless deeply sympathetic to the 'religious sentiment' and—children of Romanticism—to religion as *inner experience*.

However this may be, one seeks in vain in nineteenth-century France for any widespread adoption of Hinduism's more mystical concepts. Isolated occultists undoubtedly found analogies with their own esoteric beliefs: in its pantheism and its idea of a 'univer-

---

[1] H. F. Amiel, *Fragments d'un journal intime*, Sandoz et Thuillier, 1883–4, 2 vols., ii. 191, 279 (28.8.1875 and 31.5.1880).
[2] S. Radhakrishnan, *Eastern Religions and Western Thought*, Oxford, Clarendon Press, 1939, pp. 20–22.

sal soul'; in its doctrine of reincarnation—very close to the notion of metempsychosis adopted by Ballanche, Reynaud, and others; in its hope of a final harmonious unification of all creatures in 'le Grand Tout'. As Viatte notes, 'toujours les amateurs de recherches mystiques avaient tourné leurs regards vers les sanctuaires de l'Orient'.[1] Saint-Martin and Ballanche, for example, both remarked '[l'identité] des idées métaphysiques qui reposent au fond des doctrines indiennes avec celles qui sont enfermées dans les écrits de nos théosophes modernes', whilst Fabre d'Olivet reiterated the common idea amongst occultists that India is the source of all man's religions, 'notre berceau cosmogonique et intellectuel', in Ballanche's words.[2] Other stray thinkers shared this interest. Lamartine, for example, was to some extent attracted to Buddhism by 'le spiritualisme déjà raffiné des Sages de l'Inde', by its mysticism, which he described as '[le premier] caractère divin de cette philosophie'. Yet he adds that the second 'caractère divin' lies in its moral code, 'la douceur envers l'homme et envers toute la nature',[3] and he was also drawn, especially in later life, by its pessimism, which he used in his attacks on the notion of human perfectibility. Victor Cousin, too, not surprisingly, was sympathetic to Indian 'idealism' rather than to the 'sensualism' he also discerned. One of the first nineteenth-century philosophers to study and help to popularize Indian thought—by virtue of his *Cours* of 1820—he admired above all the *Bhagavad Gita*, 'monument du plus haut prix, et qui renferme tout le mysticisme indien'.[4] Yet it cannot be said that he was a disciple of this creed. His treatment was curtailed on his own admission by lack of translations and studies of Buddhism and Vedantism. Moreover, unlike many of his contemporaries, he was distinctly cool about Indian ethics: he noted in the *Bhagavad Gita* 'le dogme de la prédestination, destructif de toute liberté et de toute moralité' and claimed that the outcome of its moral theory is 'un absolu quiétisme, une complète indifférence, le renoncement à l'action et à la vie ordinaire'. Even worse, its 'sensualist' teachings end in 'materialism,

---

[1] Viatte, *Les Sources occultes du romantisme*, ii. 171-2.
[2] Cited by Viatte, ibid., ii. 172-3, 182, 221.
[3] Cited by Citoleux, op. cit., pp. 75, 68.
[4] *Histoire de la philosophie au 18e siècle*, p. 156.

fatalism, atheism'.[1] And when he knew more of Buddhism, after Burnouf's *Introduction*, he judged it 'very inferior' to Brahmanism and summed up its two central tenets as philosophical sensualism and the transience of the individual spirit.[2]

Occultists apart, the 'Buddhism' that attracted the nineteenth century was almost wholly naturalistic, as one can see in examining transitory and long-committed admirers alike. Vigny epitomizes the former group. He became curious about Buddhist thought from about 1855, and especially after reading Saint Hilaire's *Le Bouddha et sa religion*. He disliked its rejection of action and its cult of contemplation, but he still considered it purer than Christianity—for three main reasons.[3] First, it is not preoccupied with our self-preservation in a future world; secondly, it does not believe in the resurrection of the body; and thirdly, it does not invoke fear of divine punishments. It is instructive to note the terms in which he praises it in 1862:

Bouddha lui seul n'a point parlé de récompenses célestes. *La charité* est l'âme de sa religion, la plus profonde abnégation de soi-même, et il ne prononce même pas le nom incertain de Dieu.

Not one of these characteristics involves belief in the supernatural.

Michelet, a more devoted adherent, gives the Indians first place in his *Bible de l'humanité* (1864), as the earliest of the 'sons of light', 'in the cradle of our race'. It is the 'glory' of the eighteenth century, he declares, to have rediscovered 'la moralité de l'Asie, la sainteté de l'Orient, si longtemps niée, obscurcie'.[4] Reading the *Ramayana*, he finds the Hebrew religion dry and harsh by comparison. This sacred Indian poem offers what he seeks, he tell us— 'la bible de la bonté', '[poème] vaste comme la mer des Indes, béni, doré du soleil, livre d'harmonie divine où rien ne fait dissonance'. He continues:

Une aimable paix y règne, et même au milieu des combats une douceur infinie, une fraternité sans borne qui s'étend à tout ce qui vit, un océan

---

[1] *Histoire de la philosophie au 18ᵉ siècle*, pp. 149, 130.   [2] ibid., pp. 114, note 1, 121, note 2.
[3] Cf. G. Bonnefoy, *La Pensée religieuse et morale d'A. de Vigny*, Hachette, s.d., pp. 390–1.
[4] *La Bible de l'humanité*, pp. 5, 12, 17.

(sans fond ni rive) d'amour, de pitié, de clémence. . . . Ce n'est qu'amour, amitié, bienveillance réciproque, prières aux dieux, respect aux brahmes, aux saints, aux anachorètes.[1]

He goes on to praise Indian art and the primitive Indian family— India gave us '*la famille* dans la pureté naturelle et l'incomparable noblesse que nul âge n'a pu dépasser' [2]—and he then considers the earliest forms of Indian religion. His central point is highly significant:

C'est le caractère grandiose de cette race . . . qu'en adorant toujours elle sait bien qu'*elle a fait les dieux.* . . . Donc, nulle superstition. Si le Dieu s'oubliait, devenait un tyran, voulait enténébrer l'imagination de terreurs serviles, l'esprit . . . dirait: 'Qui t'a créé? c'est moi.' Noble culte, de haute et fière conception, qui, en donnant tout, garde tout. Les dieux bénis, aimés, ne s'émancipent pas tout à fait de leur créateur, l'homme.[3]

Leconte de Lisle may regret in *La Paix des Dieux* that the gods are only the 'anciens songes de l'Homme', but Michelet welcomes this fact; as a result, this is '[une] religion souriante, d'amitié sans terreur', source of a high and gentle morality—the opposite, to his mind, of Catholic Christianity.[4] It was only later, he thinks, that this religion became debased by being formulated as a law and a cult: 'cette loi va se chargeant de prescriptions tracassières, vexatoires'; 'ce sacerdoce devient tyrannique et stérile'.[5] Michelet's hated clerics were at work for the first but far from the last time! He concludes this section of his *Bible* by praising the Hindu ethic, which unites 'la vertu brahmanique' and 'le haut dévouement du guerrier', and also its respect for Nature and its elevation of animals. Nor should we think that the dogma of the transmigration of souls—once again Michelet skirts the supernatural—is responsible for Hindu love of animals; on the contrary, the dogma was invented because of this love.[6] This is typical of Michelet's treatment of Hinduism; at no point, in his version, does it commit us to any supernatural belief. Rather are we offered a high ethic of charity, and it is noteworthy that for him 'l'activité morale comprend

[1] ibid., pp. 12, 14.   [2] ibid., p. 6.   [3] ibid., p. 37, my italics.
[4] ibid., p. 38.   [5] ibid., pp. 45-46.   [6] ibid., pp. 54, 59.

la religion et n'y est pas comprise'; his 'bible', he remarks, 'pour-suit uniquement les grands résultats moraux'.[1]

Another mid-century popularizer of Indian thought was Taine—chiefly through his influential article on 'Le Bouddhisme' in the *Journal des débats* in March 1864. He gives a far fuller and more balanced account than Michelet, and in particular he notes the change in Buddhism from the 'poetic naturalism' with which Michelet deals to 'a mystical pantheism'.[2] What are the main beliefs he picks out? First, all existence is shot through with the suffering which results from desire, and to escape this suffering man must renounce all desire, 'se délivrer de la soif de l'être'. Secondly, the world of appearances is illusory: nothing really exists, and fully to realize this—and especially one's own un-reality—is to achieve *Nirvana*. This self-renunciation is the begin-ning of charity and compassion, for now we are free to relieve others of their sufferings—and here he draws a contrast with the 'solitary egotism' of the Brahmin ascetics and their caste-distinc-tions. In the Buddha's teaching, he stresses, 'nulle théorie, nulle philosophie, nulle liturgie; il n'exige point d'études, il ne prescrit pas de pratiques; il ne demande que l'apaisement et la mansuétude du cœur'.[3] The basis of its doctrine is 'la pensée morale', and whilst Taine prefers the more active and optimistic ethic of Chris-tianity, less conducive to 'inert quietism' and 'sombre resignation', he is glad to note that the Buddhist does not invoke the ideas of an 'autocratic God' and of divine rewards and punishments: 'par sa propre nature, le bonheur s'attache à la vertu, et le malheur au vice'.[4] Hence Taine, like Michelet, admires above all the fine moral life and practice inspired by this religion and, linked with them, the Buddhist tolerance of other races and creeds.[5]

Taine was not an adherent of Buddhism in any explicit sense; in the same article he advances trenchant criticisms of its idolatry, its superstitions, and its deadening of personality. Yet both the moralist and the poet in Taine seem to be attracted by some of its other features, and although the logician in him may find little

---

[1] *La Bible de l'humanité*, pp. 5, 53.
[2] *Nouveaux essais de critique et d'histoire*, 13ᵉ éd., Hachette, s.d., p. 265.
[3] bid., pp. 277-82.   [4] ibid., pp. 285-6, 293-4.   [5] ibid., pp. 305-6.

satisfaction, he can remark that the Indians are 'les seuls qui, avec les Allemands, aient le génie métaphysique' [1]—a leaning Taine himself fully shared. Without wishing to press them unduly, one can find several analogies between his own thought and Buddhism: its pantheism, matching the lyrical passages on the unity of Nature in 'Sainte-Odile' and others of his writings; its cult of resigned fortitude, close to his own stoicism; its determinism combined, none the less, with a belief in moral responsibility, exactly paralleled in his own thought; its doctrine of the world as appearance—not without affinity with his own view of the world and the self as composed of the flow of phenomena ('rien de réel dans le moi [he writes], sauf la file de ses événements' [2]); and, lastly, its pessimism, not unlike his own later sombre view of life. Here, at least, are suggestive resemblances, and, as with Michelet, it is solely Buddhism's naturalistic elements that are involved.

Leconte de Lisle's Indian poems offer a still more striking instance. Ménard may tell us (in 1887) that his friend in his later years was 'panthéiste et bouddhiste',[3] but we shall see within what severe limits this is true. For just as any 'pantheism' he may hold is strictly materialist—the cold neutrality of Nature may offer us self-forgetfulness but cannot satisfy our religious longings—so his borrowings from Indian religion are devoid of supernaturalism, and the Indian poems composed at intervals throughout his career suggest (as Carcassonne remarks) 'la promenade d'un dilettante, plutôt que le progrès d'une initiation'.[4] The omissions in his evocation of the Buddhist faith are especially revealing.

He presents for preference the outlook of the *Vedanta*, the most naturalistic of the Indian texts. The unreality of the world and the self; the dominance in our life of desire, suffering, and evil; death as our sole means of escape from the world of 'Will'—these are the teachings he takes up. He largely ignores the more mystical tenets of orthodox Buddhism—such as the idea of the Supreme Being, into whom the believer may be absorbed, if he renounces desire and practises austerity and devoutness of life; the notion of

[1] ibid., p. 298.　　[2] *De l'intelligence*, 16ᵉ éd., Hachette, s.d., 2 vols., i. 7.
[3] L. Ménard, 'Lettre à Pillon', *La Critique philosophique*, 1887, t.i., p. 315.
[4] E. Carcassonne, 'Leconte de Lisle et la philosophie indienne', *R.L.C.*, xi, 1931, p. 623.

'paradise' in 'Lower Buddhism', the *Nirvana* of 'Higher Buddhism'; the belief in reincarnation. He conceives *death* to be the goal of the Indian ascetic, giving a finality to physical disintegration that it does not have for the Buddhist, emptying even *Nirvana* of its transcendental meaning. And this is true even of those poems which derive from the *Bhagavata Purana*. In *Bhagavat* (1852)—one of his widest evocations of Buddhist tenets—the three believers are saved by the sight of Bhagavat (whereas on the Indian view both human sight and Bhagavat himself are illusory), deliverance comes to them in the form of physical death, and the poem ends with praise of 'l'invisible Mâyâ, créatrice du monde'—of 'illusion' itself, not of the 'reality' behind it. *La Vision de Brahma* (1857) portrays a vision of the Eternal Being, Vishnou, given to one of the personal and hence illusory gods of the Indian pantheon. But Vishnou is evoked as a physical being—he appears like some Oriental monarch, indeed—whilst Brahma resembles a human being rather than a god. A similar suppression of the mystical is found in his other poems. In *Çunacépa* (1855) it is death that the old sage offers to the young lovers as a way of release. *La Mort de Valmiki* (1881) ends as an apostrophe to the immortality of poetry, and Valmiki attains 'l'ineffable paix où s'anéantit l'âme' by contemplating not the Supreme Being but his own work. *La Mâyâ* (1881) interprets the world of 'illusion', 'le mirage immortel', as the only reality.

This non-supernatural version of Buddhism may derive in part from Leconte de Lisle's sources of knowledge: Burnouf, for example, presents an atheist as well as a theist conception of *Nirvana*.[1] But the significant fact is that Leconte de Lisle normally portrays—and can be thought to accept—only those Buddhist teachings which are compatible with a naturalistic philosophy. In so far as he may hold a Buddhist outlook, it is (in Fusil's words) 'une manière de bouddhisme scientifique'.[2]

Much the same is true of other thinkers who concerned themselves with Buddhism, such as Challemel-Lacour and Brunetière.

[1] E. Burnouf, *Introduction à l'histoire du buddhisme indien*, 2ᵉ éd., Maisonneuve, 1876, pp. 16-17.
[2] C. A. Fusil, *La Poésie scientifique de 1750 à nos jours*, Scientifica, 1918, p. 64.

The latter, whilst thinking of the Hindus as 'par excellence' 'la race religieuse' and considering the spread of Buddhism to be 'l'événement qu'on peut appeler, avec l'apparition du christianisme, le plus considérable de l'histoire du monde',[1] could yet single out as its main tenet the belief in man's universal sinfulness and unhappiness. As to Renan, he was distinctly non-committal in the two scholarly articles he devoted to recent works on Buddhism.[2] He thinks any serious mind should study a doctrine that has consoled a large part of humanity for twenty-four centuries, and he praises its high, charitable ethic which he finds similar to the Christian: 'c'est le catholicisme sans Dieu'. But he can go no further. The later theistic Buddhism became 'le plus grossier des cultes populaires', decked in '[les] extravagances d'une mythologie effrénée'. He perhaps betrays a certain sympathy with the earlier naturalistic form—this was '[la religion] la plus philosophique à son commencement'—but he is astonished that a creed compounded of atheism, materialism, and scepticism should have developed into a religion, and finds it vague and unsatisfying. He notes that 'certaines écoles modernes affectent d'y trouver le dernier mot de la sagesse'; it is clear that he does not.

The general conclusion one can advance is that Indian religion was for nineteenth-century thinkers all things to all men. Each admirer picked out what he wished to find. The occultists stressed its mysticism, its theory of metempsychosis, its doctrine of the expiation of evil through suffering. The philosophical naturalists were drawn more to Buddhism as a moral creed and to its atheist and pessimistic elements, and one can remark also the concurrent popularity of Schopenhauer, often regarded (in the title-words of Challemel-Lacour's famous article of 1870 on him) as 'Un Bouddhiste contemporain'.[3] To both groups, however, Buddhism appealed by virtue of its pantheism. It coincided at this point

---

[1] Cited by Clark, op. cit., pp. 157, 57.

[2] E. Renan, *Nouvelles études d'histoire religieuse*, Calmann Lévy, s.d., pp. 41–166. Even scholars of Buddhism are often highly critical—as witness, for example, Barthélemy-Saint Hilaire, who writes: 'Au fond, le bouddhisme n'est pas autre chose que l'adoration et le fanatisme du néant. . . . Je demande s'il est au monde quelque chose de plus contraire au dogme chrétien . . . que cette aberration et cette monstruosité' (in Burnouf, op. cit., p. xxiii.).   [3] *R.D.M.*, 15.3.1870, pp. 296–332.

with one of the salient features of the non-Christian religious thought of the age, and especially with the metaphysical ideas coming into France from Germany. It is this coincidence which Quinet, amongst others, is stressing when he writes:

Voilà la grande affaire qui se passe aujourd'hui dans la philosophie. Le panthéisme de l'Orient, transformé par l'Allemagne, correspond à la renaissance orientale, de même que l'idéalisme de Platon, corrigé par Descartes, a couronné, au dix-septième siècle, la renaissance grecque et latine.[1]

And the same recognition of a common pantheism often lay behind the frequent designation of India as 'l'Allemagne de l'Orient'—and of Germany as 'l'Inde de l'Occident'.[2] In France at this period, one may well conclude, Hinduism, and particularly Buddhism, provided a religious dress for ideas that were already independently held. Like the borrowings of the syncretists over a wider area, they consecrated beliefs that might otherwise have seemed non-religious. They lent an aroma of the divine to high-minded but, for the most part, non-supernatural philosophies of life.

[1] *Le Génie des religions, Œuvres*, i. 74.
[2] For example, V. Hugo, *William Shakespeare*, Charpentier et Fasquelle, s.d., p. 70, and J. Michelet, *Introduction à l'histoire universelle*, in *Précis de l'histoire moderne*, etc., Flammarion, s.d., p. 429. The poet Henri Cazalis (Jean Lahor), omitted here for chronological reasons, offers a little later a further good illustration of the fusion of pantheism, nihilism, and an ethic of charity; cf. R. Petitbon, 'Un dévot de la Maya brahmanique: Jean Lahor', *Cahiers de l'Association Internationale des Études Françaises*, xiii, 1961, pp. 103–16.

VII

The Cult of History and Progress (1)

1. Introduction

PHILOSOPHY of history is both an ancient and a comparatively new field of thought. Throughout civilized time men have sought to find a meaning in human history, to make sense of the events befalling them. It is no coincidence that the world-religions all offer an interpretation of the historical process—the cyclical theory of Buddhism, for example, whose doctrine of eternal recurrence preaches that history lacks any ultimate significance; more optimistically, the Hebrew and Christian doctrine of Providence, of God working out His purposes in history. Yet as a self-conscious, self-contained study philosophy of history is only a newcomer, and this is not surprising, for history itself hardly graduated as a serious discipline before the late-eighteenth century. The Neapolitan thinker Vico (1668–1744) and such French *philosophes* as Turgot and Condorcet were virtually the first philosophers of history who were independent of theological orthodoxy, and the full flowering of what Vico bravely called this 'new science' came only with Herder and Kant in the last decades of the eighteenth century.

The term 'history' has two meanings: it may refer to the events of the past or to men's accounts of these events. To these usages correspond the two distinct meanings of 'philosophy of history'. It may signify, first, *speculative* theory of history, which discusses the claim that events are directed towards a rational purpose, that they reveal a meaningful pattern which transcends the intentions of individuals and even communities. Or, secondly, the term may be applied to *analytical* or *critical* philosophy of history, the study of the methodology of history in the second sense, of its theory of knowledge, attempting to answer such questions as: what kind of knowledge is historical knowledge? can there be wholly objective history? what is the nature of historical explanation?

In the first half of the nineteenth century the former was dominant. Apart from isolated discussions of the historical method such as Comte's, critical philosophy of history was ignored prior to the work of Renouvier and Cournot in the 1860's—ignored with regrettable consequences for the speculative systems we are to survey. In our own century the roles have been somewhat reversed: the speculative approach persists in writers like Spengler and Arnold Toynbee and in Marxism, but, especially in Britain, many thinkers countenance historical theory only in its critical form.[1]

Around 1815, however, the mood was very different. Historical study in general enjoyed a marked expansion at this time, inspired mainly by nationalism and also by the Romantic vogue for 'local colour' and *exotisme* and for the novels of Walter Scott. First encouraged by Napoleon, it was further stimulated by the Restoration government, which created chairs of history in every university, reorganized the École des Langues Orientales, founded the École des Chartes and the École d'Athènes, protected historical monuments, and subsidized archaeological missions to the Near and Far East. Renan could even write of the 'revolution', 'qui depuis 1820 a changé complètement la face des études historiques, ou pour mieux dire qui a fondé l'histoire parmi nous'.[2] And whilst some of the new scholars were narrative historians, others were philosophers by predilection. Agnostics who could find no meaning in the universe set themselves to discover one in the human realm; Christians and metaphysicians who claimed to know the purpose of the universe were convinced that it must be manifest in history also. Hence, from every side, came vast interpretations of the past and comprehensive predictions of the future. Most of these speculative systems centred on the idea of progress; if one believes that history is 'going somewhere', one may think it is going downhill, but the greater temptation is to argue that it is going up, that human development is and has been in a desirable

---

[1] For a recent discussion of present-day views, cf. W. H. Walsh, *An Introduction to Philosophy of History*, London, Hutchinson, 1951; cf. also R. G. Collingwood, *The Idea of History*, Oxford, Clarendon Press, 1946.

[2] E. Renan, *L'Avenir de la science*, 23ᵉ éd., Calmann Lévy, 1929, p. 132.

direction. And if (as especially the metaphysicians of this period maintained) progress is an historical inevitability, the way is open for history to be, in a sense, deified, to form the basis of a new faith in place of a discarded religious creed. For history gives us a purpose (to move with it), a criterion of moral value (whatever triumphs in history is right), and even offers us a perfect, if impersonal, deity to worship (since history, on this theory, is always right). Renan, as we noted, was very close to this position in his 'religion of the ideal', and he was preceded by numerous others in accepting (in Isaiah Berlin's words) one of those 'metaphysico-theological theories of history, which attract many who have lost their faith in older religious orthodoxies'.[1]

Progress was indeed to prove, in Bury's words, 'a guiding spiritual force of the nineteenth century'.[2] Javary could declare in 1850 that in principle it was no longer contested by anyone and that the only remaining question concerned the conditions in which it is realized, and a little later Paul Janet could speak of 'la passion du progrès, à laquelle personne de notre temps ne peut échapper absolument'. It was a passion evidenced even in the titles of several reviews of the age—*Le Progresseur* (1828), the *Revue du progrès social* (1834), the *Revue du progrès politique, social et littéraire* (1839–42), *Le Progrès, revue démocratique* (1849–50), and others. Nor did contemporary observers fail to remark the religious overtones of this enthusiasm. The Liberal Protestant Colani was only one amongst many when he declared in his *Revue de théologie* in 1853: 'Le progrès est la religion de tous ceux qui, en dehors du christianisme, ne sont pas rongés par le doute.'[3] Only isolated writers reacted against the general mood—Baudelaire attacking the 'infatuation' with progress as '[une] idée grotesque, qui a fleuri sur le terrain pourri de la fatuité moderne', or Gautier exclaiming: 'Mon Dieu! que c'est une sotte chose que cette prétendue perfectibilité du genre humain dont on nous rebat les oreilles!' They opposed to their contemporaries' trust in progress a belief in

[1] I. Berlin, *Historical Inevitability*, London, Oxford U.P., 1954, p. 76.
[2] J. B. Bury, *History of Freedom of Thought*, 2nd ed., London, Oxford U.P., 1952, p. 181.
[3] A. Javary, *De l'idée de progrès*, Orléans, Coignet-Darnault, 1850, p. 74, Paul Janet, *Les Problèmes du dix-neuvième siècle*, 2e éd., Michel Lévy, 1873, p. 332, and T. Colani in *Revue de théologie*, vi, 1853, p. 286.

the *decadence* of modern civilization.[1] Yet even this was to pay allegiance to the underlying assumption of the age that history has pattern and direction.

2. *The Idea of Progress before 1815*

Broadly speaking, nineteenth-century France inherited two different traditions of thought about historical development— that of the French *philosophes* and that of the German idealists, traditions that intermingled as the century advanced. The former stemmed from the later seventeenth century. For as long as men lived under the authority of the past, of age-old Church and of Greek philosophy, believing that the purpose of life lay in a future realm and that this world was a mere backcloth against which man's essentially spiritual drama was being enacted, for so long the idea of historical progress was hardly entertained, except by isolated thinkers such as Jean Bodin. Moreover, men had a limited time-sequence to survey, and what they knew of the remoter past chiefly concerned its 'peaks'—Greek, Roman, and Hebrew civilization—whilst its 'valleys' were hidden: hence the view that Nature and man are the same in all ages, an idea that still lingers in Voltaire. It is true that the Hebrew and Christian religions, unlike most other world-religions, see history not as a recurrent cycle but as a movement towards a divinely ordained consummation and the universal triumph of good, and that they entertain a hope for the future that other creeds consider a delusion. But it is hard to accept the contention (found in Becker and Baillie[2]) that the *philosophes'* belief in progress has a Christian origin. Analogies between progress theories and Christianity's doctrine of history undoubtedly exist, and the latter may have suggested the former. These analogies are well summarized when Baillie says of the *philosophe*:

[1] C. Baudelaire, 'Exposition universelle de 1855', *Curiosités esthétiques*, Conard, 1923, p. 227, and T. Gautier, *Préface, Mademoiselle de Maupin*, Charpentier, 1927, p. 23. Cf. A. E. Carter, *The Idea of Decadence in French Literature, 1830–1900*, Univ. of Toronto Press, 1958.

[2] C. L. Becker, *The Heavenly City of the 18th Century Philosophers*, New Haven, Yale U.P., 1932, pp. 29–31, and J. Baillie, *The Belief in Progress*, London, Oxford U.P., 1951, p. 113. For the contrary view, cf. M. Ginsberg, *The Idea of Progress*, London, Methuen, 1953, pp. 7–10.

All he could do . . . was to transfer his hope from the eternal to the temporal scene, to shift attention from the glorified future life of those already born and dead to a possible better earthly life for those yet to be born, to replace the desire for immortality with the desire to influence future generations and if possible to be remembered by them, to transpose paradise from heaven to earth, and to make posterity rather than God the final judge.[1]

But this is far more than what he terms 'a Christian heresy'. It is to banish God from His world and Christ from the centre of human history, and to replace a God-centred hope in a heavenly future by a man-centred faith in a terrestrial future. Such a view could arise only in the scientific and rationalist atmosphere of the late-seventeenth century and amongst thinkers already doubting the existence of God and immortal life and thus more ready to look for earthly joy than for the problematic bliss of heaven. By 1650 scholasticism and Catholic authority had been challenged by Bacon, Descartes, and Gassendi, and Cartesian mechanism had threatened to reduce God to a first cause, a mere 'chiquenaude' (as Pascal alleged against it), in a universe of invariable physical laws. Soon, too, the splendour of court life and literary and artistic achievement under Louis XIV led men to reconsider the assumption that the Ancients had reached a cultural level that could never be regained. 'Les anciens sont les anciens; nous sommes les gens d'aujourd'hui,' Molière urged, and implicit here was an assertion that we might do even better than they, which, during the *Querelle des Anciens et des Modernes*, was made explicit in Perrault's *Siècle de Louis le Grand* (1687):

> La docte Antiquité dans toute sa durée
> À l'égal de nos jours ne fut point éclairée.

Both he, in his *Parallèle des anciens et des modernes* (1688–97), and Fontenelle, in the *Digression sur les anciens et les modernes* (1688), appealed to the idea that learning and experience accumulate over the ages, so that progress through knowledge becomes virtually inevitable—an idea confirmed by the concurrently popularized

---

[1] Baillie, op. cit., pp. 113–14.

successes of science. As the eighteenth century began, the sensationalist philosophy of John Locke and his many French followers provided a fertile soil for this concept of progress. If man is born a 'blank sheet', we can develop him as we will. Given the right education and environment he can in theory be made perfect; we may even be able to produce geniuses at will, thinks Helvétius. And in the same way as sensationalism was rejecting the notion of a divine determinism of human nature (as fallen and sinful and irredeemable save by God's grace), so historians like Voltaire were jettisoning the notion of a divine determinism of history. For a seventeenth-century theologian of Providence like Bossuet history was a family affair, the story of God's dealings with His children, especially in Israel and Europe, and the Day of Judgement, the end of all history, was still an imminent possibility. In marked contrast, the *philosophes* looked out upon the wider world revealed by explorers, missionaries, and Oriental scholars and to an unbounded earthly future, and they believed that, within the limits of natural determining factors like 'climate', man's history springs from his own thought and will. We are the masters of our own fortunes, and if this is our only life, we have all the greater incentive to mould it to our own desires. Some went even further: in his lectures on 'universal history' (1750) Turgot alleged that mankind is necessarily moving to greater perfection from age to age—by virtue of a force of progress that can utilize even those human passions and vices which seemed to Voltaire to make advance wholly contingent on human choice. But all were agreed in linking the notion of progress with political reform; they employed it to stimulate men to social action, urging (like the Abbé de Saint-Pierre) that good government can bring in a golden age.

Yet for all they did to naturalize the idea of progress in European thought, the *philosophes* did not offer a detailed theory of its workings or give more than a perfunctory glance at its manifestations in the past. This was true even of Turgot and of Condorcet's inaccurate and highly conjectural *Esquisse d'un tableau des progrès de l'esprit humain* (written in 1793), although this last work —the furthest development of the idea by the *philosophes*—did analyse man's past into nine 'epochs' of progress. In reality (and perhaps to their credit) the *philosophes'* interest was in the future rather than the past, in practical social improvements rather than a comprehensive survey of history. Progress was a battle-cry, not a subject for scholarly research, nor did most of them consider it inevitable. Hence it was left to other more metaphysically minded thinkers to develop a speculative philosophy of progress and to seek its 'laws'. The Italian thinker Vico had taken some steps to this end in his *New Science* (1725), fusing the cyclical theory and the notion of progress in his conception of history as a slowly ascending spiral. But though his ideas were to influence later theoreticians like Michelet, it was German thinkers who first provided a full-fledged theory.

Here Christian thought was far more important. The idea of progress was taken out of the agnostic and even atheistic atmosphere of French *philosophie* into the still religious environment of later-eighteenth-century Germany, and was re-interpreted in terms of Divine Providence. And, equally noteworthy, progress was located less in the social realm than in men's inner, psychological and moral development. Lessing, in his *Education of the Human Race* (1780), saw Old and New Testaments as the story of a continuous education of man by God and looked towards a new and yet higher gospel to further the process. Herder, in his *Ideas towards a Philosophy of the History of Humanity* (1784-91), argued that God is now inactive and has left this education in the hands of man himself—but, he added, God established the laws by which it develops. Kant's *Idea of a Universal History* (1784) defined the goal of progress not as happiness but as man's complete obedience to the moral law and discerned here a working out of God's purposes for man. Indeed, unless history has significance, belief in Divine Providence must be abandoned, he contended, for 'what use is it to glorify and commend to view the splendour and wisdom of Creation shown in the irrational kingdom of nature, if . . . human history is to offer a standing objection to our adopting such an attitude?'[1] He also tentatively suggested (in the *Critique of Practical Reason*) that man's moral development cannot be completed on earth. We must postulate a future life in which progress

[1] Cited by Walsh, op. cit., p. 123.

continues—a significant extension indeed! Hegel's *Lectures on the Philosophy of History* (delivered in 1828, published in 1837) went still further. Where Fichte, Schelling, and their predecessors had thought of God as existing outside the process of development, Hegel identified them: God, termed the Absolute, Absolute Spirit, is immanent in the world, and historical development *is* the Absolute moving towards complete self-awareness. Hegel concluded his lectures by saying: 'That the History of the World, with all the changing scenes which its annals present, is this process of development and the realization of Spirit—this is the true Theodicaea, the justification of God in History.' [1] Here is the first major change in the idea of progress effected by the German idealists. From a primarily ethical and practical ideal, as it had been for the *philosophes*, they transformed it into a metaphysical ideal having close affinities with an immanentist religion: the way was here prepared for a religion of progress such as Renan's. Secondly, they stressed the idea of development (*Entwicklung*) almost more than that of progress, seeing each stage of history as the logically necessary unfolding of potentialities contained in the preceding stages. This evolution is towards a greater good, they thought, but more important for Hegel in particular were its logical inevitability and its independence of human choice. He was little concerned with the future, believing that the Absolute had achieved full self-consciousness in his own system and declaring himself content with the existing Prussian state; philosophy, in any event, 'always comes too late' to influence events.[2] Here is the source of a further new idea: later thinkers, such as Scherer, would accept the notion of development whilst rejecting that of inevitable progress.[3]

3. Social Theories of Progress

Coming now to the nineteenth-century French scene, one finds so great a profusion of differing theories that a completely adequate selection is perhaps impossible. Almost every thinker takes up the idea of progress and utilizes it in the service of his own

---

[1] Hegel, *Philosophy of History*, transl. Sibree, London, Bell, 1878, p. 477.
[2] Hegel, *The Philosophy of Right*, transl. Knox, Oxford, Clarendon Press, 1942, pp. 12–13.   [3] Cf. pp. 189–93 below.

special preoccupations. The *philosophes* had in general united it with rationalism and political action, arguing that advance depends upon applying reason to social problems. The Germans had linked it with metaphysics, viewing it less as a social than as an intellectual process—a movement, in Hegel's case, towards the 'realization' of the Absolute. The same is true of nineteenth-century French theorists. Christians interpret progress as the work of Divine Providence. Metaphysicians like Cousin connect it with the Hegelian dialectic. Sociologists like Saint-Simon and Comte seek to transform it into one of the 'scientific' laws of history they purport to announce. Other social reformers proclaim that the very goal of history, of man's age-long advance, lies in the achievement of the particular principle they themselves advocate. For libertarians like Quinet, Michelet, or Victor Hugo, all history is moving towards greater liberty; for egalitarians like Proudhon and Leroux, towards greater equality; whilst for socialists like Louis Blanc, Cabet, and Karl Marx, its end is fraternity and a classless society. Yet it would be wrong to regard these 'coincidences' too cynically or to suspect these thinkers' sincerity. One should recall how often these theories are set in a prophetic and even eschatological context, are embodied in a religious system, be it the Catholic orthodoxy of Joseph de Maistre, one of the social religions of humanity, the messianic faith in history of Karl Marx, or Renan's religion of the ideal.

French eighteenth-century thought about progress was developed very significantly by Comte. Both his famous *loi des trois états* and his concept of historical method have already been discussed, however, in relation to his faith in science. As representative of a social philosophy of history that tries to establish a scientific law of progress we shall therefore take Comte's master, Saint-Simon, whilst to illustrate the common fusion at this time of utopian socialism and the idea of progress we shall outline the truly remarkable ideas of Charles Fourier.

L'âge d'or du genre humain n'est point derrière nous, il est au-devant, il est dans la perfection de l'ordre social; nos pères ne l'ont point vu, nos enfants y arriveront un jour, c'est à nous de leur en frayer la route.[1]

[1] *Œuvres de Saint-Simon et d'Enfantin*, Dentu et Leroux, 1865–78, 47 vols., xv. 248.

Saint-Simon's famous assertion plunges us at once into an atmosphere quite different from that of the German idealists. Progress is once again a rallying cry of the social reformer, and the mood is that of Holbach and Condorcet. Concern with the Absolute, with the growth of man's reason and spirituality, with metaphysics, yields to a utilitarian call to action. We are not invited to contemplate the workings of Providence over the centuries, but to take our destinies into our own hands. The goal does not lie in some distant future but is even now in sight, to be attained by a final, united effort. For an idealist like Herder man was still 'raised . . . but a short step above the brute'.[1] Saint-Simon shared the confidence of Condorcet, who had contended that humanity had already passed through the first nine epochs of progress and was entering the tenth and final age. Mankind resembles an individual entering his forties, ripe for his finest achievements. The 'industrial age' that is beginning will be the final period, the consummation of history. Nor, yet again, are we offered as our reward the somewhat intangible benefits of 'complete consciousness' or 'the realization of Spirit'. Condorcet had foreseen technological improvements, more food, longer life, less disease, equality of the sexes, social security against old age and sickness. Saint-Simon in his turn advocated a scientific administration that would satisfy our material wants, improve education and help us to attain 'le plus haut degré de félicité que [l'espèce humaine] puisse atteindre pendant sa vie terrestre'.[2]

Saint-Simon's chief writings on the philosophy of history were the *Introduction aux travaux scientifiques du dix-neuvième siècle* (1807–8) and his *Mémoire sur la science de l'homme* (1813). He divides the 'science of man' into two parts: the first deals with the individual under his physical and psychological aspects, the second with the human race. This latter is the science of history, he claims, and its position amongst the sciences is as high for him as is sociology for Comte. Condorcet has so far done most to establish it, but whilst he was right to maintain that man exists as a species no less than as an individual and that the species' development is

[1] Cited by F. E. Manuel, *The New World of Henri Saint-Simon*, Cambridge, Mass., Harvard U.P., 1956, p. 163.   [2] *Œuvres*, xxiii. 148.

subject to laws, he was too little concerned to discover these laws. Science, Saint-Simon stresses in common with Comte, consists not only of observing facts but also of generalizing from them and discerning their regularities. History is only now in process of moving from a conjectural to a properly scientific state—a transition made in turn by all the sciences—and still awaits a new Newton to study the operation of progress. Saint-Simon casts himself in this role. Rejecting both the *a priori* approach of the Germans and the mere 'empiricism' of the *philosophes*, he will transform the *philosophy* of history into the *science* of history. Not that he is interested in knowledge for its own sake; he wants to establish the laws of historical movement because they alone can provide a predictive basis for future action. Whilst we cannot understand our present situation unless we know the past which has produced it, Saint-Simon declares that the main benefit of historical study is 'to profit from the experience so dearly bought there'.[1] His boldest aim is to deduce the future from historical studies and thus achieve a scientific politics.

To believe that historical analysis can give scientifically reliable predictions is to presuppose that the course of events is rigorously determined. Saint-Simon does not hesitate to make this assumption; his belief in 'the necessary course of things' underlies his whole conception of an historical science.[2] And since progress constitutes the very substance and meaning of history, in his view, he is led to maintain that every age improves on the past, that protracted decline and stagnation are impossible. Here he takes issue again with Condorcet and his fellow *philosophes*, Turgot alone excepted. They had seen the Middle Ages and the religion that dominated them as an interruption of progress; indeed, this very belief had prevented them from accepting that progress is inevitable. Saint-Simon, like Comte, and in this at one with the Romantics' rehabilitation of the medieval period, argues that even these centuries played a definite, necessary role in the drama of human advance. He claims that the Middle Ages were 'the veritable cradle of our modern civilization' and that it was 'impossible to establish a better political system at that time' than existed.[3]

[1] ibid., xxii. 14.   [2] ibid., xviii. 66.   [3] ibid., xx. 73–74, 6.

Against the *philosophes* he maintains that religion is an intimate part of any social order and is in reality the science of the age clothed in a form suitable to the emotional needs it has to satisfy. Saint-Simon has been justly praised for his reassessment of medieval civilization. Yet one of its basic suppositions is disquieting. So deep is his trust in the process of history that he slips from the idea that 'whatever will be will be' to the faith that 'whatever will be will be right', justified by its historical necessity at the moment it occurs. In the light of this principle, any age can be praised since, *ex hypothesi*, it can only come prompt on its historical cue, and Saint-Simon therefore finds merit alike in Christianity and the *Encyclopédie*, in slavery and liberalism, in the Church Fathers and Luther, in Machiavelli and Montesquieu. He embraces a thoroughgoing moral relativism in his discussion of the past just as much as Hegel or Cousin: historical necessity justifies everything.[1] And a salient difficulty of his system, as of any system of historical determinism, lies in finding a place for moral exhortation. If history is a moving staircase bearing us inevitably upwards to perfection, what need is there for social activism, for political self-help? Saint-Simon's answer is that the movement can be speeded if only men will henceforth 'do consciously, by direct effort, and with more fruitful results' what they have hitherto been doing 'as it were unintentionally, slowly, indecisively, and with little success'.[2] For whatever may be the ultimate motive force behind history— a problem that, unlike the Germans, he does not discuss—its efficient causes are ideas. Institutions, policies, organization are all products of the state of knowledge and thought at a given time and can never move in advance of this state. Hence, to hasten the development of ideas is to hasten social progress.

His belief in the directive power of ideas in history also underlies his conception of the universal law which rules over historical change. For a time he contended that gravitation was the law of both history and other spheres of life, but from 1814 he seems to abandon this curious notion and substitutes something approach-

---

[1] Cf. W. M. Simon, 'History for Utopia: Saint-Simon and the Idea of Progress', *Journal of the History of Ideas*, xvii, 1956, p. 327.

[2] *Œuvres*, xviii. 166.

ing a law of alternation of organic and critical periods.[1] The two chief operations of the mind are analysis and synthesis: each age will be critical or organic according to which predominates in its intellectual life. In the critical epochs men scrutinize existing institutions and try to change them, and they abandon accepted creeds. The resultant lack of a united social purpose leads to conflict of selfish interests, bitter competition, a society that is restless, changeful, and near-anarchical: these are the ages of revolution. In the organic epochs a society is bound together by a common faith and enjoys stable and ordered government: these are the periods of construction and organization. Greece before Socrates was organic, after him critical; Lucretius and Cicero mark a similar turning-point in Roman history. In our own era, the period from the sixth to the sixteenth century was organic; the Reformers and Renaissance philosophers inaugurated a new critical age which reached its anarchical climax in the French Revolution. In the nineteenth century our task is to lay the foundations for an organic period in which social order and cohesion can be regained. Unfortunately, the religious outlook of the Middle Ages is no longer adequate to the intellectual level of the times. The unity of the new organic society must therefore come from the scientific attitude, albeit clothed for the sake of the masses in religious dress, and he urges that if society, and especially industry, are scientifically organized in the interests of the working classes, we shall see the dawn of a new era of happiness. This will, moreover, be a *permanent* 'golden age', for—by a happy coincidence that recurs in most nineteenth-century theories of progress, including Marxism —we are entering the final and culminating epoch of history. The industrial system is the one 'towards which mankind has always been moving'; this will be the final system, and all other political systems that have existed 'should be considered as merely preparatory'.[2] Saint-Simon does not explain why the law of alternation

---

[1] It has recently been argued by F. A. Isambert ('Époques critiques et époques organiques', *Cahiers internationaux de sociologie*, xxvii, 1959, pp. 131–52) that this notion is not found in Saint-Simon's works in the fully developed form attributed to him by his disciples but was derived by Buchez from Ballanche. Even Isambert's own references do, however, seem to justify the view that Saint-Simon, here as elsewhere, grasped the elements of an idea that others would clarify and expand.   [2] *Œuvres*, xxi. 166.

is about to fall into abeyance. As one commentator drily re-marks, 'the illusion that the present occupies a special, if not unique place of honour at the banquet of history, is one that dies hard';[1] Saint-Simon yields to it as readily as Hegel, Comte, or Marx.

The reason is not far to seek: Saint-Simon was a social reformer and prophet rather than a social scientist, and however fertile and stimulating one may find his philosophy of history, he did not achieve the science which he announced. He offered quite in-adequate factual evidence for his theories (entirely confined to Europe, moreover), failed to verify what facts he did adduce, and never justified his basic assumption that history is determined by laws. He recommends historians to adopt 'a vantage point suffi-ciently elevated' to enable one to take in 'at a single glance the whole course of civilization'.[2] Such a love of the general, bird's-eye view is symptomatic of the great weakness of his system—that it is philosophical, speculative, not historical.

The same criticisms apply to Charles Fourier (1772–1837) who offered an even vaster and more complex theory than Saint-Simon. 'His imagination [Flint nicely comments] was strong and exuberant but unchastened and unregulated.'[3] Perhaps the best-known illustrations of this fact are his beliefs that the world will improve to such a degree that the oceans will consist of lemonade and that human nature will advance until there are at any one time—and at an approximate estimate—37 million poets equal to Homer, 37 million philosophers equal to Newton, and 37 million writers equal to Molière.

Fourier's most influential ideas concerned his theory of the human passions and his advocacy of *phalanstères* in which men will live together in communal harmony: these views we noted earlier. But he also put forward a philosophy of history, well expressed in *Le Nouveau Monde industriel et sociétaire* (1829–30), that is not with-

---

[1] R. V. Sampson, *Progress in the Age of Reason*, London, Heinemann, 1956, p. 159.

[2] *Œuvres*, xxiii. 48.

[3] R. Flint, *History of the Philosophy of History*, Edinburgh and London, Blackwood, 1893, p. 409. Like all other students of the subject, I am much indebted to this very com-prehensive factual survey.

out interest despite its unscientific extravagance.[1] He divides history into four great periods, corresponding to the infancy, youth, manhood, and old age of an individual. Although we are still in the first of these, he tells us that the first and final periods will last for 5,000 years each and the second and third for 35,000 years each. Fourier was one of the few thinkers of his time to follow to its conclusion the analogy between history and the individual's life, and he adds that whilst the first two periods will in general be ages of ascent, the last two will bring decline. He thus rejects the notion of limitless progress, and he also denies that progress is continuous and uninterrupted even during the earlier periods. He sub-divides the first period into lesser ages: *édénisme*, the primitive golden age, followed by a descent into *sauvagerie*, *patriarcat*, *barbarie*, and *civilisation*, the stage that has now been reached by the more advanced nations. The age of *civilisation* itself mirrors the rise and decline of the individual. It falls into four sub-periods—feudalism; the rise of social liberty; the expansion of commerce, which leads to a class-ridden and evil capitalism; and— the age of senility—economic despotism, when the majority is enslaved by a wealthy oligarchy. Fourier's analysis here foreshadowed Marxist and socialist thought. The age to follow will be one of progress, however—*garantisme*—for nations will enter federations and individuals will be guaranteed by society against poverty and want. This will lead in turn to the age of *sociantisme*, in which a federation of *phalanges* on the Fourierist model will come into being and an era of idyllic prosperity, of *harmonisme*, dawn for mankind. Fourier's social thought was primarily directed to ushering in these two happier ages with which the first great period of history would end. Of the later periods he says little in detail. The second and third will be eras of respectively increasing and decreasing happiness, whilst the fourth will witness a relapse into misery and savagery.

Fourier thus resists the temptation to proclaim that the social utopia he preaches is to be permanent. Yet he does offer alternative consolations, as we saw earlier. Not only do we enjoy

[1] Cf. C. Fourier, *Le Nouveau Monde industriel et sociétaire*, Brussels, Librairie Belge-Française, 1840, 2 vols., Avant-Propos and t. ii, sections 6 and 7.

reincarnation in this world, but, when the earth disintegrates, our souls will be transported to a planet of a higher order, and there human history will recommence—following the same path of ascent and descent. Thus we may look forward to an unbounded future of reincarnations here and elsewhere, most of which— seven-eighths, to be exact—will be happy. This belief in the trans-migration of souls allowed him to be an historical optimist even though denying that earthly progress is either continuous or dur-able; he offered at this point a somewhat unusual fusion of worldly realism and extra-terrestrial idealism. The same is perhaps true of his historical philosophy as a whole. The social and economic criticisms it embodied were often incisive and pertinent—and on these his fame justly rests. Unfortunately they were combined in his too fertile mind with long-term prophecies, made almost entirely without evidence, that recall nothing so much as an astrological almanac.

With minor variations for the most part, other social thinkers of the time offered similar sketches of world history. Louis Blanc (1813–82), for example, divided human progress into the three ages of authority, individualism (inaugurated by Luther), and fraternity (announced by Revolutionary thinkers but still lying in the future). The first led to the suppression of personality; the second has led to anarchy; only in the third can we hope for a union of personal freedom and social harmony. Proudhon (1809–1865), though an ardent individualist who denied the reality of any impersonal 'force of history', nevertheless believed that the past reveals a pattern. This pattern derives not from a divine Provi-dence or from some creative drive within a divinized Nature, ideas he dismissed with contempt, but from the spontaneous development of man as a collective being. In *De la création de l'ordre dans l'humanité* (1843) he erected a *loi des trois états* identical with Comte's: 'Religion, Philosophie, Science; la foi, le sophisme, et la méthode: tels sont les trois moments de la connaissance, les trois époques de l'éducation du genre humain.' Each of these stages is necessary, but we have now entered, to Proudhon's relief, the third: 'la théologie est tombée, la sophistique est frappée à mort'.[1] Yet progress is not to be measured by material, economic, or even scientific advance. Its true criterion, as he especially argued in *De la justice* (1858), is the increase in what is essential to full humanity, namely, liberty and justice, which he interprets as equality. Past 'crises' have extended this equality: Christ taught men's equality before God; the Reformation and rationalist philosophy won equality before conscience and reason; the Revolution achieved equality before the law. But social and economic equality remain for us to establish: hence his fervent attacks upon property and the Church and his advocacy of a form of anarchy. Pierre Leroux (1797–1871), though he left the Saint-Simonians, shared their belief in the unity of mankind.[2] He even reinforced it, for on the basis of his doctrine of metempsychosis he claimed that the men of past, present, and future are quite literally united: they consist of the same souls in different bodies. Mankind's history— the central subject-matter for philosophy, in his view—reveals a continuous progress, since whilst at a given moment man may be static in one realm (the intellectual, say), he will be advancing in another (for example, the emotional). Nor has this improvement any limit, for humanity is immortal. Leroux, like Proudhon, defined progress as a ceaseless development towards equality, and this he divided into three stages, marked by man's self-deliverance, first, from the patriarchal despotism of Eastern civilizations, secondly, from the state despotism of Greece and Rome, and thirdly, yet to be achieved, from the tyranny of property and economic privilege which still abounds in the nineteenth century. The family, the state, and property are not evil in themselves but have produced class distinctions we must seek to abolish. The Revolution consecrated the idea of a society based on universal equality; now we are on the threshold of history's third and finest age.

4. *Metaphysical Theories of Progress: The Eclectics*

Meanwhile, in less politically preoccupied thinkers the German

---

[1] *Œuvres complètes de Proudhon*, nouv. éd., Marcel Rivière, 1923–59, 19 vols., vi. 42–43, 126.

[2] Cf. P. Leroux, *De l'humanité*, Perrotin, 1840, 2 vols., liv. i, ch. 3, 4, and, on metempsychosis, liv. v, ch. 12, t. i, pp. 137–56, 270–1.

metaphysical philosophies of history were exerting their influence. These were first popularized in France by Madame de Staël just before our period begins. She was also a warm admirer of Condorcet, and for a moment the French and German currents mingled in her—only to diverge again before their final confluence in later writers, and supremely in Karl Marx. But after 1815 the most effective intermediary between Hegelian philosophy and France was Victor Cousin, supported by certain of his eclectic disciples. His contribution to the philosophy of history consisted, first, in his work as a popularizer of German thought and, secondly, in his own historical theories, propounded in lectures given in 1828 and derived in large part from Hegel himself, whom he first met in 1817.

Like Hegel he claims that history is determined by the development of human reason. He therefore analyses reason's 'elements' and concludes that they are three in number: the idea of the infinite, the idea of the finite, and the idea of the relation between the two.[1] These fundamental notions determine all our thinking about life and society, but any given age is dominated by only one of them, a fact which differentiates it in countless respects from other ages.

[L'identité du genre humain] est celle des trois éléments de la conscience du genre humain. Les différences viennent de la prédominance de l'un d'eux sur les autres. Ces différences constituent les différentes époques de l'histoire.[2]

Nor is the dominance of a particular idea a matter of chance; by logical necessity human history is ruled in turn by the idea of the infinite, the idea of the finite, and the idea of their relation. It follows that there are 'trois époques de l'histoire, ni plus ni moins'. As Cousin says in a passage which makes clear his *a priori* approach:

Il est clair qu'il doit y avoir autant d'époques qu'il y a d'éléments; et s'il n'y a que trois éléments, il n'y a et il ne peut y avoir que trois grandes époques.[3]

---

[1] V. Cousin, *Cours de l'histoire de la philosophie moderne: 2e série*, t. i, nouv. éd., Didier et Ladrange, 1847, 5e leçon, pp. 95 ff.   [2] ibid., p. 88.   [3] ibid., p. 159.

In the first period, that of Oriental civilization, man is over-whelmed by a sense of his weakness in the face of the universe,[1] that is to say, by the idea of the infinite dwarfing him, an idea reinforced in his mind by the geographical area in which he lives—Asia, 'un continent haut et immense'. His religion will be pantheistic, focused upon the great unity that stretches all around him, and will preach the nothingness of man—as does Indian religion, for example. His society will be static, living from day to day, without a developing industry, its government a form of theocratic despotism. With the growth of reflection man comes to feel his own freedom and power, and the second age begins, that of the idea of the finite. It was born and flourished in Ancient Greece, in a setting of sunshine and profusion, where the world appeared more friendly, in an area of islands and enclosed sea where Nature's immensity was less overwhelming than on the Asian plateau. Man begins to feel the charm and pleasure of life, to feel secure, and thus to plan for the future and his own advantage: hence industry and commerce become progressive and highly advanced. In the religious sphere, likewise, the finite rules: the gods are reduced to the measure of man, and the mystical self-denial of the Buddhist yields to Greek humanism. As to government, men cherish their liberty and no longer permit the infinite power of the Oriental despot; they replace it by a more democratic system in which the ruler's authority is limited, finite. In the third and final age man achieves (in the Hegelian manner) a synthesis between the infinite and the finite: this epoch is determined by the idea of their relation to one another. It is above all the age of Christianity—for which the deity is Christ, both God and man in one—and it has unfolded in Western Europe, territorially limited but looking out over the vast Atlantic, in a land less amiable than the Greek but more bountiful and less desolate than Asia.

History, on this once-famous theory, is not only determined by the evolution of spontaneous reason but also, and behind even this, by the action of God. History is 'the government of God made visible', and this leads to a significant conclusion. Cousin

[1] ibid., 8e leçon.

deduces that everything in history is for the best and that this is the best of all possible worlds. Even wars, he argues, following Hegel, are necessary and useful; through them truth triumphs over error and a higher civilization over a lower. Unfortunately, this belief that 'right is might' can too easily turn into the view that 'might is right'.

His optimistic determinism was also based upon wholly inadequate historical evidence. Cousin claims in his fourth lecture that philosophy of history must be both speculative and empirical, but although his division of history into three ages may have, at first sight, a certain plausibility, it fails to cover the facts. It ignores, for example, the materialism of much Chinese religion and of Indian Vedantist creeds, and the existence of Greek and Roman mystery-religions; it can find no place for the history of the African and American continents; it quite fails to explain the complexities of West European civilization in terms of its dominant 'idea'. Cousin's approach, we saw, was *a priori*, and he was in fact reading into history what he expected to find. This was no less true of his basic assumption that history springs from the progress of the human mind. Even the vagueness of his definition of 'spontaneous reason' cannot hide the fact that he was ignoring the role played in human life by man's passional and emotional nature and reducing history to a neat, over-simple and dogmatic scheme.

Some at least of the necessary corrections were attempted by his fellow eclectics, of whom the best-known was Théodore Jouffroy (1796–1842). He held that man differs most from animals by being involved in 'un mouvement perpétuel de transformation', and he defined philosophy of history, on which he wrote a number of essays, as the study of the causes and laws of this mobility.[1] One of these essays was on 'Bossuet, Vico, et Herder', all of whom he castigated for ignoring facts, but more important were his 'Réflexions sur la philosophie de l'histoire'. Man's conduct—and hence his history—are determined by two factors, his passions and his ideas. However, though he does recognize that passion may influence events, he contends that this is much less true in national

---

[1] T. Jouffroy, *Mélanges philosophiques*, 5ᵉ éd., Hachette, 1875, p. 36. The first section of this collection is devoted to philosophy of history.

than individual life. In a nation personal passions tend to be balanced and thus neutralized by opposing passions, and this is particularly the case in a democracy as opposed to a despotic society which may be dominated by the emotional whims of a dictator. Jouffroy therefore concludes that in general 'passion acts only on the surface of the history of nations', and from this it follows that 'mobility' in history must be principally due to changes in ideas, to 'the intellectual development of mankind'. This is the central subject of history, to understand it is 'the glory of our age', and once its 'constant laws' are found, history will graduate as a new science.[1]

At this point an ambivalence appears in his thought. The recognition that passion may influence history, to however limited an extent, is sufficient in his view to invalidate any claim that events inevitably reflect the progress of ideas and to undermine any pretence to predict the future exactly. He also disavows the doctrine of historical inevitability. Yet at the same time he speaks of 'the fatality of intellectual development' and argues that progress is not merely an empirical fact but also a 'law'. This mental growth is 'spontaneous' in the masses and 'voluntary' in the philosophers, but both are moving in the same direction, albeit at different speeds: 'ils obéissent à la même loi, qui est celle du progrès'.[2] His attitude to human freedom is especially puzzling. He claims not to deny our liberty of thought and action, but he also refers to 'les lois nécessaires du développement intellectuel', and in another essay ('De l'état actuel de l'humanité' (1826)) he asserts that God has traced out man's path for him. God is at work in history, not through direct intervention perhaps, but acting, as in Nature, through the fixed laws He has established, in this case the laws of man's intelligence.[3] It is true that Jouffroy adds that within God's broad design there is room for human virtue and folly: 'ce que nous ne pouvons ni empêcher ni faire, nous pouvons du moins le retarder ou le précipiter par notre mauvaise ou notre bonne conduite'. Yet this is still a form of historical determinism that seems to deny man's ultimate freedom of choice.[4]

[1] ibid., pp. 37–41.   [2] ibid., pp. 53, 46.
[3] ibid., pp. 53, 41, 102.   [4] ibid., pp. 102–3.

5. Summary

Having studied representatives of both the metaphysical and the social, positivistic approaches to historical philosophy, we may well pause briefly to note the strikingly wide area of agreement between them, far wider than their differences of interest and methodology would lead one to expect. All agree on the importance of historical study for an understanding of man: to know what man is and is to be we must examine what he has been. All agree that history is valuable less for its own sake than for some ulterior end—metaphysical for the Germans and Cousin, sociological for the political thinkers. All or almost all agree that history is a unity, the manifestation of a single design, the product of a single motive force that far transcends human reflection. All agree that this force makes for improvement, that the law of history is a law of progress. Almost all, furthermore, tend towards a belief in historical determinism: the great advance of history cannot be changed, except in minor detail, by human choice and intervention. Some even add that historical change is only beneficent when it is independent of rational planning, when it comes spontaneously from the impetus of history itself. All agree, too, that this determinism operates in accordance with discoverable laws, whether these be deduced from the nature of reason, as for Hegel and Cousin, or from allegedly empirical study, as for Saint-Simon and Comte. All or almost all agree, lastly, that humanity is more than a collection of individual men; it is an organic whole and has a superior reality—and superior rights—to the reality and rights of the isolated human being.

It is noteworthy that many Christians of the age concurred in several at least of these ideas. Traditionalist Catholics like Bonald, Maistre, and Lamennais in his *Essai sur l'indifférence* totally rejected the notion of progress held by the *philosophes*. The Revolution has shown how rapidly men can descend to viciousness when they trust their own reason alone. It has shown the bankruptcy of a humanism built on an optimistic, sensationalist view of man, and Maistre can even assert that 'contempt for Locke is the beginning of wisdom'.[1] Yet history is certainly not fortuitous in his eyes. It is guided by God, and the Revolution, for instance, was a 'Providential event', God's punishment of man's arrogant reliance upon himself.[2] History reveals the 'laws' by which God controls His people's journey along the pathway to salvation, laws whose operation we should obediently accept. Societies, he adds, are natural organisms, and 'normal' social movement is 'unconscious'; man's planned interference can only retard God's working out of His purposes. One can also note that Maistre explicitly links these views with a doctrine of the unity of mankind. Other aspects of the traditionalists' rather savage orthodoxy may be unacceptable to their fellow Christians, but many of them can endorse these beliefs, and some admit, where Maistre cannot, the reality of progress in realms other than the purely spiritual. An historian like Mignet affirms that there are laws of history established by God. Tocqueville claims in his *De la démocratie en Amérique* (1835–40) that progress towards equality is 'un fait providentiel'; 'il est universel, il est durable, il échappe chaque jour à la puissance humaine'. Chateaubriand, in his *Études historiques* (1836), accepts Bossuet's historical system, but with one correction: the idea that 'le genre humain tournerait dans une sorte d'éternité sans progrès et sans perfectionnement, n'est heureusement qu'une imposante erreur'.[3] It is true that he claims to reject fatalism, yet even so, in his *Préface*, he surveys with interest the Hegelian notion of 'un enchaînement providentiel dans l'ordre des événements', interprets Vico's *New Science* as 'une démonstration historique de la Providence', and reviews Ballanche's *Palingénésie sociale* (1827–9) with especial approval.[4] Significantly, Ballanche drew his ideas in part from Maistre. History, he thinks, is ruled by a divine law and manifests a progressive rehabilitation of mankind from the evils of the Fall. This is achieved by successive initiations or

[1] J. de Maistre, *Les Soirées de Saint-Pétersbourg*, 8ᵉ éd., Lyon and Paris, Pélagaud, 1862, 2 vols., i. 442; cf. his prolonged attack on Locke in the 6ᵉ *Entretien*.

[2] Cf. J. de Maistre, *Considérations sur la France*, nouv. éd., Lyon and Paris, Pélagaud, 1862, ch. v, vi.

[3] A. de Tocqueville, *De la démocratie en Amérique*, 6ᵉ éd., Gallimard, 1951, 2 vols., i. 4; Chateaubriand, *Œuvres complètes*, Pourrat, 36 vols., 1836–9, t. iv—*Études historiques*, t. i, p. 139.

[4] ibid., pp. 43, 46 (quoting Michelet), 50–51.

'palingeneses', and Ballanche also adds that progress will continue indefinitely, for each soul will pass on after this life to a series of ever finer existences in other worlds.

These beliefs, held in common by Christians and agnostics, metaphysicians and sociologists, summarize the most formidable theory of history produced by earlier-nineteenth-century thinkers, the more formidable for commanding assent in such diverse intellectual quarters. It has proved formidable in practice also, for whilst, as we noted, philosophers quickly rejected such speculative interpretations and turned to 'critical' philosophy of history, this has been far from true with others. Historians may in general have refused to be transformed into social scientists or metaphysical *aides-de-camp*, but political and social thinkers have often adopted the doctrine of historical inevitability, and have argued that men's lives and behaviour are determined by some vast impersonal force—be it material environment, a race or nation, a civilization, a class, or the Hegelian Absolute. Some have also drawn the conclusion that it is morally right to sacrifice individuals to the interests of this greater entity. This doctrine is still vigorous in our own day. It is probable that in the present century more political murders have been accomplished—by Nazis, Fascists, and Marxists—in the name of 'History' and its dubious 'necessities' than in any other cause. And in the quieter, academic world, to take England alone, Isaiah Berlin thought it necessary as recently as 1953 to devote a long lecture—ironically, in memory of Comte—to attacking the fatalistic view of history, whilst in 1957 Popper could declare that the 'historicist' belief in the existence of historical 'laws' and 'trends' is 'at bottom responsible for the unsatisfactory state of the theoretical social sciences'.[1]

Critical discussion of these ideas would transcend the limits of this survey and would in any case be superfluous in view of the detailed attacks on them just mentioned and of other similar discussions.[2] It is perhaps more pertinent to consider by implication a contrary assumption that is not uncommon in our own day. This

[1] Berlin, op. cit.; K. R. Popper, *The Poverty of Historicism*, London, Routledge, 1957, p. 3.
[2] For a selection of recent criticism, cf. *Theories of History*, ed. P. Gardiner, Glencoe, Ill., Free Press, and London, Allen & Unwin, 1959, Part II.

is that the entire belief in progress depends upon the authoritarian, 'holistic', 'historicist' position held by Hegel, Comte, Joseph de Maistre, and Marx alike, and that if we refute the latter, we should abandon the former.[1] But it is noteworthy that in addition to the metaphysical and sociological schools of thought we have surveyed, there was in nineteenth-century France a third, less coherent body of thinkers whose theories of history had precisely this as their central concern: if historical fatalism be rejected, how much of the belief in progress remains? These 'liberal' philosophers are perhaps unduly neglected in the discussions of historians and sociologists, and unjustly so. With them we pick up again one of the most insistent assertions of nearly every French *philosophe*: that progress has in fact occurred, yet is not preordained and depends on human choice and action. Here is a contention shared by just as wide a diversity of thinkers as hold the fatalistic view—by later eclectics, by a Christian social thinker such as Buchez, and by radicals like Quinet and Michelet. These writers are less famous than their predecessors, for their more tentative theories were necessarily less all-embracing and impressive, but with them we perhaps return to healthier, more realistic, and less metaphysical ideas on progress and history. This is a comparative statement, however: only with Scherer shall we finally escape from the influence of a speculative metaphysic of history.

[1] For a discussion of 'holism', which considers social 'wholes' rather than individual social phenomena as the proper objects of historical and sociological theory, cf. Popper, op. cit. As to ' historicism', two American critics have distinguished at least five current and even contradictory meanings of the word; it is doubtful if it is any longer useful as a philosophical term. (Cf. D. E. Lee and R. N. Beck, 'The Meaning of Historicism', *American Historical Review*, lix, 1954, pp. 568 ff.)

VIII

The Cult of History and Progress (2)

1. *Liberal Theories of Progress*

'. . . At no time during the two hundred years in which the idea
of progress has been influential in Western thought has the fatalistic interpretation been universal or even general.'[1] This judgement of Morris Ginsberg is certainly true of England, and even in
mid-nineteenth-century France, despite the numerous thinkers
who, as we have seen, accepted historical necessity, there was a
powerful libertarian current of opinion. Even certain of the
writers here assigned to the fatalist camp were in an ambiguous
position—Jouffroy; Leroux; Ballanche; Proudhon, who rejected
alike the notions of Providence, of an Hegelian world-spirit, and
of an impersonal 'force of history', and was himself a necessitarian
only through his belief that human action is determined by the
spontaneous, non-rational development of humanity as a whole.

Every historical philosopher at this time was agreed that history
is not a matter of chance. It is determined in the sense that all
events have their causes; a causal chain links the present to the past.
The crucial question concerns the role of men's free choices.
Fatalists accepted that human choices are amongst the causes determining history, but they went on to argue that these choices are
themselves the product of a greater cause—the *Zeitgeist*; the inevitable intellectual advance of mankind, whether according to the
Hegelian or to the Comtian plan; the fusion (as for Taine) of *race*,
moment, and *milieu*; the purposive *élan vital* of Nature, as for many
pantheists; and other alternatives. They also alleged that if human
choices should run counter to the movement of progress, they are
negated, rendered insignificant, by the historical inevitability they
foolishly oppose; they agreed with Marx that our only 'freedom'
lies in 'the recognition of necessity', in willing co-operation with
history. The paramount counter-assertions of the libertarians were

---

[1] M. Ginsberg, *The Idea of Progress*, London, Methuen, 1953, p. 4.

that human choices are really free, not predetermined, and that they make a significant and ultimately decisive impact on what actually happens. If this be so, it follows that history is far from being entirely foreordained and that future events cannot be predicted with the degree of accuracy and reliability that characterizes the predictions of the natural sciences. In that case, can there be a worth while science of history at all? Here is a question that greatly preoccupied the libertarians and whose disquieting possibilities confirmed the fatalists in their fatalism.

Some writers, perhaps wisely, fought shy of such wide speculations, and this is especially true of the professional historians—Thierry, Fustel de Coulanges, and others. Tocqueville, for example, preferred to concentrate upon more specific problems like the growth of American democracy or the causes and achievements of the French Revolution. The same was true of Guizot (1787–1874), politician and historian and broadly sharing the eclectics' outlook. Despite the titles of such works as *Histoire générale de la civilisation en Europe* (1828) and *Histoire de la civilisation en France* (1829–32), he did not try to work out a full philosophy of history. Rather he analysed in detail the development of Christian civilization, especially in France from the fourth to the tenth centuries, in order to show its causes and phases. He did not doubt that European history is a unity or that progress is a reality. In fact he even equated civilization and progress—progress in two realms, the amelioration of social life and the development of the individual's inner life. Moreover, these two realms are interrelated, so that advance in the one brings advance in the other, though he sided with Cousin in thinking that the latter is the true end and social progress a means to it. But his great achievement was that, unlike the eclectic philosophers, he validated this theory by detailed reference to a past age.[1] Thereby he also bequeathed a method that others could apply to different periods, none more than Michelet, his disciple and successor at the Sorbonne. He himself divided Christian civilization into three epochs—the age of

---

[1] Baillie even concludes that he and Cousin above all effected 'the astonishingly complete naturalization of the notion of developmental progress within nineteenth-century thought'. (*The Belief in Progress*, London, Oxford U.P., 1951, p. 134.)

confusion after the fall of the Roman Empire, which he discussed at length, the feudal age, and the modern age, which his political duties prevented him from treating. But by his work on the first period he did more than any historian of his time except Michelet to demonstrate that a civilization is a developing organism. What he did not establish, however, was that its development must necessarily be progressive, as he claimed.

It was precisely the inevitability of progress that was to be questioned by later eclectics. Auguste Javary (1820–56) combats in De l'idée de progrès (1850) Cousin's fatalism and excessive optimism, especially the view that whatever happens in history is necessarily good. After reviewing past theories of progress with special reference to Turgot, Condorcet, Herder, and Kant, he contends that moral and social advance depends on human choice, that it is therefore not assured and that there can be no 'law' as to its occurrence. Whilst he recalls Cousin in defining progress in terms of the fuller realization of man's spiritual nature, he insists that this relies upon the triumph of reason and the moral will over the passions. A similar view was held by François Bouillier (1813–1899) and expounded in his Morale et progrès (1875).[1] He accepts the fact of intellectual advance by means of the gradual accumulation of knowledge over the ages. But moral progress is limited to individuals (as opposed to societies as a whole), depends on our use of our free-will, and is certainly not transmissible to future generations or to other individuals. Nor can there be any law even of intellectual progress, for this too relies on human choice.

But not all libertarians abandoned so readily the prospect of discovering a law of progress. A good example is Philippe Buchez (1796–1866), who began his career as a Saint-Simonian, then broke with Enfantin, and thereafter developed a form of Catholic socialism. A warm-hearted reformer, he helped to found the first working-class co-operatives, edited a socialist review, L'Atelier, and was elected President of the National Assembly in 1848, and his thought influenced, amongst others, Vigny, for several years his friend, John Stuart Mill, and the English Christian Socialists. He

---

[1] On Bouillier, cf. R. Flint, History of the Philosophy of History, Edinburgh and London, Blackwood, 1893, pp. 512–16.

published his first and best-known book, *Introduction à la science de l'histoire*, in 1833. As this title indicates, he seeks to make history scientific and argues that it can discover the causes of the social upheavals and miseries he sees all around him and can then prescribe remedies for them. He rejects historical fatalism, however; man's free choices are the principal factors in history. Yet he also agrees with Saint-Simon that the distinctive task of any science, including history, must be to make predictions. How can this be? His answer is that social trends, being the result of men's choices, are determined by human nature, that this is reasonably stable, and that the trends it initiates are therefore predictable. The new science can never offer certainty or be as reliable as the natural sciences, but it can attain a high degree of probability.

Unfortunately, some of his other views were not entirely compatible with this vindication of man's freedom. He contends that God's intervention is the primary force behind human progress and thinks specifically that each civilization is united and determined by a particular divine 'revelation'. There have been four such revelations, he believes, and hence four main periods in history. These revelations were vouchsafed by Adam, Noah, an unknown prophet whose influence spread over both the Oriental and the Greco-Roman cultures, and, lastly, Christ. Furthermore, each period can be sub-divided into three stages, determined in their turn by the manner in which the human mind inevitably works. These are not unlike Comte's *trois états*: the stage of theology when the revelation is expressed doctrinally; that of rationalism; and that of practical application. Each stage, Buchez adds, is also divided—into a theoretical and a practical phase. He believes that we have now entered the practical phase of the final stage of the Christian period—an era dating from Bacon and Descartes. We must proceed to the full application in social life of the Christian ideas of charity, equality, and fraternity, a task the Church has failed to accomplish. This will be the culminating epoch of human history and has an indefinite future before it.

There are moments when this scheme seems almost too tidy to be the product of human free-will, nor is one reassured when Buchez, in stressing that the entire human species is united by a continuous tradition—an 'education of mankind' in Lessing's sense—goes on to maintain that the individual is conditioned by his nation and the nation in turn by the race. Buchez's philosophy thus escaped from fatalism to only a limited extent. No more than other Christian thinkers at this time—a liberal Catholic like the Abbé Gratry, for example, as well as the traditionalists earlier[1]— did he succeed in resolving an age-old dilemma: if God be the King of history, what ultimate freedom remains to man?

2. Edgar Quinet and Jules Michelet

The two most distinguished liberal philosophers of history during these mid-century years began from neither a Christian nor an eclectic position, but from the theories advanced in the previous century by Vico and Herder. They were Edgar Quinet (1803–75) and Jules Michelet (1798–1874), friends from youth, 'frères . . . de cœur et de pensée' in the former's words. Quinet was especially drawn to Herder, for him 'the Herodotus of the philosophy of history',[2] and Michelet to Vico, but their systems differed only in emphasis and starting-point. In 1827 Quinet published his translation of Herder's *Ideen*, a work he describes as 'une source intarissable de consolations et de joie',[3] with an important *Introduction à la philosophie de l'histoire* of his own, and in 1828 he added an *Essai sur les œuvres de Herder*. In 1827 Michelet produced his translation of Vico's *Scienza Nuova*, preceded by a *Discours sur le système et la vie de Vico*, and in 1831 appeared his *Introduction à l'histoire universelle*.

From Vico, Quinet takes above all the ideas that there are laws governing human history and that each civilization springs from a unifying religious belief—a view he was to develop in *Le Génie des religions* (1842). The two notions are linked for Vico, since he holds that the concept of a divine Providence first gave history a philosophical character: God's control of our life results in regularities in history from which we can deduce 'the universal laws of mankind'. Herder's approach is different, as Quinet points out. He

[1] On Gratry, cf. Flint, op. cit., pp. 389–93.
[2] Quinet, *Essai sur les œuvres de Herder* (1827), *Œuvres complètes*, Pagnerre, 1857–60, 12 vols., ii. 437.
[3] *Introduction à la philosophie de l'histoire de l'humanité* (1825), ibid., ii. 379.

borrows from it the ideas that the world is an organism so designed as to develop within itself ever higher organisms—first mineral, then vegetable and animal, and finally human—and that universal history has moved and is still moving towards the completer 'unfolding of the flower of humanity'. Herder believed that the impetus behind this progressive development comes from God. Quinet, a lover of human freedom, opposes him on this point and asserts that man's own free-will underlies his spiritual and secular advance over the ages. Indeed, he erects the search for greater liberty as the 'law' of history, 'fondement et substance de l'histoire civile'.[1]

L'histoire, dans son commencement comme dans sa fin, est le spectacle de la liberté, la protestation du genre humain contre le monde qui l'enchaîne, le triomphe de l'infini sur le fini, l'affranchissement de l'esprit, le règne de l'âme. Le jour où la liberté manquerait au monde serait celui où l'histoire s'arrêterait.[2]

Two consequences follow from this standpoint. First, since men have free-will, progress is neither certain nor unwavering. A survey of the past reveals a movement that is in general one of advance, he thinks. This has been from man's subservience to Nature in Asiatic civilizations, through his gradual emancipation from it during the Greek and Roman eras, to the still developing liberty of the spirit he has attained in the Christian civilization, an age during which one sees 'le règne de la conscience s'élevant au-dessus des règnes aveugles de la nature'. Quinet also thinks there is much in human history to encourage our hopes for the future.

Poussé par une main invisible, non seulement le genre humain a brisé le sceau de l'univers et tenté une carrière inconnue jusque-là, mais il triomphe de lui-même; il se dérobe à ses propres voies, et, changeant incessamment de formes et d'idoles, chaque effort atteste que l'univers l'embarrasse et le gêne. . . . Ainsi, captif dans les bornes du monde, l'infini s'agite pour en sortir; et l'humanité qui l'a recueilli, saisie comme d'un vertige, s'en va, en présence de l'univers muet, cheminant de ruines en ruines, sans trouver où s'arrêter.[3]

Yet in man's past we also find periods of decadence which in *La*

[1] ibid., ii. 355 ff., 346. [2] ibid., ii. 366. [3] ibid., ii. 346, 366.

Création later he compared to the decline of certain animal species as revealed by Darwin. Hence, as well as historical fatalism, he strongly opposes, secondly, the optimistic trust that everything in history is for the best. Both fatalism and optimism seemed to him to stem from a pantheistic attitude—supremely illustrated in Hegel and of which even Herder was guilty in common with other German thinkers.[1] He agrees that the actual present has followed from the actual past, but both could have been different if men had chosen differently. Nor is it true that the better has always vanquished the worse: to hold this is to have stifled moral conscience in one's historical judgements. Quinet is no less antagonistic, as a liberal, to the attempts of Hegel, Cousin, Comte, and others to subordinate individual man to the 'Absolute' or to 'humanity'. Criticizing Strauss's *Life of Jesus*, he brands as pantheistic (as opposed to Christian) the common tendency to 'dépouiller l'individu pour enrichir l'espèce, diminuer l'homme pour accroître l'humanité'.[2] Against this totalitarian way of thought he constantly upholds the independent existence and rights of the individual.

Quinet thus offers a version of the Germanic metaphysical view of history in which religion and the development of mind and spirit are no less central, but without its fatalism, amoral optimism, and authoritarian tendencies. Responsibility for progress is not to be vested in a metaphysical or religious entity, the Absolute or Providence, but in man himself. Not that Quinet is without religious feeling. Behind men's free acts he discerns the guiding (but not dictatorial) hand of God, and as he contemplates their past achievements, he yields to 'un respect profond et pour ainsi dire religieux'. 'Au-dessus de toutes les volontés intelligentes, l'Être des êtres seul n'a point d'histoire,' he declares—at times seeming to fall himself into a pantheistic equation of this Being with Nature. And hearing '[les] harmonies des âges' or surveying 'la marche lente et majestueuse des siècles', he rises to a note of religious elevation:

Chaque peuple qui tombe dans l'abîme est un écho de la voix de l'Infini. Chaque cité n'est elle-même qu'un mot interrompu, qu'une

[1] *Introduction à la philosophie de l'histoire de l'humanité* (1825), ibid., ii. 377; cf. *Essai sur Herder*, ibid., ii. 432.   [2] 'Examen de *la Vie de Jésus*' (1838), ibid., iii. 338.

image brisée, un vers inachevé de ce poème éternel que le temps est chargé de dérouler.[1]

Michelet's views were closely allied to those of his friend but owed more to Vico. 'Pendant que la foule suivait ou combattait la réforme cartésienne, un génie solitaire fondait la philosophie de l'histoire.'[2] With Vico 'social science' began, for he perceived the analogies between the fortunes of different civilizations and was thus led to seek for the 'laws' behind them. He also saw, Michelet stresses, that individual geniuses do not achieve improvements in their own strength; they are but the symbols and expressions of their age, and, indeed, were this not so, history would be a matter of chance, dependent on the appearance of isolated great men. Vico's 'new science' thus went beyond these heroes to study the civilization they represent, seeking 'knowledge of its principles' as the primary end. 'Jusqu'ici on n'a parlé que de théologie naturelle; la science nouvelle est une théologie sociale, une démonstration historique de la Providence.' For Michelet agrees with Vico that God rules over human history—and he favourably contrasts this view with the fatalism of the Stoics and the belief in chance of the Epicureans. Writing in 1827, he can invoke the 'existence of a divine Providence' as one of his 'three fundamental principles'. He also accepts Vico's thesis that religion is the central feature of any civilization, the creative agent behind every aspect of a society's life, and in his own historical writing he tries above all to 'resurrect' the past in its full organic and spiritual reality. In contrast to religion, he notes, 'l'athéisme n'a rien fondé'.[3]

Michelet also emphasizes the organic growth revealed by the history of humanity, and like so many other writers he divides it into three periods, a 'divine or theocratic age', an 'heroic age', and a 'human or civilized age'.[4] He assures us that even in the eras we call 'barbarian'—better called 'religious and poetic' in his view—'toute la sagesse du genre humain y était déjà dans son ébauche et dans son germe'. And in each social revolution men find 'in the very corruption of the preceding stage' the elements of 'the new

---

[1] *Introduction à la philosophie de l'histoire*, ibid., ii. 386, 389–90.
[2] J. Michelet, 'Discours sur le système et la vie de Vico', *Œuvres choisies de Vico*, Flammarion, s.d., p. 9.   [3] ibid., pp. 19–20, 32.   [4] ibid., p. 22.

civilization which can redeem them'.[1] Yet Michelet is not a determinist. Mankind itself works out its destiny; this is the central message of the *Scienza Nuova: 'l'humanité est son œuvre à elle-même'*. Providence is active but does not compel us, a distinction he stresses by claiming that 'Dieu agit sur elle [l'humanité], mais par elle'. [2] His definition of progress, like Quinet's, consecrates this libertarian viewpoint. It consists in man's gradual self-freeing from the forces of Nature, and he traces this process, like Cousin, Quinet, and others, from the resigned servitude of India through Persian, Egyptian, Jewish, and Greco-Roman civilization to the present day. For him history is a ceaseless battle between man and Nature, spirit and matter, liberty and fate. It follows that men can hasten their self-liberation if they choose to do so, and part of the value of the 'new science' is that it can teach us 'les moyens par lesquels une société peut s'élever ou se ramener au plus haut degré de civilisation dont elle soit susceptible'.[3] Nor is man limited even by the fact of death, for Michelet envisages the continuation of our progress after this life: the individual survives by means of transmigration to other worlds.[4]

In later years Michelet's attitude to Christianity radically changed, and in particular he came to regard the Middle Ages as responsible for '[de] longs retards' and '[une] halte de stérilité' in mankind's advance. He also grew more sympathetic to the morality of the Asiatic peoples, 'fils de la lumière'.[5] Yet his philosophy of history remained unchanged in general, and he abandoned nothing of his faith in liberty and 'la Justice éternelle' or of his optimism for the future. He can still conclude his *Bible de l'humanité* (1864) by saying: 'Soyons, je vous prie, *hommes*, et agrandissons-nous des nouvelles grandeurs, inouïes, de l'humanité.' And celebrating 'l'accord victorieux des deux sœurs, Science et Conscience', he asserts that the 'morbid' medieval outlook can and must now be forgotten.[6]

[1] ibid., pp. 10, 22, 42–43.   [2] ibid., p. 3.
[3] ibid., p. 19. For a further statement of his views, cf. *Introduction à l'histoire universelle*, in *Précis de l'histoire moderne*, etc., Flammarion, s.d., pp. 403 ff.
[4] Cf. G. Monod, *La Vie et la pensée de J. Michelet, 1798–1852*, Champion, 1923, 2 vols., ii. 80.   [5] *La Bible de l'humanité*, Flammarion, s.d., pp. 383, 5.
[6] ibid., p. 385.

Quinet and Michelet clearly belonged to the metaphysical tradition of thought about history and progress, but far more boldly than the followers of Hegel and Cousin they affirmed the claims of human liberty. They did so, first, by their very interpretation of freedom, far closer to that of nineteenth-century political liberalism than to that of the German idealists; secondly, by their rejection of fatalism in history and their consequent belief that man can learn from his past and influence his future; yet again, by their concern for the individual; and, lastly, by their denial that whatever is is right and their contention that moral judgements can and ought to be applied to present social action and past history alike. As with Jouffroy, there perhaps remains an ambiguity in their systems as regards individual free-will. What is its extent if even great men merely 'represent' their own age, if (in Quinet's phrase) each race that passes away offers only 'un écho de la voix de l'Infini'?[1] Quinet discerns in Herder's thought 'la lutte de deux principes distincts, le génie de l'Europe moderne, et une âme sortie de l'Orient', pantheistic and fatalist;[2] there are moments when one may wonder whether he himself wholly escaped the same influence. Yet, despite these unresolved problems, their distinction in an age of authoritarian and fatalistic historical theory lies in their life-long defence of freedom. Moreover, although they may seem to us to be reading into past events their own *a priori* interpretations, they did attempt, far more than Cousin or the Germans, to justify their ideas by reference to facts: theirs was a metaphysical theory in the last analysis, but it had sought in some degree an empirical basis.

3. Edmond Scherer

With Edmond Scherer (1815–89) one moves still further from the Hegelian philosophy of history, so far that he might well be omitted here, were it not that he was an influential exponent of Hegel's thought during the Second Empire. His ideas on progress and history thus have a certain relevance at this point. Although he admires much in Hegel, Scherer firmly rejects both his fatalism

---

[1] Quinet, *Introduction à la philosophie de l'histoire, Œuvres,* ii. 389.
[2] *Essai sur Herder,* ibid., ii. 425.

and his notion of the Absolute—that is, in short, the essentials of his theory of history. He embraces the German's idea of *Entwicklung*; the universe, he asserts, is 'only the eternal flux of things', everything in it being purely relative. But this agreement cannot hide the fact that he has stood Hegel's thought on its head—nowhere more clearly than when he concludes that its greatest result has been to show that 'the absolute is dead'.[1] Moreover, change and even development are for Scherer far from synonymous with progress. 'Un changement n'est pas toujours un pas en avant, une révolution n'est pas nécessairement une évolution.'[2] Looking at contemporary France he finds visible evidence of change for the worse. 'La démocratie c'est la médiocrité', he can declare, or again: 'nous allons à l'américanisme'. The rise of a mass society may bring benefits, but he adds like another Tocqueville: 'je ne puis m'empêcher parfois de me demander si l'humanité elle-même, en définitive, ne perdra pas d'un côté ce qu'elle gagne de l'autre'.[3]

Scherer's approach to historical philosophy, well described in an essay on 'Le Progrès' written in 1864, is determined by his rejection of all religious and metaphysical beliefs. He correctly sees that a full-blown theorist of progress is in fact 'un croyant'—'un homme qui croit que le monde a un sens, et la vie humaine un idéal'.[4] He cannot share this faith, be it in God or an impersonal Absolute, and hence he concedes the reality of progress only in certain clearly defined realms where the evidence is conclusive. He fully accepts the fact of advance in the positive sciences and the 'useful arts', operating by the gradual accumulation of knowledge. 'La capitalisation incessante des résultats acquis, telle est la cause et la loi du progrès.' But where this 'capitalisation' can only be partial, 'où l'homme ne pourra s'approprier qu'imparfaitement les travaux de ses devanciers', progress will be merely 'relative'— for example, in the historical sciences and, still more, in literature, the fine arts and politics, where knowledge is only one operative

[1] E. Scherer, 'Hegel et l'hégélianisme', *R.D.M.*, 15.2.1861, p. 855.
[2] 'Émile Zola' (1881), *Études sur la littérature contemporaine*, Calmann Lévy, 1863–95, 10 vols., vii. 195.
[3] 'L'Ère impériale' (1868), ibid., iv. 22–23.
[4] 'Le Progrès' (1864), *Mélanges d'histoire religieuse*, 2ᵉ éd., Calmann Lévy, 1865, p. 416.

factor amongst many. Turning to the question of moral progress, he distinguishes two determining elements in moral behaviour: first, ethical ideas and, secondly, human nature. In regard to the former, progress is possible; humanity acquires over the ages 'un fonds de sagesse pratique', and consequently there can be 'un progrès réel et continu'. But human nature is always the same 'dans son fond', he claims; 'en ce sens donc, il n'y a point progrès'. Challenging a crucial belief of the *philosophes* and numerous nine-teenth-century social thinkers, he maintains that even education and an improved environment cannot alter man's nature 'd'une manière définitive'. Thus Scherer's conclusions are :'Progrès, au sens absolu du mot, dans les sciences exactes et dans l'industrie; progrès purement relatif dans les lettres et les beaux-arts; progrès fatalement limité par l'imperfection humaine dans les institutions sociales et dans la moralité.' [1]

Writing over twenty years later his opinions are similar but even more opposed to the necessitarian view of progress.[2] 'Il y a, cela est incontestable, progrès social au sens matériel du mot; . . . plus de souffrances écartées, plus de jouissances mises à la portée d'un plus grand nombre de nos semblables'—and the value of these advances must not be minimized. But it is an error to believe this true of the 'moral order' also, to imagine that 'la société croît en droiture, en équité, en modération, en pudeur, en délicatesse de sentiment, par une évolution nécessaire et un développement automatique'. This mistake stems from confusing 'le bien-être' and 'le bonheur'. The former is merely a prerequisite of happiness; 'le bonheur est, avant tout, état de l'âme, affaire de disposition, philosophie de la vie, si bien qu'on peut être heureux avec peu de jouissances. . . .' He concludes, in direct opposition to a whole cen-tury of social thinking: 'le progrès social ne saurait donc assurer le bonheur de personne, encore moins nous promettre celui du genre humain'.

Scherer's thought thus illustrates a highly significant moment in the history of the idea of progress. He wholly accepts the concept of development, even interpreting Hegel's 'Absolute' not as a 'substance', 'force', or 'activity' but as 'un changement sans repos,

---

[1] ibid., pp. 417–27.   [2] *Études sur la littérature contemporaine*, t. viii, pp. viii–ix.

une transformation sans fin'.[1] But, we have seen, he is far from assuming that this ceaseless flux necessarily brings improvement. The fact of development leads him less to historical optimism than to a half-regretful sense of the transience and relativity of every philosophy, religion, idea, or moral judgement—a discovery he regards as 'le fait capital de l'histoire de la pensée contemporaine'.[2] This is the consequence of Hegelian thought that he stresses in his famous article on Hegel of 1861, in which Hegel's *Philosophie der Geschichte* is not even mentioned or described, much less commended. In Scherer the Germanic theory of history, deprived of its optimistic metaphysical basis, has, as it were, lost heart. He believes in the historical necessity of evolution but not of progress. At the same time, he is untempted by the equally metaphysical theory to be advanced by future German thinkers like Spengler, that history moves in a cyclical pattern and that predestined decline follows the predestined rise of each civilization. In contrast to both theories he adopts a moderate, undogmatic, and empirical approach to the philosophy of history which, if less impressive at first sight, is refreshingly realistic.

Not that he is without hope for the future. He admits, we saw, the reality of scientific and industrial progress and even a limited advance in other realms. And in one field in particular, close to his own intellectual and emotional preoccupations, that of religious belief, he shares the fuller confidence of his radical contemporaries. This is true especially of his outlook shortly after his break with orthodox Protestantism. Quinet sees humanity as advancing from religion to religion in an endless spiritual quest. Scherer applies this idea to the history of Christian doctrine and spirituality. Writing on 'La Crise de la foi' in 1851 he even adopts something like the fatalist view we have seen him later reject. Dogmas are not absolute truths but groping approximations to the truth, not the essentials of religion but the expressions, varying from age to age, of man's eternal sensitivity to the religious. Dogma evolves, and in this evolution Scherer sees a progression. Even the doctrinal orthodoxy of Protestantism was an improvement upon the complete submission demanded by the Roman Church, and in the

[1] 'Hegel', loc. cit., p. 831.   [2] ibid., p. 855.

future, he believes, the transitory 'externals' of religion will be separated still further from its 'essence':

La métaphysique, les questions de critique, le droit ecclésiastique finiront par être considérés comme plus étrangers encore à la foi que l'observation rituelle du jeûne et du sabbat ne l'est à la morale.

A 'ceaseless and organic reformation' is leading us away from authoritarianism. 'Il y a progrès . . . dans la spiritualité, c'est-à-dire, au fond, dans la conscience de la relativité des formes et des idées; il y a, par suite, progrès dans la tolérance et la fraternité, et ce progrès est une des lois de l'histoire.' He even concludes with a far-reaching prophecy as to the outcome of this trend:

Le tout doit aboutir et aboutira certainement à un christianisme plus universel parce qu'il sera plus spirituel, à une religion plus religieuse, à un protestantisme plus conséquent. A mesure que le culte devient davantage un culte en esprit et en vérité, on comprend mieux aussi qu'il y a salut hors de l'orthodoxie comme il y a salut hors de l'Église, parce que l'Évangile est quelque chose de plus grand que toute église et que toute formule.[1]

He was perhaps less sanguine in later life,[2] but even this prophecy has not been wholly belied by actual events.

Scherer's general attitude was not unlike that of Cournot and Renouvier, the two greatest antagonists of historical fatalism during the century, the former in his *Considérations sur la marche des idées et des événements dans les temps modernes* (1872), the latter in his fourth and fifth *Essais de critique générale* (1864 and 1896). Postulating as their axiom the reality of individual freedom, they rejected the notion that there are any ineluctable laws of history, and they also denied that the facts themselves support such a notion. There is, Renouvier asserts, an equal possibility of progress or deterioration for both societies and individuals. They believed, like Scherer, that our destiny lies in our own hands. The full development of their critique falls outside our period, however; it formed part of the 'critical reaction' of the later-nineteenth century. They also post-dated—and commented on—a further major

---

[1] *Mélanges de critique religieuse*, Cherbuliez, 1860, pp. 13-15, 18-19.
[2] Cf. *Mélanges d'histoire religieuse*, pp. 243-4.

influence upon historical speculation, so far undiscussed: that of biological theories of evolution, as propounded by Lamarck, Geoffroy Saint-Hilaire, and, supremely, Charles Darwin.

4. Biological Evolution and Progress

The notion of the evolution of biological species was by no means original in the nineteenth century.[1] Even in the late-seventeenth century in England John Ray and Locke had discussed the relationships of different species and noted the vagueness of the boundaries between them. The great eighteenth-century naturalist, Buffon (1707–88), went much further, as did also, less systematically, Diderot. Seeking for the 'Newtonian laws' of biology, Buffon rejected in his *Histoire naturelle* the idea that the species are immutably fixed and separated by divine design. He also studied the different stages of the earth's history (which he believed to be far longer than the mere 6,000 years calculated from the Old Testament) and contended that no special act of creation was required to produce man. Life is a potentiality of matter, and from this beginning all the species we know, including the human, have evolved without supernatural help. Buffon thus saw man as an integral part of Nature, and this fundamental challenge to the Christian view of man opened the way for completer biological theories about man's development from animal origins. Not all biologists in the early-nineteenth century accepted this standpoint, as witness Georges Cuvier (1769–1832), a leading geologist and biologist of his day, who keenly defended the Linnaean theory of the fixity of species (except where natural catastrophes had intervened). Yet the victory of transformism was gradually assured by such scientists as J.-B. de Lamarck (1744–1829) and Étienne Geoffroy Saint-Hilaire (1772–1844), building on Buffon's work. As early as his *Philosophie zoologique* (1809) Lamarck expounded his theory of descent and argued that species have been slowly but ceaselessly modified under the influence of environment. (Balzac, one can recall, drawing on Saint-Hilaire—to whom *Le Père Goriot* is dedicated—transfers these ideas into the human realm and depicts in his novels the variations amongst men

[1] Cf. H. Butterfield, *The Origins of Modern Science*, London, Bell, 1949, ch. xii.

produced by social environment.) Changes in environment stimulate modifications in individual members of the species, and
these are transmissible to their offspring. Thus the ancestors of the
giraffe gradually acquired longer necks by reaching up to branches
beyond their normal reach, and this development was passed on
and intensified by inheritance.

Lamarck's belief in the inheritance of acquired characteristics
not only accorded with the sensationalist stress on the importance
of environment; it also gave fresh impetus to the search for progress. For, on this theory, improvements in our physical and
mental make-up are not lost when we die but can be inherited by
future generations. 'Nurture' is as formative as 'nature'. This in
part explains the tenacity with which certain thinkers defended
Lamarck's theory even after Darwin—amongst them, Le Dantec,
Spencer, Samuel Butler, and Shaw—but it is also noteworthy that
Darwin himself thought it possible that the Lamarckian process
might be a minor factor in evolution.

It was Darwin's theory, however, which diffused transformist
ideas most effectively. His Origin of Species (1859) was first translated into French in 1862, and his thought was also popularized by
T. H. Huxley and German thinkers like Hartmann and Haeckel.
Looking back to his youth, Anatole France can say: 'alors les livres
de Darwin étaient notre Bible';[1] Sully Prudhomme, equally inspired by Darwin, can write of 'l'ineffable grandeur' of transformism;[2] Brunetière can set himself, when introducing his Évolution de la poésie lyrique, to follow Haeckel and Darwin in his approach to literature.[3] Such reactions were typical and widespread.

Darwin's greatest achievements were, first, to present such a
wealth of evidence for the evolution of species as to discredit completely the opposing theory of their fixity, and, secondly, to offer
a comprehensive explanation—natural selection—as to the operation of this evolution. Where Lamarck had held that variations
are acquired in response to environmental conditions, Darwin

---

[1] A. France, La Vie littéraire, Calmann Lévy, 1924-5, 4 vols., iii. 56.

[2] Cited by P. Flottes, Sully Prudhomme et sa pensée, Perrin, 1930, p. 167.

[3] F. Brunetière, L'Évolution de la poésie lyrique en France au 19ᵉ siècle, 9ᵉ éd., Hachette,
s.d., 2 vols., i. 7-8. For some account of the early reception in France of Darwin's theory,
cf. A. Laugel, 'Darwin et ses critiques', R.D.M., 1.3.1868, pp. 130-56.

argued that they are fortuitous. Some of these chance 'changes' favour survival in a given environment, others lead to elimination. The resultant variations are handed on to offspring, and those which possess 'survival value' tend to spread throughout the entire species, for the individuals lacking them are gradually extinguished. As a consequence the species is slowly modified. Inspired by Malthus's theory of population, Darwin saw in Nature a perpetual struggle for survival in which the more poorly adapted are conquered by the better adapted. It is by means of this process that the evolution of the entire animal world, from the amoeba to man, has been effected.

Something of Darwinism's impact on religious thought was seen earlier;[1] what influence did it exert on ideas about progress? At first sight it might seem to offer clear, scientific confirmation of the fact of progress. Man's development from the lower mammals surely represents a qualitative advance. This is, admittedly, a value-judgement, but one to which most men—if not most lower mammals—can assent. Again, Darwinism, by apparently weakening the Christian position, threw men back, in their search for an alternative ethic, upon the notion (amongst other possibilities) of progress. Some thinkers, indeed, advanced an ethic based upon evolution—the 'evolutionary ethics' of Herbert Spencer; the 'superman' ethics of Nietzsche;[2] the systems, in our own century, of Lloyd Morgan, Alexander, and Smuts—each of them picking out certain tendencies in biological evolution as the criterion of moral value: the production of more varied or abundant 'types'; greater independence and control of environment; the development of greater complexity of organization or of greater individualization; the growth of solidarity and co-operation fostered by certain moral instincts, which are thus said to have 'survival value'. Darwin's thought also popularized notions that could be applied in other fields—history of languages; history of literature, as in

[1] Cf. pp. 21, 23 above.
[2] One effect of Darwinism on French thought is illustrated by Paul Bourget's sketch —in the *Préface* to *Le Disciple* (1889)—of a type of young man of the day, the 'struggle-for-lifer': 'Il a emprunté à la philosophie naturelle de ce temps la grande loi de la concurrence vitale, et il l'applique à l'œuvre de sa fortune avec une ardeur de positivisme qui fait de lui un barbare civilisé . . .'; 'sa religion tient dans un seul mot: jouir, — qui se traduit par cet autre: réussir.' (*Le Disciple*, Fayard, 1946, pp. xvi–xvii.)

Bruntieère's theory of *l'évolution des genres*; history of man's religious development; sociology; psychology; anthropology; theory of religious dogmas, alleged by some thinkers (such as, again, Brunetière) to be evolving in time; even theory of knowledge, as when Karl Pearson argues, in *The Grammar of Science* (1892), that certain axioms and ideas have 'survival value'.[1]

Yet many of Darwin's admirers fell into the serious error of equating evolution and progress, of assuming that evolution is necessarily in a morally desirable direction, towards 'higher' forms of life. This position is tenable only if one's sole criterion is that by which biological development is determined—namely, survival. But mere survival seems a dubious standard of moral worth, and one that contradicts the moral judgements we do in fact make. Nor is it clear in what way the ethical philosopher can know in advance which developments will in reality encourage survival and thus tell us which are, on this theory, good. Secondly, biologists make clear Nature's wastefulness and (from a human viewpoint) its savage cruelty—facts which seem to clash not only with the Christian idea of a morally perfect Creator but also with any pantheistic assertion that Nature and evolution are unambiguously good. Darwin himself was optimistic and even declared at the end of his book: 'As natural selection works solely by and for the good of each being, all corporeal and mental endowments will tend to progress towards perfection.' [2] But by 1893, in a famous Romanes lecture on 'Evolution and Ethics', his hardly less influential contemporary, T. H. Huxley, would contrast the struggle for life in Nature with human altruism and warn against any attempt to derive an ethic from it:

The practice of that which is ethically best . . . involves a course of conduct which, in all respects, is opposed to that which leads to success in the cosmic struggle for existence.[3]

Thirdly, biology reveals regression and decay in Nature as well as

[1] Cf. *Darwin and Modern Science*, ed. A. C. Seward, Cambridge U.P., 1909, ch. xxi-xxvii.
[2] C. Darwin, *The Origin of Species*, London, Murray, 1897, p. 402.
[3] Cf. T. H. and J. Huxley, *Evolution and Ethics, 1893-1943*, London, Pilot Press, 1947, pp. 81-82. The grandson comes to the view that in general evolution is in a morally desirable direction.

apparent advance. Many species have become extinct—the reverse face, indeed, of the struggle for survival. Furthermore, since our earth is itself evolving towards an uninhabitable condition, even successful species will ultimately die out. Evolution, in short, is a story of decline as well as advance. Moreover, historical study of former civilizations pointed the same lesson and suggested that European civilization might in turn follow its predecessors into oblivion. Nor were moralists lacking to argue that the nineteenth century was itself an age of decadence, a view also embraced by various literary writers who were repelled by the age's materialism and cultural indifference. Vico and, in the nineteenth century, Carlyle had already put forward a cyclical view of history, and in the later years of the century the theme of our civilization's mortality was to be increasingly taken up—to reach its fullest expression, in our own day, in the theories of Oswald Spengler and Arnold Toynbee.

In the long term, therefore, Darwinism tended to undermine rather than encourage the belief in inevitable progress: it described an amoral *development* from which no conclusions and no confidence about *progress*, other than purely biological advance, can be deduced. In this way it reinforced ideas like those of Scherer, Cournot, and Renouvier, for, it would seem, Darwin's theory can only discourage any optimistic worship of the historical process.

It would be quite misleading, however, to conclude by giving the impression that by the second half of the century the belief in an inevitable progress was dead, that only a hesitant hope of improvement and relativism in the manner of Scherer remained. This was true of the best philosophers of history in the later years of the century, men like Cournot and Renouvier. But amongst other writers the enthusiasm for progress was not a whit less buoyant—as witness, for example, the trust in science and its future benefits held by Renan, Berthelot, Zola, and many others. 'L'éclosion future, l'éclosion prochaine du bien-être universel, est un phénomène divinement fatal.' Thus writes Victor Hugo in *Les Misérables* (1862), and later in the novel he declares:

Le progrès est le mode de l'homme. La vie générale du genre humain s'appelle le Progrès; le pas collectif du genre humain s'appelle le Progrès. Le progrès marche; il fait le grand voyage humain et terrestre vers le céleste et le divin. . . .[1]

A host of other thinkers held similar beliefs, and they were not all by any means social progressivists. An idealist like Fouillée could conclude his *Histoire de la philosophie* by declaring that the idea of progress 'se vérifie par l'histoire même de la philosophie',[2] whilst Vacherot affirmed in 1869:

L'esprit humain tend toujours à s'affranchir et à s'élever, et . . . ce progrès est une loi de son activité, dans la sphère de la religion comme dans celle de la science.[3]

A little earlier, Eugène Pelletan had taken man's advance towards an ever fuller, richer life as the central theme of his *Profession de foi du dix-neuvième siècle* (1852), a work that is now forgotten but was highly characteristic of its time. Progress is 'la loi générale de l'univers', 'l'évangile vivant de notre destinée'. The nineteenth century is 'un siècle missionnaire chargé d'une révélation': if men will cultivate the complete range of their faculties, physical, mental, emotional, and moral, they can rise to the perfection of God Himself. His exalted conclusion was typical of a still widespread enthusiasm:

Vivre, et vivre sans cesse davantage, voilà la loi de Dieu et son commandement. Aspirer, attirer à soi la vie infinie, c'est-à-dire la Divinité, à chaque pas, à chaque instant . . . La vie! la vie! environs-nous de cette parole, car c'est l'ivresse sacrée . . .[4]

Yet if this mood of confidence persisted in some writers throughout the century (and into our own age), it was being increasingly challenged, as we have seen. The disillusioning political and military events of 1870–2, as our period ends, were further to strengthen the tendency towards a less assured, less golden vision of the future of mankind.

[1] *Les Misérables*, 4ᵉ Partie, vii, 4 and 5ᵉ Partie, i, 20; Charpentier et Fasquelle, 1926, 8 vols., v. 236 and vii. 89.
[2] A. Fouillée, *Histoire de la philosophie*, Delagrave, 1875, p. 489.
[3] É. Vacherot, *La Religion*, Chamerot et Lauwereyns, 1869, p. 463.
[4] E. Pelletan, *Profession de foi du dix-neuvième siècle*, Pagnerre, 1852, pp. 27, 440, 410.

IX

Conclusion: The Critical Reaction

THE previous chapter studied the emergence of a more cautious, pragmatic opposition to the confident historical fatalism inspired alike by Hegel, Comte, and the Saint-Simonians, and which was implicit also in the belief in God's directive providence held by the traditionalist Catholics. This formed only one part of a wider reaction against most of the principal doctrines of the first half of the century. Chronological divisions are always imperfect, but by the 1860's, if not earlier, new moods, new antagonisms were evident. Over an extremely broad intellectual front—in science, philosophy, and literature—this opposition was to be intensified in the following decades.

This is not to imply that resistance to scientism, fatalism, materialism, or authoritarian political thought had ever died throughout our period. Few genuine scientists, for example, had ever accepted the extravagant claims for science advanced by Saint-Simon, Comte, Renan, and Taine; their outlook was far better represented by the great physicist Ampère's modest *Essai sur la philosophie des sciences* (1834 and 1843, 2 vols.), which argued that scientific laws cannot be more than those hypotheses which give the best account of phenomena in the existing state of knowledge. In philosophy of history, as we have seen, almost as many thinkers defended the reality and rights of human liberty as subordinated the individual to some greater entity above him. In literature likewise, rejection of materialism and concern for an 'Ideal' were as strong in the Romantics and in Parnassians like Leconte de Lisle and Louis Ménard as in Baudelaire and his fellow-Symbolists. In metaphysics Maine de Biran and, less effectively, certain of the eclectics—Royer-Collard, Jouffroy, only partially affected by Cousin's Hegelian sympathies—defended libertarian positions. And, turning to later thinkers, one can note that Ravaisson's first major work appeared as early as 1838, Cournot's in 1851 and

Conclusion: The Critical Reaction

Renouvier's in 1854—prior, that is to say, to the completed version of Comte's *Système* and his *Synthèse* and to all or almost all the works of Littré, Renan, and Taine.

Yet it is fair to say that the critical reaction which these thinkers initiated had achieved greater coherence, influence, and self-consciousness by the late-1860's—witnessed, for instance, by the confident tone in which both Ravaisson and Renouvier surveyed contemporary philosophy in 1867.[1] Not that these writers (to make the converse reservation) were attacking merely a previous generation, a now dying outlook; their concern was with systems that were still powerful and were to remain so. The worship of science and progress in particular persisted quite unequivocally in Littré, Berthelot, Le Dantec, Zola, and other Naturalists, and in sociologists like Espinas, Izoulet, and Durkheim, while Renan and Taine were to lose their earlier confidence only towards the very end of their lives. Heightened controversy was the natural outcome.

This is not the place to survey the many aspects of this reaction as it developed during the remaining years of the century. In the realm of literature, for example, it was manifest in the Symbolists' pursuit of a less material, more suggestive poetry that should evoke the *Idéal* and serve as a means of insight into the metaphysical unknown; in the Catholic revival initiated in poetry by Baudelaire (however ambiguously) and Verlaine, in the novel, more arrestingly, by Bourget, Huysmans, and Barrès, in criticism by Brunetière, and that was to come to fruition in our own time in the writings of Péguy, Claudel, Psichari, and others;[2] in the increasing rejection from about 1885 of the Naturalists' preoccupation with material reality, and, linked with this, the rising influence in France of Russian novelists like Tolstoy and Dostoïevski with their distinctive awareness of man's spirituality;[3] in the theatre, in the later plays of Dumas *fils*, still more in Symbolists like Maeterlinck

[1] F. Ravaisson, *Rapport sur la philosophie en France au dix-neuvième siècle*, and C. Renouvier, 'De la philosophie du dix-neuvième siècle en France', *L'Année philosophique—Première Année (1867)*, 1868, pp. 1–108.
[2] Cf. works by Calvet, Giraud, and Guillemin in Bibliography, pp. 219–20 below, and also M. Tison-Braun, *La Crise de l'humanisme*, t. i, Nizet, 1958, 2e Partie.
[3] Cf. F. W. J. Hemmings, *The Russian Novel in France, 1884–1914*, London, Oxford U.P., 1950.

and Villiers de l'Isle-Adam, and in many later dramatists, in whom the 'idealist reaction' was equally marked.[1] To read Huysmans's *A Rebours* and *En Route*, Bourget's *Le Disciple* and *L'Étape*, *Les Déracinés* by Barrès, Villiers's *Axël*, Verlaine's *Sagesse*, Rimbaud's *Lettres du voyant*, the *Manifeste des Cinq*, and Vogüé's *Le Roman russe*, even to study the growing popularity in late-nineteenth-century France of Wagner or of English writers like Carlyle, Tennyson, and Ruskin, or the concurrent 'revival of Pascal',[2] is at once to perceive an atmosphere, preoccupations, views of human nature, that are far removed from the scientific self-sufficiency of Saint-Simon or Comte, the metaphysical abstraction of Cousin or Vacherot, the optimistic planning of the socialists, Renan, Taine, or Littré. Other writers bear witness to the same renunciation of the cult of science and social and material prosperity, but in a different manner—those, like the young Anatole France or the Barrès of *Le Culte du moi*, for example, who rejected scientism and materialist values but lacked the mental vigour—or, perhaps, the credulity—to replace these fallen idols, and who therefore relapsed into scepticism and pessimism, into a *fin de siècle* cult of the self. Bourget can note amongst the youths of 1889 the existence of both 'brutal positivists' and also another type, 'un épicurien intellectuel et raffiné'.

A vingt-cinq ans, il a fait le tour de toutes les idées. Son esprit critique, précocement éveillé, a compris les résultats derniers des plus subtiles philosophes de cet âge. Ne lui parlez pas d'impiété, de matérialisme. Il sait que le mot *matière* n'a pas de sens précis, et il est d'autre part trop intelligent pour ne pas admettre que toutes les religions ont pu être légitimes à leur heure. Seulement, il n'a jamais cru, il ne croira jamais à aucune, pas plus qu'il ne croira jamais à quoi que ce soit, sinon au jeu amusé de son esprit qu'il a transformé en un outil de perversité élégante. Le bien et le mal, la beauté et la laideur, le vice et la vertu lui paraissent des objets de simple curiosité.[3]

[1] Cf. D. M. Knowles, *La Réaction idéaliste au théâtre depuis 1890*, Droz, 1934.
[2] Cf. D. M. Eastwood, *The Revival of Pascal—A Study of his relation to modern French thought*, Oxford, Clarendon Press, 1936, and R. Francis, *Les Pensées de Pascal en France de 1842 à 1942*, Nizet, 1959.
[3] P. Bourget, *Le Disciple*, Fayard, 1946, p. xvii. For a brief survey of the early stages of the literary 'reaction', cf. G. Michaud, *Message poétique du symbolisme*, Nizet, 1947, 4 vols., t. i, ch. vi.

Conclusion: The Critical Reaction

The philosophical opponents of the systems we have discussed could certainly not be accused of this kind of scepticism, least of all about morality. Yet their mood was no less at variance with the self-assurance of their predecessors.[1] They too wished to re-build, to find a unifying philosophy as a basis for a stable society, but their claims were far more moderate and undogmatic. This was true of the Idealist group of philosophers—Ravaisson, Lachelier, Boutroux, and Fouillée—and of theoreticians of the scientific method like Claude Bernard in his *Introduction à l'étude de la médecine expérimentale* (1865) and Théodule Ribot in *La Psychologie anglaise contemporaine* (1870).[2] It was evident above all in the neo-criticists, small in numbers but considerable in stature. Since they were already active during the last twenty years of our period, and thus have a chronological as well as an intellectual priority, we may well take them as a brief illustration of the more tentative approach to philosophical problems that prevailed in the later years of the century.

Antoine-Augustin Cournot (1801–77) was above all a philosophers' philosopher; none of his works is easy to read, but his reputation has remained high to our own day.[3] Rejecting his predecessors' dreams of an integrated synthesis, he concentrates upon philosophical analysis and believes that philosophy must be first and foremost a critique, especially of the sciences; in this he is similar in mood to present-day logical analysts. He does not despise metaphysics, but he denies that it can be scientific or that it should be philosophers' central concern. Deeply influenced, like

[1] For the philosophical reaction, cf. A. Aliotta, *The Idealistic Reaction against Science*, translated McCaskill, London, Macmillan, 1914, D. Parodi, *Du positivisme à l'idéalisme*, Vrin, 1930, 2 vols., G. Fonsegrive, *L'Évolution des idées dans la France contemporaine*, Bloud et Gay, 1920, A. Fouillée, *Le Mouvement idéaliste et la réaction contre la science positive*, Alcan, 1896, and J. A. Gunn, *Modern French Philosophy (1851–1921)*, London, Fisher Unwin, 1922.

[2] For a brief discussion of Bernard and Ribot, cf. my *Positivist Thought in France during the Second Empire, 1852–1870*, Oxford, Clarendon Press, 1959, ch. v.

[3] His principal works are: *Essai sur les fondements de nos connaissances*, 1851; *Traité de l'enchaînement des idées fondamentales dans les sciences et dans l'histoire*, 1861; and *Considérations sur la marche des idées et des événements dans les temps modernes*, 1872. On Cournot, cf. the special no. devoted to him in *R.M.M.*, xiii, 1905, pp. 293 ff., F. Mentré, *Cournot et la renaissance du probabilisme au XIXe siècle*, Rivière, 1908, Parodi, op. cit., and (as an introduction) S. W. Floss, *Outline of the Philosophy of Cournot*, Univ. of Philadelphia Press, 1941.

all neo-criticists, by Kant—in his case by Kant the logician—his primary interest is in the theory of knowledge, particularly of scientific knowledge. Even Kant held too rigid a concept of a scientific law, he claims, for he tended to equate all science with mathematics and physics. Since Kant's time both biology and sociology have developed, and the old notion that laws can be known with complete certainty must now yield to the view that they can have no more than greater or lesser probability. Kant was mistaken in his *Critique of Pure Reason* in searching for absolute certainty; this epistemological attitude of 'all or nothing' led him to utter scepticism. Cournot himself, who began his career by working on mathematical theories of chance and probability, takes a middle way between over-confident dogmatism and Humean scepticism; he conceives of a critique 'qui procéderait par voie d'induction probable, et non de démonstration positive'. For him, therefore, the essential problem of scientific knowledge—and of knowledge in general from the moment it passes beyond observation and seeks to generalize, explain, and make inductions—lies in the evaluation of probabilities. Although these will always be exposed to 'sophistical doubt', he does believe they offer what can fairly be called knowledge—what is, indeed, apart from logical and mathematical knowledge, the only kind of knowledge we can attain. For we must accept that 'l'absolu nous échappe', that we can never 'pénétrer l'essence des choses et en assigner les premiers principes'. But if we concede that our knowledge is limited to at best high probabilities, the way is open for us to affirm conclusions even in metaphysics, albeit they must always be tentative.

These and other submissions made by Cournot, if accepted, plainly shake the dogmatic assurance common alike to positivists like Saint-Simon, Comte, Littré, and Taine, and to confident metaphysicians like Hegel and Cousin, not to add the traditionalist Catholics. His arguments were to be reinforced, moreover, by Renouvier, Bernard, and Ribot, and such Idealist works as Lachelier's *Du fondement de l'induction* (1871) and Boutroux's *La Contingence des lois de la nature* (1874). Cournot also alleged that man has free-will, here again in sharp contradiction to both the pantheistic metaphysicians and the scientific fatalists of his time.

And still more attention was given to this question of human liberty by another neo-criticist, Jules Lequier (1814–62), a lonely and sometimes mentally unbalanced man, who was befriended by Renouvier at the École Polytechnique. His thought was little heeded by his contemporaries, though its influence was effective through Renouvier's own works, but today he is widely admired as a precursor of existentialism, being sometimes compared, particularly in his personal life, to Kierkegaard.[1] Renouvier himself acknowledged an 'incomparable obligation' to Lequier and regarded him as the founder of French neo-criticism, while Ravaisson judged him the only major thinker of his day on the subject of free-will.[2]

This problem was in fact Lequier's chief preoccupation. In a fragment entitled *La Feuille de charmille* he tells that he was challenged by it even as a boy.

Un jour, dans le jardin paternel, au moment de prendre une feuille de charmille, je m'émerveillai tout à coup de me sentir le maître absolu de cette action, toute insignifiante qu'elle était. Faire, ou ne pas faire! Tous les deux si également en mon pouvoir! . . . Je ne suffisais pas à mon étonnement; je m'éloignais, je revenais, mon cœur battait à coups précipités. J'allais mettre la main sur la branche, et créer de bonne foi, sans savoir, un mode de l'être, quand je levai les yeux et m'arrêtai à un léger bruit sorti du feuillage. Un oiseau effarouché avait pris la fuite. S'envoler, c'était périr: un épervier qui passait le saisit au milieu des airs. C'est moi qui l'ai livré, me disais-je avec tristesse.[3]

But, the boy now wonders, was his action perhaps only the fated outcome of a sequence of events outside his control? The man devoted much of his career to seeking an answer and, though he was a Catholic, he declined on this subject to make an appeal to Christian orthodoxy. His *Recherche d'une première vérité*, published by Renouvier in 1865, vividly describes his struggle to reach a conclusion independent of his religious faith.

[1] On Lequier, cf. the useful introduction in J. Wahl, *Jules Lequier: Introduction et choix*, Genève-Paris, Traits, 1948, J. Grenier, *La Philosophie de J. Lequier*, Belles-Lettres, 1936, and G. Séailles, 'Un Philosophe inconnu—Jules Lequier', *Rev. Philos.*, xlv, 1898, pp. 120 ff.

[2] Renouvier, cited by L. Dugas in his edition of Lequier's *Recherche d'une première vérité*, Colin, 1924, p. 54; Ravaisson, op. cit., 5ᵉ éd., Hachette, 1904, p. 237.

[3] *Recherche d'une première vérité*, ed. Dugas, p. 71.

His first goal is complete certainty, and to this end, like Descartes, he will doubt all that can be doubted 'in good faith'. Yet in the resultant mood of scepticism he realizes that he is quite unable to reach a first truth by any deductive method—for a first truth is by definition that which cannot be deduced from any other. Indeed, he becomes increasingly doubtful about the reality of even free-will, and despite an 'inner feeling' of liberty he concludes: 'Il est impossible de constater par l'expérience la nécessité ou la liberté.' [1] There are no convincing proofs of free-will, nor can it be deduced from any observational data; the case for determinism is, if anything, the stronger, as he argues in the fourth Part of *La Recherche*. But at this point in his discussion he is seized by 'a revolt of feeling'. He now develops an idea he had mentioned earlier: that liberty is an essential pre-condition of the very search for knowledge.[2] If all is determined, even the assertion that all is determined, for example, would be determined; it would be impossible to make any affirmation that could be known to be prompted solely by a judgement as to truth and error. The hypothesis of determinism thus leads not only to an overthrow of the notion of moral responsibility but also to total scepticism about the possibility of an impartial search for truth; 'c'est une chimère qui renferme le doute absolu dans ses entrailles'. Yet this is far from proving the reality of free-will, and he is forced to conclude that one cannot find any first truth without an appeal to belief of some kind. We must *choose* to *believe* in free-will, he urges, in a passage strongly reminiscent of Pascal's 'wager'. What are the rival merits of asserting necessity and liberty? If universal determinism is in fact true, then,

si j'affirme la nécessité, je l'affirme nécessairement, mais sans être en état d'en garantir la réalité, et voilà le doute qui revient; si au contraire j'affirme la liberté, je l'affirme encore nécessairement, et de plus je trouve dans le parti que je prends l'avantage d'affermir en moi les fondements de la connaissance et de la morale.

If, on the other hand, we are in fact free, then, he continues,

[1] J. Lequier, *La Liberté*, textes inédits présentés par J. Grenier, Vrin, 1936, p. 80.
[2] *Recherche*, p. 134; cf. pp. 111–12.

si j'affirme la nécessité, je l'affirme librement, je suis dans l'erreur au fond, et je ne me sauve pas même du doute, tandis qu'en affirmant la liberté, je suis à la fois dans le vrai et je recueille les mérites et les avantages de mon affirmation libre.

Hence he concludes, in distinctly 'existentialist' terms:

Je préfère affirmer la liberté, et affirmer que je l'affirme au moyen de la liberté. Mon affirmation me sauve, m'affranchit. Je renonce à poursuivre l'œuvre d'une connaissance qui ne serait pas la mienne. J'embrasse la certitude dont je suis l'auteur. . . . C'est un acte de la liberté qui affirme la liberté.[1]

Choice, belief, liberty: these are the major themes of his thought; he chooses to believe in liberty.

Charles Renouvier (1815–1903), the leader and chief exponent of neo-criticism, began from these ideas.[2] As a youth he was a Saint-Simonian, helping Leroux with his *Encyclopédie nouvelle*, and an ardent republican. He was even a determinist, until, about 1850, he was won over by the views of Lequier, his 'master'; later he would say of his own philosophy: 'elle ramène et subordonne tout à la reconnaissance de la liberté humaine'.[3] Renouvier also accepts the strict positivist theory of knowledge. Though in other ways a disciple of Kant, he thinks it wrong to assert the existence of 'things in themselves; 'substance', for example, is no more than a convenient word. We only know phenomena, and the claims of Hegel and other metaphysicians to know 'ultimate reality' are false. But he criticizes his positivist predecessors: they failed to make an exact analysis of notions like phenomena and law; they opposed the belief in free-will far too dogmatically; and they tended to illiberalism in their social and religious ideas. In reality,

---

[1] ibid., pp. 134–5 and 138.

[2] Of his many books and articles the most important are: his *Essais de critique générale*, 1854–97, *La Science de la morale*, 1869, and (as a summary of his final philosophy) *Le Personnalisme*, 1903. Of many studies of his thought, cf. G. Milhaud, *La Philosophie de Renouvier*, Vrin, 1927, Parodi, op. cit., A. Darlu, 'La Morale de Renouvier', *R.M.M.*, xii, 1904, pp. 1 ff., R. Verneaux, *L'Idéalisme de Renouvier*, Vrin, 1945, G. Séailles, *La Philosophie de Ch. Renouvier*, Alcan, 1905, O. Hamelin, *Le Système de Renouvier*, Vrin, 1927, and L. Prat, *Ch. Renouvier philosophe*, Hachette, 1937. For English readers helpful introductions are in Gunn, op. cit., and L. S. Stebbing, *Pragmatism and French Voluntarism*, Cambridge U.P., 1914, pp. 92 ff.

[3] 'De la philosophie . . .', loc. cit., p. 107.

they fell into the very metaphysical dogmatism they condemned in others, embraced pantheism in one form or another, and subordinated the individual to a greater whole. In opposition to them Renouvier stresses the relativity of human knowledge, urging in particular that we are never passive in the act of knowing but that our entire personality and especially our will are inevitably involved in both perception and intellection. He even claims that all certainty is based on an act of will to choose; it is always a form of belief, 'une affaire passionnelle'. This is above all the case when we turn from science to philosophy, and Renouvier sums up philosophical problems—such as that of free-will—as a series of dilemmas between which choice must be made; in each instance we have to make a 'moral wager'. He himself opts for belief in free-will and in the independent reality of each human personality, and he asserts that this is a pluralist world, in which not one supreme cause (as the pantheist thinks) but many different causes are operative, amongst them individual wills. He is no less convinced of the possibility of a 'science of ethics', based on the 'categorical imperative' of which we are aware through our conscience. He formulates this ethic in Kantian terms, but it can be more simply described as 'personalist': our supreme duty is to persons and the fulfilment of human personality. This is the position he defends against Comte, Hegel, Catholic orthodoxy, pantheism, and every other creed that, in his view, exploited human beings as a mere means to an end. He likewise resists any theory that would make the individual subservient to historical necessity. Believing in free-will and also claiming that there was in fact a regression during the Middle Ages, he denies the existence of inevitable progress. His religious position is similar: he founded a periodical, *La Critique religieuse*, in order to combat Catholicism, and the Protestantism he advocated in later life is extremely liberal. He even refuses to accept that man is subject to a deity of infinite power, for in order to resolve the problem of unmerited suffering he postulates that God is finite.

The thought of Cournot, Lequier, and Renouvier may seem a tentative, modest, and unemphatic reply to the vast systems we have surveyed. But its primary merit lies precisely in their attitude of sceptical interrogation, their refusal to be impressed by the big, all-inclusive, high-flown abstractions, their insistence upon the limitations of human knowledge and the elements of fallibility and belief it can never wholly exclude. Moreover, to accept their contentions is to reject alike the claims to metaphysical certainty made by Hegel and Cousin, to scientific certainty made by the *scientistes*, to theological certainty made by the Catholics. It is to perceive that fatalism, materialism, pantheism, evolutionism, and the cults of history, the Absolute, and science have no higher status than any other metaphysical conjectures. It is also to be reminded of values usually overlooked in the monolithic systems of both the Comtian and the Hegelian types, the values of human personality and individual liberty.

Not all the thinkers who preceded them ignored these values, clearly enough. One recent historian rightly claims, for example, that 'the underlying motive of social romanticism is the liberation of the individual personality, and hence the moral and spiritual emancipation of mankind'. [1] Certainly, moreover, almost every writer we have discussed was marked by altruistic vigour, humanitarian sympathies, and ardent seriousness. Even today, a century later, their idealism can refresh, challenge, and reproach. Theirs was a positive, utterly sincere attempt to meet a changed intellectual and political situation, and virtually every one of them persisted in unorthodox and unpopular views despite the fact or the threat, at one time or another, of imprisonment, loss of career and position, or forced exile from France. Yet, when that is said, many, though certainly not all, of them were over-confident and authoritarian in their outlook. They give weight to Talmon's remark, when discussing 'political messianism': 'This is the curse on salvationist creeds: to be born out of the noblest impulses of man, and to degenerate into weapons of tyranny.' [2] In part this resulted from an excessive optimism about educated human nature, a belief that the élite of scientists, philosophers, or intelligent idealists they wished to establish in power would inevitably be benevolent—

---

[1] D. O. Evans, *Social Romanticism*, Oxford, Clarendon Press, 1951, p. 81.

[2] J. L. Talmon, *The Origins of Totalitarian Democracy*, London, Secker & Warburg, 1952, p. 253.

and should thus be given supreme social control. In part it stemmed from a kind of apocalyptic obsession with historical change and crisis and the dangers of social and philosophical disunity. Only strong action by resolute leaders, they felt, was adequate for the troubled times. This is understandable enough, perhaps, given the background of Revolutionary disorder, Napoleonic centralization, the recurrent revolutions in Europe throughout the first half of the century, and the rapid transformation of France from an agrarian to an industrial economy. It was also strengthened by an inner need for dramatic conflict and action: Saint-Simon or Comte, for instance, would have been bored by the perfectly organized and united society to which they looked forward. But, whatever its causes, this vision of history made them over-hasty and over-assertive in their conclusions. Furthermore, they took it as axiomatic that social order must wait upon intellectual order: hence their urgent—too urgent—search for a unifying synthesis, for what Saint-Simon, aspiring to be (in a significant comparison) 'the Napoleon of the sciences', called 'the integrating principle for organizing all disciplines of learning'. And in their earnest, well-intentioned, but sometimes too humourless confidence in intelligence, they never doubted that this principle could rapidly be found, had indeed been discovered by their own efforts, or that it would be right to impose upon other men what they knew—with certainty —was good for them. And lastly, their tendency towards authoritarianism derived from the precedents which, given their situation, came naturally to their minds—the strong central government of Napoleon and the unyielding religious authority of the Roman Church. It was not only Comte who regarded Catholic unity as 'the masterpiece of human wisdom'. Saint-Simon and his followers, for example, were hardly less indebted to the Catholic assumption that all authority, to be fully effective, must be absolute, and it is noteworthy that so many of their number—and of the Fourierists also—should eventually have returned to the Roman faith.[1] The spirit of Joseph de Maistre—openly praised by Saint-Simon and Comte—hovers over several of the social reli-

[1] Cf. H. Louvancour, *De Henri de Saint-Simon à Charles Fourier*, Chartres, Durand, 1913, pp. 417 ff.

gions of the time. Indeed, it is not unreasonable to conclude, as a generalization, that the period surveyed here was an age that believed in infallibility—the Papal infallibility preached by Bonald, Maistre, and Lamennais (and later proclaimed as a dogma by the Pope), the scientific infallibility announced by Saint-Simon, Comte, and other *scientistes*, the metaphysical infallibility asserted in varying forms by Hegel, Cousin, and Taine, and the infallibility of historical evolution affirmed by many theoreticians of progress.

In contrast, the neo-criticists and many of their contemporaries, whilst no less animated by a generous humanism, never forgot that even men's highest thought could be fallible. Scientific laws are 'useful hypotheses', not unquestionable certainties; metaphysics and theology deal with what is in principle the 'unknowable' and must therefore be a matter for personal speculation and belief, not for dogmatic assertion; history is as complex and as morally ambivalent as the human beings who create it. And the authoritarianism that seems almost inevitably to go with excessive confidence is as little justified intellectually as morally; Littré's warning is characteristic of the growing scepticism:

Toutes les doctrines peuvent être perverties par le fanatisme, et tous les fanatismes, qu'ils soient sacrés ou profanes, sont dangereux et féroces.[1]

'Ils ont tous échoué, en définitive.' Such is Faguet's judgement on a selection of the main religious and philosophical creeds we have studied.[2] Tested by the simple criterion of durability this is true. The nineteenth-century trust in science has been severely qualified by later generations of thinkers: not only is scientific knowledge bounded by the limits of the empirical method, but its application to human life can be no more beneficent than the men who direct it. The belief in inevitable progress appears equally ill-founded today to all save Communists. 'Nous autres, civilisations, nous savons maintenant que nous sommes mortelles.' Thus

[1] Cited from *De l'établissement de la 3ᵉ République* by G. Weill, *Histoire de l'idée laïque en France au XIXᵉ siècle*, nouv. éd., Alcan, 1929, p. 228.

[2] É. Faguet, *Politiques et moralistes du XIXᵉ siècle*, 5ᵉ éd., Société française d'Imprimerie, 1903, 3 vols., t. ii, p. xi.

wrote Paul Valéry in 1919, and a more recent writer, Albert Camus, has declared that 'l'histoire est sans yeux et qu'il faut donc rejeter sa justice. . . .' [1] These claims are as typical of their time as were the optimistic prophecies of, say, Hugo and Zola. As to the nineteenth-century religious substitutes, only Comtism managed to survive into our own age as an independent cult of any vitality —and even that with a greatly diminished following. What remains today of the cults of humanity, evolution, 'le Grand Tout', and the Ideal, of all the schismatic churches and ardent sects that flourished in France a century ago, or of the religious enthusiasts who sought Utopia in the U.S.A.? Even by 1894, to accept Jules Bois's account, the new systems of the 1830's that were to have transformed European society had become 'les petites religions de Paris', or else had been forgotten.

This was in part because, as just noted, several of these sects adopted an authoritarian attitude in a period of growing liberalism; in part because they lacked, obviously enough, the efficient organization of an established church and also the poetic appeal of distant, time-misted origins and an ancient tradition; in part because they competed so publicly and stridently with each other, wrangling like all-too-human activists as they offered their various deities, theories of the future life and plans for the political present. And above all, perhaps, they failed because what they attempted was, if not impossible, exceedingly difficult. Their dilemma (as a contemporary remarked of some of them in 1865) was that they were 'toujours à la recherche de cette pierre philosophale qu'on appelle religion scientifique, comme si une religion dont on a le secret et où l'on a mis sa main d'homme pouvait jamais être une religion'. [2] Scherer makes the same point in less tendentious terms in a review of the Oxford Essays and Reviews of 1860, when he singles out as the great question underlying the religious controversies of his day: can religion become more rational without ceasing to be religion? [3] The thinkers we have

[1] Valéry, La Crise de l'esprit, Variété I, Éditions de la N.R.F., 1934, p. 13, and Camus, 'Prométhée aux enfers', L'Été, 2e éd., Gallimard, 1954, p. 88.

[2] Massol, cited by Weill, op. cit., p. 202.

[3] Scherer, Mélanges d'histoire religieuse, 2e éd., Calmann Lévy, 1865, p. 244.

discussed were unanimous in returning an affirmative answer, utterly persuaded that religion could not only be rendered more scientifically and intellectually acceptable but would thereby gain increased efficacy in both its social and individual roles.

It must at least appear doubtful whether their own confidence was justified. It is harder than they appreciated to navigate between the Scylla of irrationality and the Charybdis of a non-religious secularism. Generalization is difficult, but for the most part the creeds they propounded are either non-scientific and even irrational or (by normal criteria) non-religious or both. It is neither scientific nor even reasonable to claim, for example, that Nature is universally good—as do the Saint-Simonians, the Fourierists, Renan and Taine, and numerous other pantheists. Again, there is not the slightest evidence for the faith in interstellar migration and metempsychosis held by the Saint-Simonians, Fourier, Leroux, Reynaud, and others—or for their other borrowings from illuminist mumbo-jumbo. Nor is there good reason to contend, alternatively, that we live on eternally as part of Nature or of humanity —for there is no justification possible for the belief that either of these will be immortal.

What of the other candidates for divinity? It is not unreasonable (though it cannot in principle be scientific, as Comte alleged) to propose humanity as an object of devotion. It must be stressed that in its present state this deity lacks moral perfection, but the Comtian might retort that he worships an ideal humanity that will at some future date come into existence through our strivings now. The deification of our abstract notion of perfection, explicit in Vacherot and implicit in Cousin and the eclectics, is no less unobjectionable on rational grounds. The problem here is the same as confronts believers in a non-supernatural form of Buddhism and, indeed, in all forms of 'naturalistic religion'—the problem posed by Scherer and hinted at by Quinet when he argued that Strauss's revised Christianity left only 'une religion de mort, un évangile de la raison pure, un Jésus abstrait, sans la crèche et le sépulcre'.[1] Is a scientific, a rational, an abstract religion a contradiction in terms?

[1] 'Examen de *la Vie de Jésus*', *Œuvres complètes*, Pagnerre, 1857-60, 12 vols., iii. 292.

The conviction of Comte, Vacherot, and many of their contemporaries, was that to reject the supernatural elements of older
creeds is not to exclude the possibility of religious commitment.
They would grant that it must differ from more primitive faiths
but would also assert that the progress of human thought has
brought a more mature, rational notion of religion. We are thus
not entitled to quote against them either a Christian conception
of religion or such anthropological definitions as, for instance,
Tylor's—'the belief in spiritual beings'—or Frazer's—'a propitia-
tion or conciliation of [conscious or personal agents] superior to
man which are believed to direct and control the course of nature
and of human life'.[1] Nor, thinking of Buddhism, surely a religion,
yet often agnostic, can we deny that, in Söderblom's words, 'real
religion may exist without a definite conception of divinity'.[2]
What, then, is the minimum definition by which we can fairly
judge? Perhaps we can accept Söderblom's conclusion that 'there
is no real religion without a distinction between holy and pro-
fane', that 'the only sure test is holiness', the holy being that
which 'inspires awe'. But even now we may differ in our understanding of 'holiness' and 'awe', and hence in our judgement of the
claim that 'the holy' can fairly be equated, as many nineteenth-
century thinkers argued, with a moral value or values quite independent of any supernatural being. The answer will clearly vary
with each man's temperament, and perhaps we ought therefore to
say, adopting a distinction of Gabriel Marcel's, that in the last
resort the definition of 'religion' poses not a solvable 'problem'
but a 'mystery' in which each of us is permanently involved, that
can only be personally decided. But perhaps two points can be
made. First, it is surely to be feared that a modified Comtian cult of
an ideal humanity of the future and a metaphysical cult of the
notion of perfection are alike too abstract and remote to command
the reverence, emotional as well as intellectual, of a substantial
group in any community—and unless this be achieved, religion
must fail in its social function. Secondly, it is surely doubtful

---

[1] Cited in *Encyclopaedia Britannica*, 1951, art. 'Religion', vol. xix, p. 103.
[2] N. Söderblom, art. 'Holiness', *Encyclopaedia of Religion and Ethics*, vol. vi, Edinburgh,
Clark, 1913, p. 731.

whether we can for long feel awe, experience 'the sense of the holy', in contemplating what we know to be our own creations, values which we have ourselves invented. And what can remain of mystery if mystery, to be acceptable to the seeker, is required to be scientifically verified and rationally understood? Deck these creeds as we may with the oratory of Cousin, the symbolism of Ménard's mystical paganism, Comte's festivals and catechism, or Renan's emotional elevation of tone, all we hear in them is the echo of our own voice.

The judgements of their philosophical successors can hardly be doubted, however, whatever the truth about these wider issues. Each answered Scherer's question in his own way. Some abandoned religion for the sake of rationality and embraced either the pessimistic scepticism or the hedonistic materialism described by Bourget, or else, more finely, persevered as idealistic but firmly secular humanists. This last reaction is found, for instance, in the group, led by Massol and supported for a time by Renouvier, which from 1865 published the journal, *La Morale indépendante*, and—challenging the almost universal assumption of the previous generation—argued, like Proudhon before them, that ethical beliefs need not be founded upon a religious faith.[1] Others abandoned rationality for the sake of religion—so it seems to the present author at least—and, like Bourget himself, returned to the Catholic Church. Only a small group remained who continued to seek for the best of both worlds, still tried to realize the hopes of Constant and the Romantics earlier. They too wished to free man's 'religious sentiment' from church authority and prescribed rituals, to shun the illiberal dogmatics of both Catholicism and secular prophets like Comte and Enfantin, to defend a tolerant, humanitarian religion that could unite Christ's own teaching and the best impulses of nineteenth-century humanist idealism. Some of them—such as Quinet for a time, Eugène Sue, and Édouard Laboulaye, for example—turned to the Unitarian faith. Others placed their hopes in liberal Protestantism—Scherer himself,

---

[1] On this journal, cf. C. Coignet, *De Kant à Bergson*, Alcan, 1911, Ière partie, ch. i, and cf. also C. Coignet, *La Morale indépendante*, Baillière, 1869. Others who collaborated included Vacherot, Charles Secrétan and Challemel-Lacour.

Renouvier from the mid-1870's, George Sand; the group, including Colani and Albert Réville, that from 1850 ran the *Revue de théologie*; Charles Dollfus and Auguste Nefftzer, who preached a 'progressive Christianity' first in the *Revue germanique*, then in *Le Temps*; Auguste Sabatier and other contributors to the *Revue chrétienne*; and Léon Richer and Henri Carle, who argued for a still wider 'rational religion' in the pages of *L'Opinion nationale*.[1] Little known even in their own day and forgotten now, they failed, however, to win any significant following. Yet on a longer view, by their influence on the Modernist movement later, they helped to inspire a marked re-direction of Christian thought and practice in the twentieth century. More generally, it is arresting to realize how many of the accusations made against nineteenth-century Christianity are irrelevant today—so far at least as most Protestant thought is concerned. Acceptance of scientific discoveries, including evolutionary theory; emphasis upon the sacramental view of the body—not unlike that 'rehabilitation of matter' for which Saint-Simon called; rejection of the belief in biblical infallibility and of the harsher forms of the doctrines of grace, eternal punishment, and the Atonement; greater stress upon Christian social action; wider doctrinal tolerance—all these and numerous other features of Protestant teaching in our own day suggest that Renouvier, Scherer, and their friends were right to believe possible a creed that would be religious, humanitarian, and compatible with reason and science. They suggest this, but they do not establish it; each reader will no doubt pass his own judgement.

[1] Cf. Weill, op. cit., pp. 134, 150 ff., 182–4. Convenient surveys of French Protestantism are found in G. Weill, 'Le Protestantisme français au XIXᵉ siècle', *Revue de synthèse historique*, xxiii, 1911, pp. 10 ff., and C. Coignet, *L'Évolution du protestantisme français au XIXᵉ siècle*, 1908.

Select Bibliography of Secondary Authorities

History of Philosophy

C. Adam, *La Philosophie en France: La Première Moitié du dix-neuvième siècle*, Alcan, 1894

I. Benrubi, *Philosophische Strömungen der Gegenwart in Frankreich*, Leipzig, Meiner, 1928

É. Bréhier, *Histoire de la philosophie*, t. ii—*La Philosophie moderne*, Alcan, s.d.

A. Cresson, *Les Courants de la pensée philosophique française*, 2ᵉ éd., Colin, 1931, 2 vols.

— *La Philosophie française*, P.U.F., 1951

P. Damiron, *Essai sur l'histoire de la philosophie en France au XIXᵉ siècle*, 3ᵉ éd., Hachette, 1834, 2 vols.

R. Daval, *Histoire des idées en France*, P.U.F., 1953

V. Delbos, *La Philosophie française*, Plon, 1919, ch. xii–xiv

M. Ferraz, *Histoire de la philosophie en France au dix-neuvième siècle*, Didier and Perrin, 1877–87, 3 vols.

A. Fouillée, *Histoire de la philosophie*, Delagrave, 1875, 4ᵉ Partie, ch. ix

L. Lévy-Bruhl, *History of Modern Philosophy in France*, London, Kegan Paul, 1899, ch. xi–xv

R. Lote, *Histoire de la philosophie* in *Histoire de la nation française*, ed. G. Hanotaux, t. xv, Plon-Nourrit, 1924

J. T. Merz, *European Thought in the Nineteenth Century*, Edinburgh, Blackwood, 1914, 4 vols.

R. B. Perry, *Philosophy of the Recent Past*, London, Scribners, 1927

G. de Ruggiero, *Modern Philosophy*, trans. Hannay and Collingwood, London, Allen & Unwin, 1921

J. Wahl, *Tableau de la philosophie française*, Fontaine, 1946

Philosophical Groups and Themes

P. Alfaric, *Laromiguière et son école*, Belles Lettres, 1929

F. Baldensperger, *Le Mouvement des idées dans l'émigration française (1789–1815)*, Plon, 1924, 2 vols.

G. Boas, *French Philosophies of the Romantic Period*, Baltimore, Johns Hopkins U.P., 1925

P. Bourget, *Essais de psychologie contemporaine*, Plon, 1926, 2 vols.
— *Pages de critique et de doctrine*, Plon-Nourrit, s.d., 2 vols.

L. Brunschvicg, *Le Progrès de la conscience dans la philosophie occidentale*, Alcan, 1927

É. Cailliet, *La Tradition littéraire des idéologues*, Philadelphia, American Philosophical Soc., 1943

C. H. Van Duzer, *The Contribution of the Ideologues to French Revolutionary Thought*, Baltimore, Johns Hopkins U.P., 1935

É. Faguet, *Politiques et moralistes du dix-neuvième siècle*, 5ᵉ éd., Société française d'Imprimerie, 1903, 3 vols.

R. Flint, *Anti-Theistic Theories*, 9th ed., Edinburgh and London, Blackwood, 1917

V. Giraud, *Le Christianisme de Chateaubriand*, t. i, *Les Origines*, Hachette, 1925

J. A. Gunn, *Modern French Philosophy (1851–1921)*, London, Fisher Unwin, 1922

A. Lalande, *Vocabulaire technique et critique de la philosophie*, 7ᵉ éd., P.U.F., 1956

D. Parodi, *Du positivisme à l'idéalisme—Études critiques*, Vrin, 1930
— *Du positivisme à l'idéalisme—Philosophies d'hier*, Vrin, 1930
— *La Philosophie contemporaine en France*, Alcan, 1919

F. Picavet, *Les Idéologues*, Alcan, 1891

F. Ravaisson, *Rapport sur la philosophie en France au dix-neuvième siècle*, 5ᵉ éd., Hachette, 1904

C. Renouvier, 'De la philosophie du dix-neuvième siècle en France', *L'Année philosophique—Première Année (1867)*, 1868, pp. 1–108

A. V. Roche, *Les Idées traditionalistes en France de Rivarol à Maurras*, Urbana, Univ. of Illinois Press, 1937

H. V. Routh, *Towards the Twentieth Century—A Spiritual History of the Nineteenth Century*, Cambridge U.P., 1937

C. A. Sainte-Beuve, *Les Grands Écrivains français—XIXᵉ siècle: Philosophes et Essayistes*, Garnier, 1930, 3 vols.

J. Vier, 'La Prose des idées au dix-neuvième siècle', *Histoire des littératures*, *Encyclopédie de la Pléiade*, Gallimard, 1956–8, 3 vols., t. iii

G. Weill, *Histoire de l'idée laïque en France au XIXᵉ siècle*, nouv. éd., Alcan, 1929

Select Bibliography

Relevant General Studies of French Literature

I. Babbitt, *The Masters of Modern French Criticism*, London, Constable, 1913

J. Bédier et P. Hazard, *Littérature française*, t. ii, Larousse, 1949

C. Beuchat, *Histoire du naturalisme français*, Corrêa, 1949, 2 vols.

R. Dumesnil, *Le Réalisme et le naturalisme*, Gigord, s.d.

J. Giraud, *L'École romantique française*, 4ᵉ éd., Colin, 1942

R. Jasinski, *Histoire de la littérature française*, t. ii, Boivin, 1947

P. Martino, *Parnasse et symbolisme*, 7ᵉ éd., Colin, 1947

G. Michaud, *Message poétique du symbolisme*, t. i, Nizet, 1951

A. Monglond, *Le Préromantisme français*, Grenoble, Arthaud, 1930, 2 vols.

P. Moreau, *Le Romantisme*, 2ᵉ éd., Gigord, 1957

A. Nettement, *Histoire de la littérature française sous le gouvernement de Juillet*, 2ᵉ éd., Lecoffre, 1859, 2 vols.

E. Scherer, *Études sur la littérature contemporaine*, Calmann Lévy, 1863–95, 10 vols.

M. Souriau, *Histoire du romantisme en France*, Spes, 1927, 2 vols.

— *Histoire du Parnasse*, Spes, 1929

A. Thibaudet, *Histoire de la littérature française de 1789 à nos jours*, Stock, 1936

Ph. Van Tieghem, *Petite Histoire des grandes doctrines littéraires en France*, P.U.F., 1946

P. Van Tieghem, *Le Romantisme dans la littérature européenne*, Michel, 1948

Numerous volumes of correspondence, memoirs, etc., cast interesting, if fitful, light upon the intellectual life of the age. The most useful of these are Sainte-Beuve's *Correspondance* and the Goncourts' *Journal*. Cf. also the general bibliographies to Chapters III–VIII below.

Catholicism

L. Baunard, *Un Siècle de l'église de France, 1800–1900*, Poussielgue, 1901

J. Calvet, *Le Renouveau catholique dans la littérature contemporaine*, Lanore, 1931

A. Dansette, *Histoire religieuse de la France contemporaine*, t. i, *De la Révolution à la troisième République*, 2ᵉ éd., Flammarion, 1952

A. Debidour, *Histoire des rapports de l'église et de l'état en France de 1789 à 1870*, Alcan, 1898

J. B. Duroselle, *Les Débuts du catholicisme social en France (1822–1870)*, P.U.F., 1951

L. Foucher, *La Philosophie catholique en France au dix-neuvième siècle*, Vrin, 1955

V. Giraud, *De Chateaubriand à Brunetière: Essai sur le mouvement catholique en France au dix-neuvième siècle*, Spes, 1938

H. Guillemin, *Histoire des catholiques français au dix-neuvième siècle (1815–1905)*, Geneva, Paris and Montreal, Éditions du Milieu du Monde, 1947

K. S. Latourette, *Christianity in a Revolutionary Age*, vol. i: *The Nineteenth Century in Europe*, London, Eyre & Spottiswoode, 1959

J. Leflon, *Histoire de l'église*, t. 20: *La Crise révolutionnaire (1789–1846)*, Bloud et Gay, 1949

B. Menczer, *Catholic Political Thought, 1789–1848*, London, Burns Oates, 1952

F. Mourret, *Le Mouvement catholique en France de 1830 à 1850*, 1917

C. S. Phillips, *The Church in France, 1789–1907*, London, S.P.C.K., 1929–36, 2 vols.

W. J. S. Simpson, *Religious Thought in France in the Nineteenth Century*, London, Allen, 1935

P. Spencer, *Politics of Belief in Nineteenth-Century France—Lacordaire: Veuillot: Michon*, London, Faber, 1954

G. Weill, *Histoire du catholicisme libéral en France, 1828–1908*, Alcan, 1909

Secular Religions: General

J. Bois, *Les Petites Religions de Paris*, Chailley, 1894

E. Caro, *L'Idée de Dieu et ses nouveaux critiques*, Hachette, 1864

A. Erdan, *La France mystique: Tableau des excentricités religieuses de ce temps*, Coulon-Pineau, s.d., 2 vols.

A. L. Guérard, *French Prophets of Yesterday: A Study of Religious Thought under the Second Empire*, London, Fisher Unwin, 1913

E. Poitou, *Les Philosophes français contemporains et leurs systèmes religieux*, 2e éd., Charpentier, 1864

L. Reybaud, *Études sur les réformateurs contemporains*, Guillaumin, 1840–3, 2 vols.

H. Tronchon, 'Une Crise d'âmes: 1830', *Revue des cours et conférences*, 27e Année, 1926, pp. 385–99, reprinted in *Romantisme et préromantisme*, Belles Lettres, 1930

J. Vinson, *Les Religions actuelles*, Delahaye and Lecrosnier, 1888, ch. ix

Select Bibliography

Religious Thought of the Romantics

General

R. Canat, *Une Forme du mal du siècle: Du sentiment de la solitude morale chez les romantiques et les parnassiens*, Hachette, 1904

H. Girard, 'La Pensée religieuse des romantiques', *Revue de l'histoire des religions*, t. 89, 1924, pp. 138–62

A. Hoog, 'La Révolte métaphysique et religieuse des petits romantiques', in *Les Petits Romantiques français*, Cahiers du Sud, 1949, pp. 13 ff.

P. Lasserre, *Le Romantisme français*, Mercure de France, 1907

P. M. Masson, *La Religion de Rousseau*, 2e éd., Hachette, 1916, 3 vols., t. iii

F. Strowski, 'Le Romantisme humanitaire et philosophique', *Revue des cours et conférences*, 21e Année, 1912–13, pp. 209–23, 521–38, and 22e Année, 1913–14, pp. 105–16, 328–37

A. Viatte, *Le Catholicisme des romantiques*, Boccard, 1922

Individual Authors

J. B. Barrère, *Hugo, l'homme et l'œuvre*, Boivin, 1952

P. Bertault, *Balzac et la religion*, Boivin, 1942

G. Bonnefoy, *La Pensée religieuse et morale d'Alfred de Vigny*, Hachette, s.d.

M. Citoleux, *La Poésie philosophique au dix-neuvième siècle—Lamartine*, Plon-Nourrit, 1905

E. Estève, *Alfred de Vigny, sa pensée et son art*, Garnier, 1923

P. Flottes, *La Pensée politique et sociale d'Alfred de Vigny*, Belles Lettres, 1927

H. Guillemin, *Lamartine, l'homme et l'œuvre*, Boivin, 1940, ch. iv

C. Lecœur, *La Pensée religieuse de Victor Hugo*, Bordas, 1951

M. Leroy, *La Pensée de Sainte-Beuve*, Gallimard, 1940

— *La Politique de Sainte-Beuve*, 6e éd., Gallimard, 1941

J. Merlant, *Senancour*, Fischbacher, 1907

G. Michaut, *Sainte-Beuve avant les Lundis*, Fontemoing, 1903

M. L. Pailleron, *George Sand*, Grasset, 1938–53, 3 vols.

J. Roos, *Les Idées philosophiques de Victor Hugo*, Nizet, 1958

P. Salomon, *George Sand*, Hatier, 1953

D. Saurat, *La Religion de Victor Hugo*, Hachette, 1929

A. Viatte, *Victor Hugo et les illuminés de son temps*, 2e éd., Montreal, Éditions de l'Arbre, 1943

Foreign Philosophical Influences

A. Baillot, *L'Influence de la philosophie de Schopenhauer en France* (*1860–1900*), Vrin, 1927

J. M. Carré, *Les Écrivains français et le mirage allemand* (*1800–1940*), Boivin, 1947

V. Delbos, *Le Problème moral dans la philosophie de Spinoza et dans l'histoire du spinozisme*, Alcan, 1893

P. Janet, 'French Thought and Spinozism', *The Contemporary Review*, xxix, 1877, pp. 1072 ff.

— 'Le Spinozisme en France', *Rev. Philos.*, xiii, 1882, pp. 109 ff.

L. Reynaud, *L'Influence allemande en France au dix-huitième et au dix-neuvième siècles*, Hachette, 1922

H. Tronchon, *La Fortune intellectuelle de Herder en France—La Préparation*, Rieder, 1920

M. Vallois, *La Formation de l'influence kantienne en France*, Alcan, s.d.

Cf. also F. Baldensperger and W. P. Friederich, *Bibliography of Comparative Literature*, Chapel Hill, Univ. of North Carolina, 1950

CHAPTER III: THE CULT OF SCIENCE

Science and Positivism

M. Caullery, *La Science française depuis le dix-septième siècle*, Colin, 1933

D. G. Charlton, *Positivist Thought in France during the Second Empire, 1852–1870*, Oxford, Clarendon Press, 1959

W. C. Dampier, *A History of Science and its Relations with Philosophy and Religion*, 4th ed., Cambridge U.P., 1948

Histoire de la Science, edited by M. Daumas, *Encyclopédie de la Pléiade*, Gallimard, 1957

F. A. Hayek, *The Counter-Revolution of Science*, Glencoe, Ill., Free Press, 1952

La Science française, edited by H. Poincaré, 2e éd., Larousse, 1933, 2 vols.

Influence on Literature

J. J. Bridenne, *La Littérature française d'imagination scientifique*, Dassonville, 1950

R. Fath, *L'Influence de la science sur la littérature française dans la seconde moitié du dix-neuvième siècle*, Lausanne, Payot, 1901

C. A. Fusil, *La Poésie scientifique de 1750 à nos jours*, Scientifica, 1918

D. L. King, *L'Influence des sciences physiologiques sur la littérature française de 1670 à 1870*, Belles Lettres, 1926

Select Bibliography

Saint-Simon—see p. 226 below

Comte

H. B. Acton, 'Comte's Positivism and the Science of Society', *Philosophy*, xxvi, 1951, pp. 291–310

E. Caird, *The Social Philosophy and Religion of Comte*, 2nd ed., Glasgow, Maclehose, 1893

G. Cantecor, *Comte*, nouv. éd., Mellottée, s.d.

A. Cresson, *Comte*, P.U.F., 1941

J. Delvolvé, *Réflexions sur la pensée comtienne*, Alcan, 1932

P. Ducassé, *Méthode et intuition chez Auguste Comte*, Alcan, 1939

G. Dumas, *Psychologie de deux messies positivistes—Saint-Simon et Auguste Comte*, Alcan, 1905

H. Gouhier, *La Vie d'Auguste Comte*, Gallimard, 1931

— *La Jeunesse d'Auguste Comte et la formation du positivisme*, Vrin, 1933–41, 3 vols.

L. Lévy-Bruhl, *The Philosophy of Auguste Comte*, translated Beaumont-Klein, with an Introduction by F. Harrison, London, Swan, 1903

É. Littré, *Auguste Comte et la philosophie positive*, 2ᵉ éd., Hachette, 1864

— 'La Philosophie positive: M. Auguste Comte et M. J. Stuart Mill', *R.D.M.*, 15.8.1866, pp. 829–66

J. S. Mill, *Auguste Comte and Positivism*, 2nd ed., London, Trübner, 1866

C. de Rouvre, *Auguste Comte et le catholicisme*, Rieder, 1928

T. Whittaker, *Comte and Mill*, London, Constable, 1908

Littré

S. Aquarone, *The Life and Works of Émile Littré*, Leyden, Sythoff, 1958

E. Caro, 'Émile Littré', *R.D.M.*, 1.4.1882, pp. 516–51, and 1.5.1882, pp. 5–46

E. Renan, 'Réponse au discours de réception de M. Pasteur', *Discours et conférences*, 9ᵉ éd., Calmann Lévy, 1928

C. A. Sainte-Beuve, 'M. Littré', *Nouveaux lundis*, t. v, Calmann Lévy, 1866

E. Scherer, 'Émile Littré', *Études sur la littérature contemporaine*, t. vii, Calmann Lévy, 1882

Taine

G. Barzellotti, *La Philosophie de Taine*, Alcan, 1900

A. Chevrillon, *Taine—Formation de sa pensée*, Plon, 1932

A. Cresson, *H. Taine, sa vie, son œuvre*, P.U.F., 1951
V. Giraud, *Essai sur Taine*, 6ᵉ éd., Hachette, s.d.
— *H. Taine—Études et documents*, Vrin, 1928
S. J. Kahn, *Science and Aesthetic Judgment—A Study of Taine's Critical Method*, London, Routledge, 1953
A. Laborde-Milaà, *Hippolyte Taine—Essai d'une biographie intellectuelle*, Perrin, 1909
R. Lenoir, 'L'Idéalisme de Taine', *R.M.M.*, xxiii, 1916, pp. 859–78
M. Leroy, *Taine*, Rieder, 1933
J. S. Mill, *Dissertations and Discussions*, vol. iv, London, Longmans, 1875
G. Monod, *Les Maîtres de l'histoire—Renan, Taine, Michelet*, Calmann Lévy, 1894
D. D. Rosca, *L'Influence de Hegel sur Taine théoricien de la connaissance et de l'art*, Gamber, 1928
P. V. Rubov, *Hippolyte Taine—Étapes de son œuvre*, Champion, 1930

Renan—see p. 227 below

CHAPTER IV: SOCIAL RELIGIONS

Social Thought: General

H. R. d'Allemagne, *Les Saint-Simoniens, 1827–37*, Gründ, 1930
D. Bagge, *Les Idées politiques en France sous la Restauration*, P.U.F., 1952
C. C. A. Bouglé, *Socialismes français*, 2ᵉ éd., Colin, 1933
S. Charléty, *Histoire du saint-simonisme (1815–1864)*, 2ᵉ éd., Hartmann, 1931
G. D. H. Cole, *A History of Socialist Thought*, vol. i, London, Macmillan, 1953
É. Durkheim, *Le Socialisme*, Alcan, 1928
D. O. Evans, *Le Socialisme romantique—Pierre Leroux et ses contemporains*, Marcel Rivière, 1948
— *Social Romanticism*, Oxford, Clarendon Press, 1951
E. Fournière, *Les Théories socialistes au XIXᵉ siècle, de Babeuf à Proudhon*, Alcan, 1904
A. J. George, *The Development of French Romanticism*, Syracuse U.P., 1955
A. Gray, *The Socialist Tradition*, London, Longmans, 1946
H. J. Hunt, *Le Socialisme et le romantisme en France*, Oxford, Clarendon Press, 1935

Select Bibliography

G. G. Iggers, *The Cult of Authority: The Political Philosophy of the Saint-Simonians*, The Hague, Nijhoff, 1958

G. Isambert, *Les Idées socialistes en France de 1815 à 1848*, Alcan, 1905

M. Leroy, *Histoire des idées sociales en France*, t. ii: *De Babeuf à Tocqueville*, Gallimard, 1950; t. iii: *D'Auguste Comte à P.-J. Proudhon*, Gallimard, 1954

C. L. de Liefde, *Le Saint-Simonisme dans la poésie française entre 1825 et 1865*, Haarlem, Amicitia, 1927

H. Louvancour, *De Henri de Saint-Simon à Charles Fourier*, Chartres, Durand, 1913

J. P. Mayer, *Political Thought in France from Sièyes to Sorel*, London, Faber, 1943

H. Michel, *L'Idée de l'État: Essai critique sur l'histoire des théories sociales et politiques en France depuis la Révolution*, Hachette, 1896

R. Picard, *Le Romantisme social*, New York, Brentano's, 1944

J. Plamenatz, *The Revolutionary Movement in France, 1815–1871*, London, Longmans, 1952

R. Soltau, *French Political Thought in the Nineteenth Century*, London, Benn, 1931

J. L. Talmon, *The Origins of Totalitarian Democracy*, London, Secker & Warburg, 1952

— *Political Messianism: The Romantic Phase*, London, Secker & Warburg, 1960

G. Weill, *L'École Saint-Simonienne*, Alcan, 1896

— 'Les Saint-Simoniens sous Napoléon III', *Revue des études Napoléoniennes*, iii, 1913, pp. 391–406

Influences Abroad

E. M. Butler, *The Saint-Simonian Religion in Germany*, Cambridge U.P., 1926

R. L. Hawkins, *Auguste Comte and the United States (1816–1853)*, Cambridge, Mass., Harvard U.P., 1936

— *Auguste Comte and the United States (1853–1861)*, Cambridge, Mass., Harvard U.P., 1938

M. Holloway, *Heavens on Earth: Utopian Communities in America, 1680–1880*, London, Turnstile Press, 1951

J. E. McGee, *A Crusade for Humanity: The History of Organised Positivism in England*, London, Watts, 1931

I. W. Mueller, *John Stuart Mill and French Thought*, Urbana, Univ. of Illinois Press, 1956

R. K. P. Pankhurst, *The Saint-Simonians, Mill and Carlyle*, London, Sidgwick & Jackson, 1957

M. Quin, *Memoirs of a Positivist*, London, Allen & Unwin, 1924

H. Roddier, 'P. Leroux, G. Sand et Walt Whitman', *R.L.C.*, xxxi, 1957, pp. 5–33

G. Weill, 'Le Saint-Simonisme hors de France', *Revue d'histoire économique et sociale*, ix, 1921, pp. 103–14

Saint-Simon

C. C. A. Bouglé, *L'Œuvre de Saint-Simon*, Alcan, 1925 (selected texts with Introduction)

G. Brunet, *Le Mysticisme social de Saint-Simon*, Presses françaises, 1925

G. Dumas, *Psychologie de deux messies positivistes—Saint-Simon et Auguste Comte*, Alcan, 1905

H. Gouhier, *La Jeunesse d'Auguste Comte et la formation du positivisme*, t. ii: *Saint-Simon jusqu'à la Restauration*, Vrin, 1936

R. Lenoir, 'Henri de Saint-Simon', *Rev. Philos.*, c, 1925, pp. 179–222

M. Leroy, *Le Socialisme des producteurs: Henri de Saint-Simon*, Rivière, 1924

— *La Vie véritable de Saint-Simon*, Grasset, 1925

F. E. Manuel, *The New World of Henri Saint-Simon*, Cambridge, Mass., Harvard U.P., 1956

F. M. H. Markham, *Henri Comte de Saint-Simon: Selected Writings*, Oxford, Blackwell, 1952 (with an Introduction)

G. Weill, *Un Précurseur du socialisme: Saint-Simon et son œuvre*, Perrin, 1894

Enfantin

S. Charléty, *Enfantin*, Alcan, 1931 (selected texts with Introduction)

Fourier

F. Armand et R. Maublanc, *Fourier*, Éditions Sociales Internationales, 1937 (with selected texts)

H. Bourgin, *Fourier: Contribution à l'étude du socialisme français*, Bellais, 1905

A. Pinloche, *Fourier et le socialisme*, Alcan, 1933

C. Gide, *Fourier précurseur de la Coopération*, Association pour l'enseignement de la Coopération, s.d.

P. Janet, 'Le Socialisme au dix-neuvième siècle—La Philosophie de Charles Fourier', *R.D.M.*, 1.10.1879, pp. 619–45

Considérant

M. Dommanget, *Victor Considérant, sa vie, son œuvre*, Éditions Sociales Internationales, 1929

Leroux

D. O. Evans, *Le Socialisme romantique: Pierre Leroux et ses contemporains*, Marcel Rivière, 1948

J. E. Fidao-Justiniani, 'Pierre Leroux et son œuvre', *R.D.M.*, 15.5.1906, pp. 320–55

P. Janet, 'La Philosophie de P. Leroux', *R.D.M.*, 15.4.1899, pp. 767–88 and 15.5.1899, pp. 379–406

H. Mougin, *Pierre Leroux*, Éditions Sociales Internationales, 1938 (with selected texts)

P. Stapfer, 'Un Philosophe religieux du dix-neuvième siècle: P. Leroux', in *Questions esthétiques et religieuses*, Alcan, 1906, pp. 91–143

P. F. Thomas, *Pierre Leroux, sa vie, son œuvre, sa doctrine*, Alcan, 1904

Comte—see p. 223 above

CHAPTER V: METAPHYSICAL RELIGIONS

Cousin

J. Barthélemy-Saint Hilaire, *Victor Cousin, sa vie et sa correspondance*, Alcan, 1895, 3 vols.

P. Dubois, *Cousin, Jouffroy, Damiron*, Perrin, 1902

P. Janet, *Victor Cousin et son œuvre*, 3e éd., Alcan, 1893

J. Pommier, 'L'évolution de V. Cousin', *Revue d'histoire de la philosophie*, avril-juin 1931

— 'V. Cousin et ses élèves vers 1840', *Revue d'histoire et de philosophie religieuses*, juillet-oct. 1931

E. Scherer, *Études sur la littérature contemporaine*, t. iv, Calmann Lévy, 1873, pp. 75–86

J. Simon, *Victor Cousin*, 5e éd., Hachette, 1921

Simon

G. Picot, *Jules Simon*, Hachette, 1897

Renan

R. Berthelot, 'La Pensée philosophique de Renan', *R.M.M.*, 1923, pp. 365–88

J. P. Boosten, *Taine et Renan et l'idée de Dieu*, Maestricht, Boosten & Stols, 1937

J. Chaix-Ruy, *Ernest Renan*, Vitte, 1956

P. Lasserre, *Renan et nous*, Grasset, 1923

— *La Jeunesse de Renan*, Calmann Lévy, 1928, 2 vols.

G. Monod, *Les Maîtres de l'histoire—Renan, Taine, Michelet*, Calmann Lévy, 1894

D. Parodi, 'Ernest Renan et la philosophie contemporaine', in *Du positivisme à l'idéalisme—Philosophies d'hier*, Vrin, 1930, pp. 198-225

J. Pommier, *Renan, d'après des documents inédits*, Perrin, 1923

— *La Pensée religieuse de Renan*, Rieder, 1925

— *La Jeunesse cléricale de Renan*, Belles Lettres, 1933

G. Séailles, *Ernest Renan*, 2ᵉ éd., Perrin, 1895

C. Smith, 'The Fictionalist Element in Renan's Thought', *French Studies*, ix, 1955, pp. 30-41

Ph. Van Tieghem, *Renan*, Hachette, 1948

M. Weiler, *La Pensée de Renan*, Grenoble, Bordas, 1945

Vacherot

P. Janet, 'Le Testament d'un philosophe [Vacherot]', *R.D.M.*, 1.6.1885, pp. 550-83

D. Parodi, 'La Philosophie d'Étienne Vacherot', in *Du positivisme à l'idéalisme—Philosophies d'hier*, Vrin, 1930, pp. 38-103

Taine—see p. 223 above

CHAPTER VI: OCCULT AND NEO-PAGAN RELIGIONS

Occultism

P. Arnold, *Histoire des Rose-Croix*, Mercure de France, 1955

P. G. Castex, *Le Conte fantastique en France de Nodier à Maupassant*, Corti, 1951

L. Cellier, *Fabre d'Olivet*, Nizet, 1953

Champfleury (pseud.), *Les Vignettes romantiques*, Dentu, 1883, pp. 232-46

H. J. Hunt, *The Epic in Nineteenth-Century France*, Oxford, Blackwell, 1941, ch. ii and v

P. M. Jones, *The Background of Modern Poetry*, Cambridge U.P., 1951

Éliphas Lévi (A. Constant), *Histoire de la magie*, Baillière, 1860

G. Martin, *Manuel d'histoire de la franc-maçonnerie française*, 3ᵉ éd., P.U.F., 1934

H. Matthey, *Essai sur le merveilleux dans la littérature française depuis 1800*, Payot, 1915

M. Praz, *The Romantic Agony*, transl. Davidson, London, Oxford U.P., 1933

A. Viatte, *Les Sources occultes du romantisme*, Champion, 1928, 2 vols.

— *Victor Hugo et les illuminés de son temps*, 2ᵉ éd., Montreal, Éditions de l'Arbre, 1943

— 'Les Swedenborgiens en France de 1820 à 1830', *R.L.C.*, xi, 1931, pp. 416–50

For individual authors, cf. the useful bibliography in Castex, and the studies of Romantic religious thought listed above.

Non-Christian World-Religions

J. Barthélemy-Saint Hilaire, 'Notice sur les travaux de M. Eugène Burnouf', in Burnouf, *Introduction à l'histoire du buddhisme indien*, 2ᵉ éd., Maisonneuve, 1876

R. Canat, *L'Hellénisme des romantiques*, Didier, 1951–5, 3 vols.
— *La Renaissance de la Grèce antique (1820–1850)*, Hachette, 1911

C. Clerc, *Le Génie du paganisme*, Payot, 1926

F. Desonay, *Le Rêve hellénique chez les poètes parnassiens*, Champion, 1928

J. Ducros, 'Le Retour de la poésie française à l'antiquité grecque', *R.H.L.F.*, 1916, pp. 328 ff., and 1917, pp. 80 ff.

P. Jourda, *L'Exotisme dans la littérature française depuis Chateaubriand*, Boivin, 1938, and P.U.F., 1956, 2 vols.

P. Moreau, 'Romantisme français et syncrétisme religieux', *Symposium*, viii, 1954, pp. 1–17

Hassan El Nouty, *Le Proche-Orient dans la littérature française de Nerval à Barrès*, Nizet, 1958

S. Radhakrishnan, *Eastern Religions and Western Thought*, Oxford, Clarendon Press, 1939

R. Schwab, *La Renaissance orientale*, Payot, 1950

Michelet—see p. 233 below

Taine—see p. 223 above

Leconte de Lisle

E. Carcassonne, 'Leconte de Lisle et la philosophie indienne', *R.L.C.*, xi, 1931, pp. 618-46

H. Elsenberg, *Le Sentiment religieux chez Leconte de Lisle*, Jouve, 1909

E. Estève, *Leconte de Lisle*, Boivin, 1923

A. Fairlie, *Leconte de Lisle's Poems on the Barbarian Races*, Cambridge U.P., 1947

P. Flottes, *Leconte de Lisle, l'homme et l'œuvre*, Hatier-Boivin, 1954

I. Putter, *The Pessimism of Leconte de Lisle*, Berkeley and Los Angeles, Univ. of California Press, 1954-61, 2 vols.

CHAPTERS VII AND VIII:
THE CULT OF HISTORY AND PROGRESS

Philosophy of History

J. Baillie, *The Belief in Progress*, London, Oxford U.P., 1951

I. Berlin, *Historical Inevitability*, London, Oxford U.P., 1954

J. B. Bury, *The Idea of Progress*, 2nd ed., New York, Dover, 1955

Philosophy and History: Essays presented to E. Cassirer, Oxford, Clarendon Press, 1936

R. G. Collingwood, *The Idea of History*, Oxford, Clarendon Press, 1946

C. Dawson, *Progress and Religion*, London, Sheed & Ward, 1936

R. Flint, *History of the Philosophy of History*, Edinburgh and London, Blackwood, 1893

M. Ginsberg, *The Idea of Progress—A Revaluation*, London, Methuen, 1953

G. P. Gooch, *History and Historians in the Nineteenth Century*, London, Longmans, 1913

L. Halphen, *L'Histoire en France depuis cent ans*, Colin, 1914

C. Jullian, *Extraits des historiens français du XIXe siècle*, 8e éd., Hachette, s.d., *Introduction*

D. E. Lee and R. N. Beck, 'The Meaning of Historicism', *American Historical Review*, lix, 1954, pp. 568 ff.

K. Löwith, *Meaning in History*, Univ. of Chicago Press, 1949

P. Moreau, *L'Histoire en France au XIXe siècle*, Belles Lettres, 1935

K. R. Popper, *The Poverty of Historicism*, London, Routledge, 1957

A. Salomon, *The Tyranny of Progress*, New York, Noonday Press, 1955

R. V. Sampson, *Progress in the Age of Reason*, London, Heinemann, 1956

H. Sée, *Science et philosophie de l'histoire*, Alcan, 1928

Select Bibliography

H. Tronchon, 'Les Études historiques et la philosophie de l'histoire aux alentours de 1830', *Revue de synthèse historique*, déc. 1922, reprinted in *Romantisme et préromantisme*, Belles Lettres, 1930

W. Walsh, *An Introduction to Philosophy of History*, London, Hutchinson, 1951

E. Wilson, *To the Finland Station*, London, Secker & Warburg, n.d.

Evolution

H. Butterfield, *The Origins of Modern Science*, 2nd ed., London, Bell, 1957, ch. xii

M. Landrieu, *Lamarck, le fondateur du transformisme, sa vie, son œuvre*, Société zoologique, 1909

A. Laugel, 'Darwin et ses critiques', *R.D.M.*, 1.3.1868, pp. 130–55

Cf. also bibliography on Science, p. 222 above.

Saint-Simon—see p. 226 above, and

S. Bernstein, 'Saint-Simon's Philosophy of History', *Science and Society*, xii, 1948, pp. 82–96

C. Renouvier, 'La Question du progrès—Burdin, Saint-Simon et Comte', *La Critique philosophique*, x, 1, 1881, pp. 337–46 and 353–68

W. M. Simon, 'History for Utopia: Saint-Simon and the Idea of Progress', *Journal of the History of Ideas*, xvii, 1956, pp. 311–31

Fourier—see p. 226 above

Louis Blanc

L. A. Loubère, 'Louis Blanc's Philosophy of History', *Journal of the History of Ideas*, xvii, 1956, pp. 70–88

J. Tchernoff, *Louis Blanc*, Société française de librairie et d'édition, 1904

J. Vidalenc, *Louis Blanc*, P.U.F., 1948

Proudhon

C. C. A. Bouglé, *La Sociologie de Proudhon*, Colin, 1911

— *Proudhon*, Alcan, 1930 (selected texts with Introduction)

D. W. Brogan, *Proudhon*, London, Hamish Hamilton, 1934

É. Dolléans, *Proudhon*, Gallimard, 1948

J. Duprat, *Proudhon sociologue et moraliste*, Alcan, 1929

G. Guy-Grand, *La Pensée de Proudhon*, Bordas, 1947

H. de Lubac, *Proudhon et le christianisme*, Éditions du Seuil, 1945

Secular Religions in France 1815–1870

H. de Lubac, *The UnMarxian Socialist*, London, Sheed & Ward, 1948
C. A. Sainte-Beuve, *P.-J. Proudhon, sa vie et sa correspondance*, 2ᵉ éd.,
    A. Costes, 1947
G. Woodcock, *P. J. Proudhon*, London, Routledge, 1956

Leroux—see p. 227 above

Cousin—see p. 227 above

Jouffroy

E. Caro, 'Jouffroy et ses œuvres', *R.D.M.*, 15.3.1865, pp. 333–76
P. Dubois, *Cousin, Jouffroy, Damiron*, Perrin, 1902
V. Giraud, 'Âmes romantiques', *R.D.M.*, 1.9.1928, pp. 219–30
L. Ollé-Laprune, *Jouffroy*, Perrin, 1899
J. Pommier, *Deux études sur Jouffroy et son temps*, Alcan, 1930
M. Salomon, *Jouffroy*, Bloud, 1907

Guizot

P. Janet, *Les Problèmes du XIXᵉ siècle*, 2ᵉ éd., Michel Lévy, 1873, livre v
J. S. Mill, 'Guizot's Essays and Lectures on History', *Dissertations and
    Discussions*, t. ii, 2nd ed., London, Longmans, 1867, pp. 218–82

Buchez

G. Castella, *Buchez*, Bloud, 1911
A. Cuvillier, *P. J. B. Buchez et les origines du socialisme chrétien*, P.U.F.,
    1948
— *Hommes et Idéologies de 1840*, Marcel Rivière, 1956, ch. i–iii
B. P. Petri, *The Historical Thought of Buchez*, Washington, D.C.,
    Catholic Univ. of America Press, 1958

Quinet

C. L. Chassin, *Edgar Quinet, sa vie et son œuvre*, Pagnerre, 1859
R. Heath, *Edgar Quinet: His Early Life and Writings*, London, Trübner,
    1881
H. J. Hunt, *The Epic in Nineteenth-Century France*, Oxford, Blackwell,
    1941, ch. vi
J. J. Kaspar, *La Révolution religieuse d'après Edgar Quinet*, Fischbacher,
    1906

R. H. Powers, *Edgar Quinet: A Study in French Patriotism*, Dallas, Southern Methodist U.P., 1957

E. Seillière, *Edgar Quinet et le mysticisme démocratique*, Société d'économie sociale, 1919

H. Tronchon, *Le Jeune Edgar Quinet ou l'aventure d'un enthousiaste*, Belles Lettres, 1937

A. Valès, *Edgar Quinet, sa vie et son œuvre*, Vienne, Aubinet, 1936

Michelet

J. M. Carré, *Michelet et son temps*, Perrin, 1926

J. L. Cornuz, *Jules Michelet*, Genève, Droz, and Lille, Giard, 1955

O. A. Haac, *Les Principes inspirateurs de Michelet*, New Haven, Yale U.P., 1951

D. Halévy, *Michelet*, Hachette, 1928

H. Kohn, *Prophets and People*, New York, Macmillan, 1947, ch. ii

G. Monod, *Les Maîtres de l'histoire—Renan, Taine, Michelet*, Calmann Lévy, 1894

— *La Vie et la pensée de Jules Michelet, 1798–1852*, Champion, 1923, 2 vols.

Scherer

É. Boutmy, *Taine, Scherer, Laboulaye*, Colin, 1901

O. Gréard, *Edmond Scherer*, Hachette, 1890

Addenda

The following have appeared since this work was completed:

A. G. Lehmann, *Sainte-Beuve: a portrait of the critic, 1804–1842*, Oxford, Clarendon Press, 1962

J. Lively, *The Social and Political Thought of Alexis de Tocqueville*, Oxford, Clarendon Press, 1962

F. E. Manuel, *The Prophets of Paris*, Cambridge, Mass., Harvard U.P., 1962

Revue internationale de philosophie, lx, 1962, fasc. 2, *Charles Fourier*

GENERAL INDEX

Principal references are indicated by italicized numerals

Q*

General Index

General Index

Pasteur, Louis, 38, 39
Paul, St., 33, 47, 67, 77, 87
Pearson, Karl, 197
Pécaut, F., 142
Pecqueur, Constantin, 79
Péguy, Charles, 201
Pelletan, Eugène, 82, 119, 131, 199
Perrault, Charles, 159
Persia, 139, 188
Persian religion, 33
Petitbon, R., 154n.
Peyre, Henri, 138n., 142n.
Phalange, La (review), 82
Philosophes (French eighteenth-century philosophical group), 6, 13, 18, 31, 44, 45, 48, 94, 106, 109, 137, 138, 140, 155, *158–61*, 162, 163, 165, 166, 176, 179, 191
Picavet, F., 7n.
Plato, 100, 142, 154
Plutarch, 140
Poincaré, Henri, 64
Poitou, E., 34, 117
Polish mystics, 131
Pommier, Jean, 27n., 99n.
Pompadour, Antoinette, Marquise de, 129
Ponsard, François, 41, 137
Pope, Alexander, 140
Popper, K. R., 178, 179n.
Prat, L., 207n.
Pressensé, Edmond de, 12, 15
Producteur, Le (journal), 70
Progrès, revue démocratique, Le (review), 157
Progresseur, Le (review), 157
Protestantism, 12, 82, 144, 192, 208, 215, 216
Protestants, 12, 14, 15, 16, 23, 67, 68, 107, 157
Proudhon, Pierre Joseph, 163, *170–1*, 180, 215
Psichari, Ernest, 201

Quakers, 23
Quin, Malcolm, 92
Quinet, Edgar, 2, 6n., 9n., 12, 22, 23, *32–33*, 34, 98, 137, 138, 139, 140, 154, 163, 179, *184–9*, 192, 213, 215

Racine, Jean, 132
Radhakrishnan, S., 146
Ravaisson, Félix, 97, 142, 143, 200, 201, 203, 205
Ray, John, 194
Reformation, 38, 171
Reid, Thomas, 23
Reign of Terror, 1, 7, 38
Renaissance, 38, 123, 127, 140, 167
Renan, Ernest, 12, 15, *16–18*, 23, 26, 29, 32, 37, 41, 44, 48, 55, *57–58*, 83, 97, *106–13*, 116, 119, 120, 121, 125, 137, 139, 145, *153*, 156, 157, 162, 163, 198, 200, 201, 202, 213, 215
Renouvier, Charles Bernard, 12, 38, 56n., 64, 117, 119, 125, 156, 193, 198, 201, 204, 205, *207–8*, 215, 216
Réveil, Le (review), 12
Réville, Albert, 12, 216
Revolutionary religions, *4–6*, 31, 65
Revolution, French, of 1789, 1, 7, 10, 28, 36, 44, 65, 90n., 167, 171, 176, 177, 181, 210
Revolution, French, of 1830, 8, 131
Revue chrétienne, 216
Revue de philosophie positive, 54
Revue des Deux Mondes, 15
Revue de théologie, 12, 15, 157, 216
Revue du progrès politique, social e littéraire, 157
Revue du progrès social, 157
Revue encyclopédique, 83
Revue germanique, 216
Revue indépendante, 83

INDEX OF WORKS

Index of Works

Index of Works

Index of Works

Printed in Great Britain by
Butler & Tanner Ltd., Frome and London